MW01235372

The Art of Letting Go of Overthinking in Relationships

3 Books in 1

Stop Overthinking and Relationship Anxiety, Discover Your Attachment Style for Better Communication in Marriage

By Robert J. Charles, Ph.D., D.Min

Download the Audiobook Version for FREE

If you love listening to audiobooks on-the-go, you can download the audiobook version of this book for FREE (Regularly $14.95) just by signing up for a FREE 30-day Audible try!

Click one of the links below to get started.

>> For Audible US <<

>> For Audible UK <<

>> For Audible FR <<

>> For Audible DE <<

Table of Contents

YOUR FREE GIFTS

Breathtaking BONUS! #1
Master the Art of Building Stronger Bonds with Loves Ones

In this Bonus, you'll find:

- How to Develop Effective Communication Strategies

- Ways to Build a Healthy Relationship Plan

- Exercises to Establish Healthy Boundaries for Personal Growth

Discover Powerful Strategies to Elevate Your Relationships to New Heights!

Click here to get this BONUS.

AMAZING BONUS! #2

Companion Worksheets
<u>7 Transformative Worksheets</u> for Cultivating a New Mindset for a Better Life

Inside this BONUS, you'll discover:

- How to Cultivate Self-Compassion for True Happiness?

- How to Unleash Your Happy Hormones?

- How to Create Your ideal Self-Care Routine?

If you want to start a better life with self-compassion and self-care

<u>Download this BONUS.</u>

Book #1

Letting Go of Overthinking in Relationships and Relationships Anxiety Workbook

Rewire Your Anxious Brain to Fix an Unhealthy Relationship, Stop Toxic Thoughts and Discover Your Attachment Style

By Robert J. Charles, PhD, DMin

INTRODUCTION

Selena had always been a kind and thoughtful partner, but her relationships were often plagued by worry and overthinking. Even when she was happy, her mind was always racing with worries and fears, especially the fear of becoming vulnerable and ending up hurt. One day, her partner, Alex, organized a surprise picnic by the lake. Selena's thoughts ran wild and began to race with questions as they sat together: "Does he really love me? What happens if something goes wrong? Is he trying to break up with me?"

Alex, sensing her discomfort, moved closer to her and took her hands in his. "You know, Selena, I've come to realize that our mind can be both our biggest ally and our most cruel critic. It has the power to make up situations that aren't grounded in reality. But if we allow this, we risk missing out on the beauty and genuineness of our relationship. I want us to be present in this moment, free from the shackles of overthinking." Selena saw that her overthinking was robbing her of beautiful moments with Alex, so she made a conscious effort to let go of her anxieties and live in the present.

Falling and being in love, as you've probably noticed, is not quite the same in reality as it is portrayed in the movies. It's messy and complicated, and the scene where you stand in the rain and blurt out your feelings to each other and then hug passionately definitely never happens. Relationships are like intricate dances that require the complete focus, patience, and dedication of both partners. Like we've all heard so many times, love is a choice. It takes time and effort. And while it might seem beautiful and rosy at the start of the relationship, it rarely stays that way for too long.

The end of a relationship also is never painless, especially if you've been treated unfairly throughout the relationship. As someone who has experienced what it feels like to be abused and taken advantage of, I know how much it hurts to let somebody go or be let go of regardless of if the person was right for me or not. And I know how much this can affect future relationships.

It might seem unfair and irrational, but projecting the fears and anxiety earned from a previous relationship is bound to occur, and if not properly addressed can cause a lot of problems in the current relationship and could even lead to the death of the relationship.

Allowing overthinking and anxiety to cast a cloud over your relationship doesn't always stem from the wounds sustained from a previous relationship, though; it can occur as a result of dysfunctions in how you were raised and the home you grew up in, or as part of a personality trait you just can't seem to shed. One thing, however, is certain: overthinking and anxiety make it difficult to find happiness and peace.

Knowing this, however, doesn't automatically make things better. I learned this the hard way when I realized that I was clinging to my anxiety and overthinking to avoid facing and working on them. Sounds weird, doesn't it? Shouldn't the fact that I understood the problem have made it half-solved already? It should have, *but* it didn't.

Let me give you an example. Isabella and her partner, Benjamin, were in a slightly heated discussion. She was calmly and rationally trying to explain that she always felt small whenever Benjamin held grudges over small issues, ultimately causing problems where there weren't any. Benjamin once held a grudge for two days because she arrived at their dinner date late. And even if she had a completely understandable and reasonable excuse, he latched onto her lateness, thinking about it over and over again until he came to the ridiculous conclusion that her arriving late meant that she just didn't care enough and was looking for ways to break it off with him.

After patiently listening to what Isabella had to say, Benjamin selfishly pointed out that he had been hurt before, and that if she was a good partner, she would understand him and accept him the way he was. So, at this point, Benjamin understood the negative effects his past relationships and experiences had had on him; he just wasn't very willing to work on those negative effects.

As I said earlier, it's not enough to just acknowledge that you have a problem with anxiety and overthinking. Don't get me wrong, it is very essential to do so—but you also have to acknowledge the fact that it could cause you to hurt your partner, whether willingly or not, *and* you have to be willing to work on yourself. After all, relationships are a two-way street. Neither of you is perfect, but you ought to strive to be the best version of yourself for you and your partner.

Overthinking and anxiety are not only painful but also exhausting for both partners.

Letting go of overthinking and anxiety in relationships is never easy, but it's well worth it. If you are tired of always overthinking things and imagining worst-case scenarios in your relationships, then this workbook is for you. Overthinking can cause you to develop a narcissistic and pessimistic mindset. You become a person others try to avoid, and you automatically think the worst not only of yourself but also of other people. Essentially, you become a "glass half-empty" person, and you can no longer find happiness and satisfaction in your daily life and relationships. In your relationship as a couple, you find yourself lashing out at your partner, and you can't seem to stop hurting them. You might eventually become a full-blown bitter person with few or no loved ones around.

Is this what you want for yourself? Absolutely not, right? Then this relationship workbook is for you. In it, I have garnered my experiences with anxiety and overthinking. I struggled with anxiety and overthinking as a child, and in my relationships as an adult, I struggled with relationship anxiety. Realizing the problem I had was the first step; working on myself to become better (and yet making mistakes along the way) was the second.

I eventually started reading books about anxiety and overthinking, carrying out exercises to help me, talking to people who had similar experiences, and most importantly, I talked to my partner. I allowed myself to become vulnerable and I showed her every part of me, even the worst parts that scared me into thinking she might leave me. We also worked on trust and learning to communicate effectively with each other, not just yelling and not listening to ourselves. It wasn't easy; she also had to learn to be patient with me and to forgive me for the times I had hurt her with actions that stemmed from my overthinking and anxiety. Cut to now: we're married and have enjoyed many years together. We've surely had our ups and downs, but by the grace of God, with what we learned while we were still in courtship, and even what we learned inside marriage, we've had a truly beautiful marriage.

We have also been able to help a few of our friends who also had problems with their relationships due to anxiety and overthinking. Ben and Suzanne were one such couple. Ben was one of my closest friends, and Suzanne, my wife's. We always spent time together at least once a month on a double date. They were over for dinner one Sunday night and my wife and I couldn't help but notice that there seemed to be tension between them. At first, we thought it was probably just a little misunderstanding going on—until we all went out the next month on a double date and the tension between them had become so much worse. They were openly snapping and taking digs at each other. It went on like that until I had to ask, "Is everything all right between you two? You've been at each other's throats all night."

Suzanne, who seemed to have been waiting for that question, immediately launched into her side of the story. They eventually came home with us and we spent the entire night discussing what must have gone wrong between them. After praying and discussing what to do, my wife and I sat them down the following morning and we had another in-depth conversation, this time about the relationship anxiety that seemed to be plaguing them both and causing a strain on their marriage. We encouraged them to be open and honest with each other, teaching them the same tips and exercises that helped us. We also encouraged them not to feel ashamed or reluctant to see a Christian marriage counselor, if necessary.

The following weeks were fraught for them and also for us, but were well worth it in the end. They both grew in love for and understanding of each other.

It might be a long and difficult process, but I can assure you that reading this book will be of great help to you, your partner, and your relationship. In this book, you'll learn:

- The overthinking and anxiety cycle
- How overthinking and anxiety impact one's life
- What relationship anxiety looks like
- Possible causes of relationship anxiety
- The negative impact of anxiety on your relationship
- Brain exercises to rewire your anxious brain

- Working on trust and intimacy issues

- Creating healthy relationship habits

- The benefits of decluttering

- Mind and space decluttering

- Healthy coping habits for the overthinker

- And a whole lot more!

Are you ready to finally have that beautiful and anxiety-free relationship you've always wanted? Then let's dive in! I hope you enjoy the book.

PART ONE

Understanding Relationship Anxiety

In this part, you'll be obtaining an in-depth understanding of:

- The anxiety and overthinking cycle

- The possible causes of anxiety and overthinking

- The impact of anxiety and overthinking on your relationship

And in doing so, you'll not only begin to understand relationship anxiety, but you'll also be able to recognize the signs of relationship anxiety in yourself and/or your partner, as well as identify and understand the negative impact anxiety and overthinking has had (and/or is having) on your life and your relationship.

This will serve as a guide in taking that critical first step in rewiring your anxious brain and repairing the damage anxiety and overthinking might have had on you, your partner, and your relationship.

CHAPTER ONE

THE ANXIETY AND OVERTHINKING CYCLE

"Anxiety in the heart of man causes depression, But a good word makes it glad."

—Proverbs 12:25

Laura found herself trapped in a never-ending cycle of anxiety and overthinking. Her thoughts seemed to have a life of their own, always dissecting scenarios and scrutinizing every little nuance of her conversations. She would analyze texts, look for underlying meanings, and repeat conversations in her brain, questioning every word she spoke. Her relationship with Mark started to suffer as a result of her incessant mental chatter, which always left her worn out and on edge.

You might think that you know what anxiety is: that person who always has sweaty palms, never makes eye contact, and just can't seem to be able to face a crowd—right? Actually, that's not quite it.

"Anxiety is your body's natural response to stress. It's a feeling of fear or apprehension about what's to come" (Holland, 2022). According to the American Psychological Association (the APA), "Anxiety is an emotion characterized by feelings of tension, worried thoughts, and physical changes like increased blood pressure" (n.d.).

At one point or another, everyone has experienced anxiety. For example, you may worry and feel anxious if you have an important presentation to make, before taking an exam, or before making a life-changing decision. When this happens occasionally, it's quite normal and happens to the best of us.

However, when it occurs too frequently, prevents you from living a normal life, and causes you to avoid situations (like missing school or faking an illness so you don't have to give a speech at your friend's wedding), then it could be that you have an anxiety disorder.

If your anxiousness feels overwhelming and is excessive and persistent, and it's not a reaction to a specific situation (like an exam or a presentation), then your anxiety symptoms may be "chronic and can interrupt [your] daily life" (Lindberg, 2021). According to the Anxiety & Depression Association of America, anxiety disorders are the most common mental health condition in the United States. The APA notes that anxiety disorders are not just the typical nerves you might feel from time to time; the anxiety is excessive and disruptive. Anxiety disorders affect nearly 30% of adults at some point in their lives.

Anxiety disorders include:

- Obsessive-compulsive disorder (OCD)
- Agoraphobia
- Post-traumatic stress disorder (PTSD)
- Social anxiety disorder
- Generalized anxiety disorder (GAD)
- Phobias
- Separation anxiety disorder
- Panic disorder

These will be discussed in more detail later on.

What is overthinking? Well, it "involves thinking about a certain topic or situation excessively and analyzing it for long periods of time" (Morin, 2023).

It simply means you are unable to turn off your mind. It's like having a committee meeting going on all the time in your head. This happens when your mind spins and you make multiple U-turns and detours without reaching your intended destination.

Imagine this scenario: As you get comfortable in bed and try to fall asleep, your mind is full of ideas. You begin to overanalyze the conversations you had during the day, obsessing over what you said and didn't say. You imagine wildly different scenarios of how tomorrow's meeting might go, and you suddenly start wondering what the meaning of life is. You have officially entered the overthinking zone. And while it might originally seem harmless, overthinking eventually leads to a lot of problems and difficulties, ranging from the physical to the emotional.

Anxiety and Overthinking: Are They Intertwined?

Anxiety and overthinking. Like two peas in a pod, they appear to complement one another. They are usually intertwined, and one cannot exist without the other. Overthinking frequently gets its start from anxiety, that well-known state of uneasiness and fear. Anxiety sounds like a persistent voice in our thoughts that constantly imagines the worst-case scenario and questions every choice we make. In the meantime, overthinking is the overeager sidekick that follows anxiety's cues and analyzes, dissects, and overanalyzes every aspect of our life.

"Anxiety makes us overthink everything in many different ways, and the result of this overthinking isn't helpful at all" (Peterson, 2015). There are several ways through which anxiety causes overthinking (the list below is inspired by Tanya Peterson, author of several books on reducing anxiety):

1. Obsessively overanalyzing every conversation you have. You can't help thinking through every conversation, doing so over and over again until you come to a wildly inappropriate and false conclusion regarding how the conversation went or what it was *truly* about.

2. Having false beliefs about yourself and imagining bad scenarios that could develop as a result of that false belief.

3. Unnecessarily imagining worst-case scenarios that could occur as a result of you carrying out the activity that causes your anxiety (e.g., facing a crowd to give a presentation).

4. Thinking "what if?" and letting your mind run wild with the bad things that could happen. *What if...* These two simple words have the power to set off a torrent of terrifying thoughts, throwing our imaginations into an uproar.

5. Anxiety trains our minds to recognize potential dangers in our surroundings. While hypervigilance can be of great value in moments of true danger, it can also lead to overthinking in normal situations. Our minds become hyper-focused on imagined threats, exaggerating them and causing unnecessary scrutiny and anxiety.

6. Anxiety often coexists with perfectionism and a fear of failure. We put immense pressure on ourselves to meet unrealistically high standards, scared of making mistakes or falling short. This fear of failure causes overthinking as we constantly examine every move we make, striving for perfection and fearing the outcome of any mistake.

I once read somewhere that anxiety and the overthinking that comes with it were more useful for our ancestors than they could ever be for us in the modern world. Imagine a man in the forest trying to hunt deer. He is extremely focused on the deer stripping off the bark of a tree just a few feet away from him when he realizes that the bushes behind him are rustling. His mind immediately goes into overdrive, thinking several thoughts at once. He tries to plan the outcome of every scenario that could develop—if the rustling is an animal hiding in the bushes, if it is a small or large animal, prey or foe, if he ought to escape or not, if he should remain still or not, what he would do if the deer got away... and so many more thoughts. Quite understandable, however, as it is the world he lives in. However, I highly doubt a rustling bush would mean a tiger is hiding and getting ready to attack you on your way home.

Anxiety and overthinking go hand in hand and almost always do more harm than good. It is up to us to figure out how to overcome it without losing touch with reality.

Ruminating and Worrying: The Overthinking Branches

Overthinking is a trap—one that most of us seem to have fallen into many times. I know I have, too many times to count. It involves "repetitively dwell[ing] on the same thought or situation over and over to the point that it disrupts your life" (Witmer, 2023). I know we all must have experienced that decision we just couldn't seem to make that kept us up at night.

It's quite normal. Everyone has had difficulty with making a decision and thinking too much about a particular thing. However, it becomes overthinking when you can't get it out of your head and it begins to affect you negatively.

Globally recognized motivational speaker Tony Robbins points out, "So when does thinking become *overthinking*? It's when you can't seem to turn your concerns off. It's when you think so much, you become paralyzed—

unable to actually make a decision or take any action" (2023). Overthinking is like a massive, sprawling tree with many branches, and the most prominent of these branches are ruminating and worrying. These intertwined aspects of overthinking can consume our minds, trapping us in cycles of repetitive thinking and constant worrying.

Rumination

You must have heard the phrase "ruminating on the past." That's exactly what rumination involves: obsessively and repeatedly thinking about events that have occurred in the past, particularly the negative ones. Rumination is defined as "engaging in a repetitive negative thought process that loops continuously in the mind without end or completion" (Scolan, 2021). It is repeated musing about past events, conversations, mistakes, etc. It's like continually pressing the rewind and play buttons on a mental movie to dissect each scene and analyze it from every angle. This tendency to overthink keeps us stuck in the past and unable to fully engage with the present. We find ourselves unable to let go of what has already happened and endlessly wondering what could have happened and what should have happened.

Worrying

Worry, on the other hand, draws our attention to the future and involves uncertainty. It's a branch of overthinking that takes us into a realm of uncertainty and conjures up countless scenarios of potential harm and negative consequences. Worry can become all-encompassing as we struggle to deal with "what might happen" and find solace in the unknown.

Rumination and worry come in many forms, but they have one thing in common: being unable to get out of the bondage of thinking too much.

Both thrive on overanalysis, dwelling on the past or the future, and magnifying potential problems. This constant cycle of rumination and worry can lead to increased stress and anxiety, and even affect your ability to make clear decisions.

Different Types of Anxiety

Anxiety, which negatively affects daily life for so many of us, manifests itself in a variety of ways and also affects people in distinctive ways. Anxiety has different aspects, each with its challenges and manners of manifestation.

Anxiety is a normal reaction to perceived dangers or pressures that serves as a protective mechanism to prepare us for impending harm. However, anxiety disorders develop when anxiety becomes excessive, invasive, and affects daily living. Several diverse forms of anxiety disorders occur within this broad spectrum, each with its own set of triggers, symptoms, and underlying causes.

By gaining a deeper understanding of the different types of anxiety, we can better recognize and address the challenges they present. From generalized anxiety disorder (GAD) with its pervasive worry, to panic disorder, characterized by sudden and intense panic attacks, and social anxiety disorder (SAD), which is accompanied by profound fear in social situations, each anxiety disorder offers its own set of experiences and complexities. Here are some of the common types of anxiety disorders:

1. Generalized anxiety disorder: This disorder involves "excessive, unrealistic worry and tension with little or no reason" (WebMD Editorial Contributors, 2023) about different elements of life, such as your job, health, relationships, and everyday circumstances. Individuals with GAD frequently struggle to regulate their anxiety,

which can interfere with everyday functioning. There may be symptoms such as "restlessness, fatigue, difficulty concentrating, irritability, muscle tension, or sleep disturbances" (DeMartini et al., 2019). GAD often manifests gradually and can have a major influence on a person's quality of life.

2. Obsessive-compulsive disorder (OCD): A person with OCD has difficulty controlling their thoughts and often engage in repetitive behaviors (Lindberg, 2021). By definition, OCD involves obsessions (invasive and unwelcome thoughts that cause harsh suffering) and compulsions (repetitive behavioral or mental acts that individuals feel forced to carry out to ease their anxiety or forestall a dreaded outcome). Contamination worries, safety concerns, and undesired violent or forbidden ideas are common obsessions. Excessive cleaning, checking, or repeating rituals are common manifestations of compulsions. OCD may negatively influence everyday functioning and such individuals often need specialist treatment, such as counseling and medication.

3. Panic disorder: According to the American Psychiatric Association (2023), "the core symptom of panic disorder is recurrent panic attacks, an overwhelming combination of physical and psychological distress." It is characterized by repeated and unpredictable panic attacks, which are intense bouts of anxiety or distress followed by physical symptoms such as heart palpitations, sweating, shaking, shortness of breath, chest pain, and a sense of impending doom. Panic attacks can occur without an obvious reason, leading to fear of future attacks and causing individuals to evade specific events or places to avoid a potential attack. Panic disorder can be extremely stressful, necessitating counseling and medication.

4. Phobia disorders: According to the National Institute of Mental Health (2023), a phobia is "an intense fear of—or aversion to—specific objects or situations." Phobia disorders are characterized by an excessive and illogical fear of certain items, events, or activities. The fear is exaggerated and not proportional to the harm that could be caused by the feared stimuli. Specific phobias (fear of spiders, heights, or flying, for example), social phobia (fear of social settings and being humiliated or embarrassed), and agoraphobia (fear of staying in locations or circumstances from which escape may be difficult, such as elevators) are examples of common phobias. Phobias can cause the individual to avoid certain situations or objects unnecessarily in a manner that could disrupt daily life.

5. Social anxiety disorder (SAD): This is "a fear or anxiety about social situations where you are exposed to judgement, scrutiny, or rejection in a social or performance situation" (Anthony, 2021). People with social anxiety often worry about embarrassing themselves or being humiliated, causing them to avoid social interactions, public speaking, or other performance situations. Physical symptoms like blushing, sweating, trembling, and rapid heartbeat are usually observed in social anxiety. Treatment options include therapy, medication, and techniques like cognitive restructuring and social skills training.

6. Separation anxiety: Separation anxiety means feeling "very anxious or fearful when a person you're close to leaves your sight" (WebMD Editorial Contributors, 2023). It is usually found in children but can also affect adults. It involves extreme fear or anxiety about separation from attachment figures or from familiar environments. Children with separation anxiety may have difficulty attending school or being away

from their parents, while adults may go through distress when separated from their significant other or home. Physical symptoms such as headaches, stomachaches, and nightmares can occur. Treatment for separation anxiety commonly involves therapy and gradually increasing exposure to separation situations.

7. Post-traumatic stress disorder (PTSD): According to the National Health Service (2023), PTSD is "an anxiety disorder caused by very stressful, frightening or distressing events." The symptoms of PTSD include intrusive thoughts about or flashbacks to the trauma, as well as nightmares, dissociation (feeling detached from reality), and feelings of sadness or guilt (Lok et al., 2018).

It is important to note that these anxiety disorders can coexist or present in different combinations. Each disorder has specific diagnostic criteria, treatment approaches, and potential causes, so you need to see a professional in order to be accurately diagnosed and treated.

The Vicious Anxiety Cycle

In medical biochemistry, there's something called the positive feedback system. In this system, the presence of a product leads to an increase in the activity of the system/pathway that led to the production of that product. Simply put, the more the presence and concentration of a certain chemical in the body, the more the body produces it... until it reaches a certain peak or crescendo, after which there is a decrease in the production of that chemical.

Take the anxiety cycle to be a positive feedback system, only a vicious one (don't let the word "positive" confuse you here!). When an event occurs that leads to you having symptoms of anxiety, you try to avoid the anxiety. This brings temporary relief—which doesn't last for long. Then the symptoms come back with a vengeance. And so, the more you try to avoid your anxiety, the stronger it gets.

Jaclyn Gulotta, PhD, LMHC, a licensed psychologist in Florida, explains, "The cycle of anxiety is when an event or situation happens and the person feels a lack of control or fear and avoids coping in order to escape intense emotions" (quoted in Mandriota, 2022).

This vicious cycle has four stages:

Stage 1: Anxiety and a desire to cope with it

Stage 2: Avoidance – trying to get out of the situation

Stage 3: Temporary relief

Stage 4: Heightened anxiety

Let's consider an example of the vicious anxiety cycle in a scenario involving a fear of flying:

Stage 1. Feeling anxious and wanting to deal with it:

Johnny has a fear of flying and has a business trip coming up that requires him to take a flight. As the travel date approaches, he starts feeling anxious about the upcoming flight and wants to find a way to cope with his fear.

Stage 2. Attempting to avoid the situation:

Johnny begins considering alternative modes of transportation to avoid flying. He explores options like driving or taking a train, believing that by avoiding air travel, he can prevent the anxiety and fear associated with flying.

Stage 3. Feeling a temporary sense of relief:

Once Johnny decides to drive instead of flying, he experiences a temporary sense of relief. He no longer has to face the fear-inducing situation of being on an airplane, and his anxiety subsides temporarily. This relief reinforces his belief that avoiding flying is an effective strategy for managing his fear.

Stage 4. Returning to a state of heightened anxiety:

As Johnny embarks on his road trip, he realizes that driving takes significantly longer and is more tiring than flying. He also becomes aware that his fear of flying has limited his ability to explore new destinations quickly and efficiently. These realizations trigger a return to a heightened state of anxiety as he worries about missing out on opportunities, facing long travel times, and not being able to fully participate in work-related activities.

Johnny's heightened anxiety may continue to reinforce his fear of flying and perpetuate the vicious anxiety cycle.

Brutal, isn't it? That's what anxiety does. The cycle eventually becomes deeply ingrained, making it harder to break free from its grip.

Signs You're an Overthinker

Overthinking is a common problem that affects some of us more than others. It entails incessantly overanalyzing circumstances, decisions, and discussions, which frequently leads to tension, worry, and indecision. If you find yourself engaged in an overthinking loop, here are some symptoms that you may be a chronic overthinker:

1. Difficulty making decisions: Overthinkers tend to struggle to make decisions, regardless of how big or small they might be. They overanalyze every possible outcome, weigh the pros and cons

excessively, and dread making the wrong choice. This indecisiveness can lead to prolonged delays in taking action or even might even lead to avoiding decisions altogether.

2. Constant analysis and second-guessing: Overthinkers have a tendency to dissect past events and conversations, endlessly scrutinizing every detail and unnecessarily looking for hidden meanings. They always question themselves, replaying scenarios and imagining other outcomes that could have occurred, often leading to self-doubt and confusion.

3. Perfectionism: Overthinkers set high standards for themselves and expect everything to be flawless. They strive for perfection in their work, relationships, and personal life, which can lead to an excessive focus on details and an inability to accept imperfections or mistakes. This pursuit of perfection can be overwhelming and lead to a constant fear of failure.

4. Catastrophizing: Overthinkers have a tendency to catastrophize events, imagining the worst-case scenario. They are too concerned with things that have not yet occurred (and may never occur), causing unneeded stress and anxiety. This negative way of thinking can be taxing and prevent individuals from appreciating the present moment.

5. Analysis paralysis: Overthinkers frequently become locked in a loop of analysis paralysis, in which they are so overwhelmed by the possibilities that they struggle to take any action at all. This can emerge in a variety of aspects of life, including job, relationships, and even routine daily tasks, resulting in missed opportunities and a sense of being trapped.

6. Seeking external approval: Before making judgments or taking action, overthinkers frequently seek reassurance and approval from others.

The Negative Effects on Your Life

Believe it or not, studies have shown that overthinking can actually impact your general sense of wellbeing (Toshi, 2023). The damaging effects of overthinking include, but are not limited to:

1. Damage to mental health: Constant overanalyzing creates a vicious cycle of mental harm (Chukuemeka, 2022). Overthinking drains you mentally, leaving you feeling listless and directionless after expending all your energy on thinking about your anxieties and worries (Nwokolo, 2022).

2. Impaired decision-making: Overthinking impairs your ability to make well-informed judgments. It's easy to get caught in the trap of indecision if you overanalyze every choice and dwell on potential consequences and alternative outcomes. As the fear of making the wrong choice increases, you'll waste great opportunities and come to dread making decisions. As a result, you may feel trapped and unable to progress in numerous aspects of your life.

3. Strain on relationships: Overthinking may have a bad influence on your relationships, which is probably why you are currently holding this book in your hands. Questioning your own behavior or the motives of others all the time can lead to misunderstandings, miscommunication, and avoidable fights. Overthinkers often interpret events incorrectly. Distance, mistrust, and tension can result in damaged personal and professional relationships.

4. Reduced creativity and innovation: Overthinking stifles creativity and innovation. When you are trapped in a cycle of overanalysis and self-doubt, it becomes difficult to think outside the box or take risks. Overthinkers tend to be overly cautious, fearing failure or criticism, which inhibits their ability to explore new ideas and approaches. This can hinder personal and professional growth, limiting your potential for success.

5. Sleep disturbances: Overthinking often causes disruptions to sleep patterns due to difficulty falling or staying asleep. The racing thoughts and worry can keep your mind active, making it difficult to get quality sleep. Lack of proper rest and sleep can also cause fatigue, irritability, and decreased cognitive functioning during the day.

Understanding Relationship Anxiety

"Relationship anxiety is when a person experiences persistent doubt, fear, or worry in a relationship" (Caporuscio, 2020). It is a common phenomenon in romantic partnerships. You may experience relationship anxiety due to "attachment difficulties in early childhood, emotional neglect, or from general anxiety that manifests as worry in your relationships" (Powell, 2022).

The most common causes include, but are not limited to:

- Low self-esteem
- Toxic past relationships
- Trauma
- Environmental factors
- Traditional and cultural norms

These will be discussed in detail later on.

Signs Your Relationship Anxiety Has Become Unhealthy

Here are some indicators that you need to get a handle on your relationship anxiety and perhaps seek professional help:

1. Constant worrying: Persistent and intrusive thoughts about the relationship or excessive worry about your partner's feelings, commitment, or potential problems, even when there is no concrete evidence to support your concerns, can be problematic.

2. Fear of rejection or abandonment: Relationship anxiety can manifest as a deep-seated fear of being rejected or abandoned by your partner. This fear may lead to clingy behavior, possessiveness, or an overwhelming need for reassurance and validation.

3. Overanalyzing and doubting: As someone experiencing relationship anxiety, you may tend to overanalyze every aspect of the relationship. You question your partner's intentions, doubt the authenticity of their love, or search for hidden meanings behind their words and actions. This constant doubt can strain the relationship and create unnecessary tension.

4. Avoidance and withdrawal: Relationship anxiety leads to a tendency to avoid or withdraw from the relationship. Scared of possible rejection or abandonment, you may create emotional distance, avoid difficult conversations, or even contemplate ending the relationship as a way of protecting yourself from perceived harm.

5. Neglecting self-care: When relationship anxiety becomes overwhelming, you may neglect self-care and prioritize the

relationship above your own wellbeing. You may excessively focus on the needs and wants of your partner, sacrificing your own interests, friendships, and personal growth. This imbalance can lead to feelings of resentment and dissatisfaction, further exacerbating the relationship anxiety.

6. If you notice these signs in yourself or your relationship, it is important to accept them for what they are (no denial) and seek support. Remember, addressing and working through relationship anxiety can lead to personal growth, improved wellbeing, and a stronger, more fulfilling relationship.

MAIN IDEAS

Remember Laura?

One day, Laura decided that enough was enough. She recognized that her anxiety and overthinking were holding her back from truly enjoying life and maintaining a healthy relationship. She started to read and learn about anxiety and overthinking, especially relationship anxiety. She looked back at her past relationships and decided to forgive those who had hurt her. She prayed, too; she talked to God about everything and held on to all the Bible had to say on anxiety. With determination and the support of therapy, she started implementing strategies to quiet her racing mind. Gradually, she learned to challenge her negative thoughts, practice mindfulness, and engage in self-care activities. As she gained control over her anxious tendencies, Laura felt a newfound sense of freedom and a deeper connection with Mark. The cycle was finally broken, and she embraced a life filled with peace, confidence, and a brighter outlook on the future.

Anxiety and overthinking frequently coexist, forming a complicated and interwoven cycle that can be difficult to break. Overthinking is a symptom of anxiety in which excessive worry and rumination take center stage. This persistent cycle of overthinking feeds worry, creating a feedback loop that worsens both mental states. We tend to overthink more when we are nervous or stressed. Overthinking has many branches, including ruminating and worrying. Ruminating is repeated attention on negative ideas, events, or memories, whereas worrying is excessive anticipation of prospective negative results. These two characteristics of overthinking can waste a large amount of mental energy and contribute to anxiety's persistence.

Understanding the many types of anxiety, identifying the indications of overthinking, and realizing the detrimental effects on one's life are all important stages in breaking free from this cycle.

Relationship anxiety can add another layer of complication. It is characterized by excessive anxiety and uncertainty about one's romantic connection, which frequently leads to insecurity, mistrust, and emotional pain. Recognizing indicators of unhealthy relationship anxiety, such as continual doubt, lack of trust, or difficulty maintaining a healthy emotional connection, is critical for obtaining help and treating these issues before they have a negative influence on one's wellbeing and relationships.

WORKBOOK ONE

Exercise 1: Self-Assessment

Take a moment to reflect on your relationship anxiety and answer the following questions:

- Do you frequently doubt the stability and future of your romantic relationship?

- Are you constantly seeking reassurance from your partner about their feelings for you?

- Do you often experience intense jealousy or possessiveness in your relationship?

- Are you overly sensitive to perceived signs of rejection or abandonment?

- Do you find yourself constantly questioning your partner's actions and motives?

Suggested Practice: Relationship Anxiety Self-Reflection

Take some time to journal about your relationship anxiety using the following prompts:

- Reflect on specific instances when you have experienced anxiety or worry in your relationship. What were the triggers for these feelings?

- How does your relationship anxiety impact your emotional wellbeing and overall relationship satisfaction?

- Consider any patterns or recurring thoughts that contribute to your relationship anxiety. Are there any underlying fears or insecurities driving these thoughts?

- Explore the ways in which your relationship anxiety affects your behavior and interactions with your partner. How does it influence your communication, trust, and ability to be vulnerable?

- Think about any previous experiences or past relationships that may be contributing to your relationship anxiety. How have these experiences shaped your current mindset?

Suggested Practice: Relationship Anxiety Awareness

Pay attention to your relationship anxiety in your day-to-day interactions with your partner. Take note of the following:

- Identify triggers: What situations, behaviors, or thoughts tend to trigger your relationship anxiety?

- Notice your physical sensations: How does your body react when you experience relationship anxiety? Are there any specific physical symptoms, such as increased heart rate or muscle tension?

- Observe your thought patterns: What kind of thoughts run through your mind during moments of relationship anxiety? Are they realistic or based on assumptions and fears?

- Monitor your behavior: How does your relationship anxiety influence your actions and reactions towards your partner? Are there any patterns of avoidance, clinginess, or seeking excessive reassurance?

- Reflect on the impact: Consider how your relationship anxiety affects both you and your partner. Does it create distance, tension, or strain in the relationship?

Remember, self-assessment and self-reflection are essential steps in understanding and addressing relationship anxiety. These exercises and practices will help you gain insights into your specific anxieties and lay the groundwork for developing healthier coping mechanisms and strategies in your relationship.

CHAPTER TWO

EXPLORING THE CAUSES

"Have I not commanded you? Be strong and of good courage; do not be afraid, nor be dismayed, for the Lord your God is with you wherever you go."

—Joshua 1:9

"Healing doesn't mean the damage never existed, it means the damage no longer controls our lives."

—Anonymous

As Raven sat on her porch swing, sipping her morning tea, her mind wandered back to the early days of her relationship with James. They'd been inseparable, always laughing and sharing their dreams. But as time passed, a veil of anxiety and overthinking seemed to settle over their once blissful connection. Raven often found herself questioning James' love and commitment, dissecting every word and action for hidden meanings. The fear of being hurt or abandoned consumed her, leaving her in a constant state of unease.

Reflecting on their journey, Raven realized that the causes of her anxiety and overthinking were rooted in past experiences. She had been hurt before, betrayed by someone she thought she could trust. Those wounds had never fully healed, and they cast a shadow over her current relationship. Raven understood that her overanalyzing was a defense mechanism, an attempt to protect herself from potential heartbreak. It wasn't James' actions that fueled her anxiety, but rather her own fears and insecurities that needed addressing.

Relationship anxiety, no doubt, places massive strain on a relationship. So much so that it can eventually cause the relationship to become toxic and emotionally draining for both partners, regardless of which partner is suffering from relationship anxiety. One of the ways by which you can understand and overcome it is to understand the underlying cause of it. Knowing and understanding the reason why you or your partner has relationship anxiety brings you much closer to overcoming it and achieving a much healthier mindset in and towards your relationship.

In this chapter, we'll be talking about possible causes of relationship anxiety in detail, so let's get right to it.

Your Past Relationships Matter

"Relationship problems occur when expectations from past relationships are applied to the current participants in a new relationship" (Woods, 2021). Your past relationships and the experiences you have had in those relationships can play a major role in shaping your future relationship(s).

Think about it: why do people who have experienced what it's like to be cheated on find it difficult to trust their new partner? Why do people who were emotionally manipulated become cold and seemingly unfeeling? Their past relationship has caused them to, in the first example, become unable to trust others, and in the second instance, develop a self-protective measure that prevents them from having true intimacy with their partners.

Exploring the causes of relationship anxiety in terms of previous relationships provides a more in-depth understanding of how past experiences influence your current mindset and behavior.

1. Trust issues: Betrayal, infidelity, or broken trust in previous relationships can cause deep-seated trust issues. The mental and sometimes physical scars left by such experiences can make it truly difficult to trust and fully open yourself in future relationships. Relationship anxiety might then develop as a protective strategy against future hurt and disappointment.

2. Abuse: Being in an abusive or toxic relationship can have a significant effect on your trust, self-esteem, and general wellbeing. Abuse, whether emotional, physical, or psychological, can cause long-term tension and anxiety in later relationships. Scars from previous violent relationships may cause hypervigilance, dread of experiencing the same thing, and anxiety.

3. Patterns and repetition: Patterns in relationships are common, especially when unresolved issues from the past go untreated. If you find yourself repeating the same relationship dynamics or attracting people who demonstrate similar bad habits, it might worsen your relationship anxiety. Recognizing and addressing these behaviors is critical for breaking the cycle and cultivating healthy relationships.

Low Self-Esteem

Your self-esteem is basically "your opinion of yourself" (Whelan, 2022). If you have low self-esteem, it "essentially means having a poor opinion of yourself" (Cherry, 2023). Individuals with low self-esteem frequently doubt their own value and believe they are insufficient, unlovable, or undeserving of love and pleasure. These poor self-perceptions can have a significant impact on our relationships and contribute to anxiety and overthinking in a variety of ways, including:

1. Constant need for validation: Low self-esteem can lead to a constant need for external validation from your partner. People with low self-esteem often rely heavily on their partner's approval to feel safe and worthy. They seek repeated affirmation of love and acceptance. This excessive need for approval can strain the relationship as the other partner begins to feel overwhelmed or unable to satisfy the insatiable need for approval.

2. Negative self-talk and overthinking: People with low self-esteem often have negative inner monologues and constant self-criticism. You may brood over past failures, ruminate on your shortcomings, and constantly fear that you are not good enough. This can lead to overanalyzing every interaction, conversation, and decision as you constantly question your partner's feelings, intentions, and loyalty.

3. Jealousy and insecurity: Low self-esteem frequently fuels feelings of jealousy and insecurity in relationships. Individuals who feel intimidated by perceived competition may continuously compare themselves to others. They may assume that their partner will eventually find someone more suitable and deserving of their affection. Jealousy and insecurity can rise to the level of possessiveness and a constant need for reassurance, straining the relationship even further.

Overcoming low self-esteem and minimizing relationship anxiety and overthinking necessitates self-reflection, self-compassion, and active self-esteem-building efforts.

"Why is he with me?" "I can't believe someone like her is with someone like me." Thoughts like this not only destroy you as a person, but can place unnecessary pressure on your partner and strain your relationship. Besides, what do you think is so wrong with you? What does the Bible say about you? What does God say about you? Do you see yourself that way?

"Because you are precious in my eyes and honored, and I love you, I give men in return for you, people in exchange for your life."—Isaiah 43:4

"For you created my innermost being; you knit me together in my mother's womb. I praise you because I am fearfully and wonderfully made; your works are wonderful, I know that full well."—Psalm 139:13–14

The Role of Trauma

This may seem to be quite similar to the first point in this chapter (your past relationships matter). However, traumatic experiences are not limited to past relationships. Trauma can occur as a result of any intensely stressful event or situation (Leonard, 2020). "Traumatic events can happen at any age and have lasting effects on your physical and mental well-being" (Ryder, 2022). In turn, this will likely affect your capacity to create and sustain good relationships.

Traumatic experiences can lead to post-traumatic stress disorder, which we discussed in the previous chapter. As a quick reminder, PTSD is "a psychiatric disorder characterized by intrusive thoughts, nightmares, flashbacks, and hyperarousal" (American Psychiatric Association, 2013). Individuals with PTSD often experience anxiety and overthinking related to their traumatic experiences, which can significantly affect their relationships (Cloitre et al., 2009).

Trauma can erode an individual's ability to trust others, especially their romantic partners. Past experiences of betrayal, abuse, or abandonment can lead to anxiety and overthinking, making it challenging to establish and maintain healthy intimacy in relationships (Feiring & Taska, 2005). Trauma can also significantly impact an individual's self-esteem and self-worth. Those who have experienced trauma may develop negative beliefs about themselves and struggle with feelings of worthlessness and inadequacy.

These feelings can, in turn, contribute to relationship anxiety and overthinking (Szymanski & Kashubeck-West, 2014). As a result, trauma survivors may use coping methods such as avoidance and emotional detachment as a form of self-protection. These strategies can hinder their ability to engage fully in relationships, leading to anxiety and overthinking (Katz & Windecker-Nelson, 2004).

Understanding the impact of trauma on relationship dynamics is critical for creating a successful therapeutic approach and support networks for those who have been traumatized.

Your Attachment Style Also Matters

Everyone has an attachment style, but not many people are aware that this is a thing (Izuakam, 2023). Your attachment style refers to how you behave in your relationships with others (Gonsalves, 2023). Attachment "is the emotional connection you formed as an infant with your primary caregiver—probably your mother" (Robinson et al., 2023). In the field of psychology, attachment theory "proposes that each and every one of us has an attachment style that developed when we were very young" (McDermott, 2023). As Robinson et al. (2023) explain, "According to attachment theory, pioneered by British psychiatrist John Bowlby and American psychologist Mary Ainsworth, the quality of the bonding you experienced during this first relationship often determines how well you relate to other people and respond to intimacy throughout life."

Basically, your attachment style comes from your experiences during childhood and plays a crucial role in shaping how you and maintain relationships. It can also impact whether or not you have relationship anxiety (Bowlby, 1969). Attachment theory suggests that early experiences with caregivers shape individuals' expectations and beliefs about relationships throughout their lives (Bowlby, 1969).

The theory identifies three primary attachment styles: secure, anxious (or preoccupied), and avoidant.

Secure Attachment Style

Securely attached individuals view themselves and other people positively (Mikulincer & Shaver, 2016). They typically had consistent and responsive caregiving during their early childhood, which helped them develop a sense of security and confidence in relationships. In romantic relationships, they are less likely to engage in excessive worrying, jealousy, or possessiveness (Simpson et al., 2007). They have a positive self-image and trust in their partners, which contributes to a sense of security and reduces the need for constant reassurance or validation. Their secure base in childhood serves as a model for secure relationships in adulthood, creating a cycle of healthy attachment patterns.

In summary, secure attachment style is characterized by a positive view of oneself and others, trust, and comfort with intimacy. Individuals with a secure attachment style experience lower levels of relationship anxiety and overthinking, leading to greater relationship satisfaction and stability.

Anxious Attachment Style

Anxious attachment style involves fear of abandonment and a simultaneous need to be close to others, as well as anxiety about relationships in general

(Mikulincer & Shaver, 2016). Individuals with an anxious attachment style frequently have a history of unpredictable, inconsistent caregiving in their early years, which leads to feelings of insecurity and a constant need for reassurance and validation in their relationships. This leads them to overthink and overanalyze their partner's behaviors (Ein-Dor et al., 2015).

Research shows that anxiously attached individuals are more likely to experience relationship anxiety (Cassidy & Shaver, 2016) because of their tendency to view normal behavior as an indication of rejection on the part of their partner. This leads to reassurance-seeking behaviors in the anxiously attached person (Ein-Dor et al., 2015). The accompanying negative thought patterns and anxious behaviors contribute to a cycle of anxiety and overthinking, which can undermine relationship satisfaction and stability.

In summary, those with an anxious attachment style have a heightened need for reassurance and tend to engage in overthinking. Their fear of rejection and abandonment can lead to maladaptive thoughts and behaviors in romantic relationships.

Avoidant Attachment Style

Those with an avoidant attachment style tend to be emotionally distant from their romantic partner, as in childhood they typically experienced unresponsive or inconsistent care from their parents or caregivers (Mikulincer & Shaver, 2016). Individuals with an avoidant attachment style value self-reliance, self-sufficiency, and autonomy, which might affect their behavior and interactions in romantic relationships.

As a result, these individuals develop a coping mechanism: suppressing their own needs and emotions (Bartholomew & Horowitz, 1991). They can use this coping mechanism to reduce the perceived hazards of emotional reliance and vulnerability. As a result, they frequently avoid seeking intimacy, rely only on themselves for support, and keep an emotional distance from their partner. They may also dismiss or suppress how they feel (Feeney & Noller, 1990). These shields act as a safeguard against potential rejection or disappointment. However, these protective systems can exacerbate marital problems by impeding open and honest communication and preventing the building of trust.

In summary, individuals with an avoidant attachment style tend to prioritize independence and self-reliance in relationships. They may exhibit emotional distancing, avoidance of intimacy, and suppression of attachment-related needs and emotions.

Understanding attachment styles and promoting secure attachment can contribute to healthier and more fulfilling relationships.

The Connection Between Physical Health and Emotional Wellbeing

Have you ever experienced something like this: you're sleep-deprived or haven't had a proper meal all day, and you find yourself snapping at people or being a grumpy bear in general. Well, this happens to almost everyone. However, intense strain on one's physical health can also cause strain on one's relationship and possibly eventually damage the relationship.

If we're physically ill, it significantly increases our risk of becoming mentally ill as well (and vice versa). According to the Mental Health Foundation (2022), "Nearly one in three people with a long-term physical health condition also has a mental health problem, most often depression or anxiety."

The Effect of Environmental Factors

"The environment and mental health are intrinsically connected. The places where you spend a lot of time—home, work, school, and even socially—can have a significant impact on your mental well-being" (Lindberg, 2023). Furthermore, "some aspects of environmental experience have long-term effects, through mechanisms that have not yet been identified, on levels of anxiety and depression symptoms" (Kendler et al., 2011).

In fact, our environment can even alter our brains—research has shown that "children raised in adverse environments tend to have hindered brain development, increasing their risk of memory issues, learning difficulties, and behavioral problems" (Lindbergh, 2023). Just as the environment can affect our brains, it can also impact us psychologically, potentially affecting stress levels, and therefore our overall mental health (Helbich, 2018).

Also, think about this ... Who are your friends? Who are the people you surround yourself with? What are they like? Think in particular about the ones whoa re currently in a relationship or married. How do they treat their significant others? When you go out, what do you notice them doing to their partners or vice versa? Are there any behaviors you normally wouldn't be comfortable with, but you've grown accustomed to and they don't faze you anymore, such as belittlement, disregard of feelings and opinions, or disrespectful behavior?

These acts are oftentimes not glaringly obvious. They are mostly subtle and might even seem like acts of love or normal behavior. You'll find that you may have begun to do the same to your partner, or perhaps you also accept such treatment regardless of how it makes you feel.

The Impact of Cultural and Societal Norms

Anxiety and overthinking in relationships can be influenced by cultural and societal norms, as these factors play a significant role in shaping individuals' beliefs, expectations, and behaviors within intimate partnerships. Cultural and societal norms encompass a range of factors, including gender roles, relationship ideals, communication patterns, and expectations regarding love and commitment. Understanding the impact of these norms can provide insights into the causes of your anxiety and overthinking.

Traditional gender roles often assign different responsibilities and expectations to each gender, which can create pressure and lead to relationship anxiety. For example, in many cultures, women are expected to prioritize caregiving and emotional support in relationships, while men are expected to be strong, independent, and provide financially (Christopher & Cate, 2018). These rigid gender roles can lead to feelings of inadequacy, anxiety about meeting societal expectations, and overthinking about one's performance in the relationship.

Cultural and societal norms that promote relationship ideals can also contribute to anxiety and overthinking. Movies, TV shows, and popular culture frequently depict idealized love relationships that may not always match reality. These idealized representations can lead to excessive expectations and put pressure on people to conform to the standards of a "perfect" relationship. Research has shown that exposure to such idealized relationships can create anxiety and dissatisfaction when real life does not meet these standards (Knobloch-Westerwick & Alter, 2017).

Anxiety and overthinking in relationships can also be influenced by the communication patterns dictated by societal conventions. In some cultures, indirect communication is valued, and people may be hesitant to voice their demands and problems directly. Meanwhile, those who dread confrontation or potential conflict may experience anxiety in cultures that value aggressively straightforward communication.

It is important to keep in mind that cultural and societal norms vary greatly across regions, and subgroups within countries. The effect of these norms on anxiety and overthinking in relationships will also differ. Furthermore, people may absorb and interpret norms differently, resulting in a range of experiences and responses within the same cultural setting.

Recognizing the impact of these societal standards can help us manage our relationships with more understanding and open discussions, resulting in happier and more fulfilling relationships.

Other Causes of Anxiety and Overthinking in Relationships

1. Lack of relationship role models: Growing up without healthy relationship role models or witnessing harmful relationship dynamics can have an impact on your attitudes and expectations about relationships. You may struggle to understand the boundaries of healthy relationships if you did not have positive models to learn from.

2. Fear of rejection or abandonment: Being rejected or abandoned can leave emotional wounds. These events can cause anxiety in relationships by instilling dread of being rejected or abandoned again. Fear of re-experiencing that hurt and humiliation might cause you to doubt your worthiness of love and generate a perpetual sense of unease.

MAIN IDEAS

Let's return to Raven for a moment. With her newfound awareness, Raven mustered the courage to have an open conversation with James. She bared her soul, sharing her struggles and the reasons behind her anxieties. To her relief, James responded with empathy and understanding, assuring her of his unwavering love and commitment. He, too, had noticed the strain in their relationship and was willing to work together to overcome it.

Embracing vulnerability, Raven and James embarked on a journey of healing and growth. They attended couples therapy, seeking professional guidance in navigating their insecurities and building a stronger foundation. Through this process, they learned to communicate more openly, practicing active listening and offering reassurances when needed. As the days turned into weeks and the weeks into months, Raven's anxiety gradually loosened its grip on their relationship. Trust flourished, and their connection blossomed into a deeper, more resilient bond. Together, they transformed their shared love story into one of resilience, reminding each other that healing and growth are possible even in the face of past traumas.

The causes of anxiety and overthinking in relationships form an intricate web of psychological, relational, and societal influences. Past events, such as prior traumas or unfavorable interpersonal dynamics, might contribute to anxiety and overthinking on an individual level. These habits might also be fueled by insecurities, low self-esteem, and a fear of abandonment or rejection. External constraints and societal expectations, such as cultural norms or media influences, can also heighten concerns about the perceived "success" of the relationship or keeping up appearances. Understanding these factors enables us to identify the underlying causes of our anxiety and overthinking, allowing us to handle them more effectively and create healthier interpersonal dynamics.

Relationship dynamics, in addition to individual considerations, can play a substantial part in the development of anxiety and overthinking. Lack of trust, poor communication, or frequent confrontations can create an unpredictable environment and foster anxious thoughts. Unresolved concerns from the past, as well as ongoing habits of emotional neglect or inconsistency, can contribute to anxiety. Furthermore, unreasonable expectations, such as demanding perfection or frequent reassurance, can lead to overthinking and further strain on the relationship.

WORKBOOK TWO

Section 1: Personal Reflection

1. Reflect on your personal history. Are there any past experiences or traumas that may have contributed to your anxiety and overthinking in your relationships?

2. Consider your self-perception and self-esteem. How does your self-image impact your anxiety and overthinking patterns within relationships?

3. Explore any underlying fears or insecurities that may be triggering your anxieties. Are there specific fears of abandonment, rejection, or failure that contribute to your overthinking?

Section 2: Relationship Dynamics

4. Analyze your current or past relationship dynamics. Have there been instances of trust being broken or inconsistent behavior that have contributed to your anxiety and overthinking?

5. Reflect on the communication patterns within your relationships. Do misunderstandings or a lack of open communication contribute to your overthinking? How do conflicts affect your anxiety levels?

6. Consider the influence of external factors on your relationship. How do societal expectations, cultural norms, or media portrayals impact your anxieties about relationship "success" or outward appearances?

Section 3: Patterns and Triggers

7. Identify recurring patterns in your anxious thoughts. Are there specific situations or triggers that consistently lead to anxiety and overthinking in your relationships?

8. Reflect on the role of control in your relationships. Do you feel a need to control outcomes or constantly seek reassurance? How does this contribute to your anxiety and overthinking?

9. Explore any perfectionistic tendencies or unrealistic expectations you may have for yourself or your partner. How do these expectations fuel anxiety and overthinking?

Conclusion:

Reflect on the insights gained from this workbook. Acknowledge the causes of your anxiety and overthinking in relationships, both personal and relational. It is a critical step in letting go of anxiety and overthinking in your relationships.

CHAPTER THREE

THE IMPACT OF ANXIETY AND OVERTHINKING ON RELATIONSHIPS

"Blessed is the man who trusts in the Lord,And whose hope is the Lord. For he shall be like a tree planted by the waters, Which spreads out its roots by the river, And will not fear when heat comes; But its leaf will be green, And will not be anxious in the year of drought, Nor will cease from yielding fruit."

—Jeremiah 17:7,8

"Anxiety is love's greatest killer. It makes others feel as you might when a drowning man holds on to you. You want to save him, but you know he will strangle you with his panic."

—Anaïs Nin

The impact of worry and overthinking on relationships is best defined as "catastrophic." Daniel had been a worrywart for as long as anyone could remember. When he was a child, it was cute to have a responsible kid who never forgot to do the dishes or pick up his younger siblings from school, but as he grew older, it became clear that his overthinking was driving people away from him, and this realization came only after his breakup with Lauren.

Being a constant worrier indicates that your relaxation switch is faulty. This means the mind of an overthinker like Daniel is always in overdrive, and for him, it was almost impossible to get his mind off the little things. Once he fixated on something, there was no room for anything else, and this slowly drove a wedge between him and Lauren.

Being an overthinker can make your relationships a bit strenuous, but it is still possible to make meaningful connections and maintain a romantic relationship if you manage your anxiety properly.

Relationship Anxiety: More Than Just Jealousy and Insecurity

It's normal to feel jealous sometimes. Jealousy tends to occur "when someone feels insecure about their relationship" (Stritof, 2022). In the context of a romantic relationship, jealousy can come in the form of resentment, hatred, worry, or uncertainty that your partner may leave you or interact with others more successfully than you do. It is caused by a lack of self-assurance and a fear of losing someone. Everyone is wired to experience jealousy, but when it gets illogical, it can be toxic. Irrational, unhealthy jealousy stems from "fear of abandonment and a worry about not being truly loved" (Rodriguez et al., 2016) and frequently results in mistreatment of one's partner.

Unhealthy jealousy is generally caused by mistrust. Individuals with anxiety tend to have less trust in people, which makes them test their partners whenever they can, leading to obsessive thought patterns about their partners being unfaithful, which then gives rise to bitterness and develops into jealousy over time. Jealousy is an irrational fear of losing something or someone which is or who's yours already. Obsessive thinking spells doom for almost every relationship. Why? Because people who overthink tend to find faults in even the littlest of things, which leads to jealousy or insecurity. For people with anxiety, jealousy and insecurity are programmed right alongside their anxiety; their lack of trust gives rise to fear, which brings about jealousy.

At some point, "jealous people feel so overwhelmed by their emotions and insecurities that they begin to exert control over their partners" (Stritof, 2022). Some of the behaviors that might show up are:

- Going through one's partner's emails, texts and call logs

- Searching one's partner's personal belongings

- Interrogating one's partner at every opportunity

- Overreacting and getting mad over small or irrelevant issues

Unfortunately, jealousy typically ends up causing resentment and defensiveness on the part of the other partner (Rodriguez, 2015) and "wreaks havoc on a relationship as the jealous person becomes more and more fearful, angry, and controlling" (Stritof, 2022).

Common Negative Behaviors Associated with These Traits

We all feel anxious at times—it's a normal part of life—but keep in mind that "chronic anxiety can interfere with your quality of life" (Cherney, 2022). It shouldn't be surprising by now to learn that anxiety and overthinking have a harmful impact on the human mind and body. The repercussions can be physical or psychological, and, if left unchecked, have debilitating implications. Negative behaviors related to these attributes are more common than most people realize, including:

1. Insomnia or poor sleeping habits: I believe we barely value the ability to sleep at will; imagine not being able to sleep even when you are thoroughly exhausted. We all like to get some good shuteye, right? But for people struggling with anxiety, loss of sleep is pretty much

normal, as they oftentimes have trouble sleeping due to overthinking. They are always lost in their thoughts, and the obsessive thought patterns make it hard for the body to relax enough to go into sleep mode.

2. Drug addiction: Constantly thinking about the same things is enough to drive someone nuts. Some people cope in healthy ways, but for others, it's more difficult, and they turn to drugs to help them unwind and relax.

3. Poor time management and a drop in productivity: Being an overthinker, or worrywart as I like to call it, implies that a person will fixate on one thing for hours and shut out everything else, no matter how urgent their other tasks that day may be. The decline in productivity is due to difficulty keeping track of time as well as an inability to concentrate.

4. Mood swings: People who suffer from anxiety tend to be irritable and quick to become depressed. This is due to their uncertainty, fear, and repetitive thought processes, which makes them more volatile and prone to melancholy and negativity (Knight, 2023).

5. Restlessness and indecisiveness: This is possibly the most common habit in people who suffer from anxiety and overthinking. This is because they overanalyze everything, making it difficult to make decisions and preventing them "from recognizing the evidence needed for problem-solving and making rational decisions" (Knight, 2023).

6. High blood pressure, illness, and exhaustion: These are some of the physical consequences of overthinking and anxiety. Overthinking "has been linked to physical health issues such as anxiety, depression,

obsessive-compulsive disorder (OCD), post-traumatic stress disorder (PTSD), chronic fatigue, insomnia and sleep disruption" (Knight, 2023).

Anxiety Issues and Codependency

Another word for having an anxious attachment style is being "codependent" (McLean, 2021). Codependency is a dysfunctional way to approach relationships—it involves one partner completely sacrificing their own needs and desires for the sake of the other. And codependency doesn't only exist in romantic relationships; it can be found between parent and child, friends, and family members just as easily.

While anxiety is defined as a feeling of uncertainty or dread, codependency in this context is an attachment or reliance on someone as a result of this anxiety.

There are two types of anxiety in relationships: isolation anxiety and relationship attachment anxiety. Individuals who suffer from isolation anxiety in relationships are withdrawn and prefer to be alone. They may be irritable and cranky. They are not inherently bad people; they simply prefer to be alone, and when they are in relationships, they expect (or rather demand) that their partners be helpful and accommodating, despite the fact that this is not how a healthy relationship should operate. People with this type of anxiety don't know how to make concessions and expect everyone else to bow and adhere to their will, which leads to the relationship becoming nearly dictatorial in nature—which no one wants.

Relationship attachment anxiety occurs when someone suffocates their partner due to anxiety or fear of abandonment. The worried person is constantly watching their partner; it's similar to jealousy without evidence of something to be jealous about. Individuals with this type of anxiety are drawn to isolated individuals, and this is where codependency begins.

Individuals with codependent traits seek the approval of others (most notably their partners) and bury their own needs and wants in an attempt to please their partners, and slowly, without either of them even realizing it, they begin to lose themselves. Some are so far gone that they cannot even distinguish their own desires from those of their partner. They are also often extremely clingy—and not the cute kind of clingy that makes you feel cherished, but one that frustrates their partners and makes them feel suffocated.

While it is obviously okay to express your affection for your partner, you must be careful not to suffocate them with your emotions. People with a tendency to be codependent spend a lot of time and resources attempting to help or "fix" their partner, and when they fail, their inner overthinker explodes and starts fretting over everything. While people may believe that the anxious/codependent individual's actions are unselfish, in reality they are not: everything they do is in an attempt to control their own anxiety. They internalize the fears, emotions, and difficulties of others, leaving them in a condition of continual anxiety and paranoia. They also find it difficult to express their feelings since they believe they are unimportant and come second to those of their partner.

Anxious people with codependent traits fear criticism and being perceived as not good enough, which is why they try their hardest to make their partner happy even at the expense of their own happiness. Certain past experiences, such as being criticized by their boss at work or being criticized by their parents as a child, can exacerbate the anxiety. These people are so focused on assisting their partner with everything that they end up feeling drained and overwhelmed, causing them to become unreasonable, irritable, and exhausted.

The Impact of Overthinking and Anxiety on Communication in Relationships

Communication is simply the exchange of opinions, ideas, and thoughts between parties—in this case, between romantic partners. Communication is the key to relationships, and it can be verbal or non-verbal, ranging from eye contact to direct conversation. Most couples, after years of being together, are able to convey information through mere gestures or expressions.

One couple I can think of, for example, were always traveling separately around the world on business, but after retirement, they discovered they had spent decades texting and video calling, which made it difficult for them to express themselves face to face. They realized they weren't good at it and went on communicating by phone. Even though they live in the same house, they spend more time calling each other and having text conversations than talking in person. Others may find it strange, but this is exactly what works for them.

Communication can make or break a relationship; without communication, you and your partner cannot talk and express your feelings. Constant, open communication builds lasting relationships, and talking about both the little things and the big things brings you closer together.

Lack of communication, on the other hand, will break the relationship. It starts slowly for most, as you start to grow distant from each other, question each other, and assume the worst when the solution to the problem might simply be to talk it out. Yes, talking it out is a way of finding solutions to arguments and everyday problems in a relationship. Lack of communication, therefore, is like a parasite which slowly eats at the relationship until it becomes a shell or husk of its former self.

A relationship is like a computer and anxiety is a computer virus, and communication is the firewall preventing the loss of files (which in this situation is the relationship). This means the more you and your partner communicate with each other, the lesser the chances of the two of you growing apart. An overthinker or worrywart is not able to express their feelings to their other half because they find it hard to have conversations without obsessing over the little things that oftentimes don't even matter, and because of that they dread conversations and avoid them—and that's a first-class ticket to being alone.

However, anxiety can really throw a wrench in your ability to communicate* effectively with your partner: "It takes a lot of mental energy to hold a conversation, even if it doesn't seem like it. So it should come as little surprise that when your mind is overwhelmed with anxiety it can impair your ability to communicate" (Abraham, 2020). To genuinely converse with others, we need more cognitive capacity than we realize. This is due to the brain's need to listen to information, comprehend it, process it, and come up with a proper response. Learning that surprised me as well, but when you think about it, it's not strange that people with anxiety find it difficult to communicate owing to the continual labor their brain is putting in due to overthinking and tension. Any relationship will suffer as a result of this.

*Click HERE to get this companion book that will help improve your communication skills.

Negative Effect on Problem-Solving in Relationships

Do you ever feel like bringing up an issue that you're supposed to discuss with your partner would result in conflict, so you ignore it? "Does telling your partner that you don't want to go to their family for the holidays feel like it might explode into an emotional drama?" (Blue, 2018). If so, this is rather typical. Conflicts are a normal part of life, and people who suffer from anxiety are no exception. However, avoiding an issue out of fear of having an argument is destructive to a relationship—such pent-up emotions will inevitably manifest in other ways. Recognizing and confronting difficulties head-on promotes a good partnership.

Unfortunately, anxious people struggle with confrontation; they often rehearse the entire conversation in their head hundreds of times before it actually happens, which leads to a worry of things going horribly wrong, so they avoid having the conversation altogether. The mistake they make here is that by not bringing it up, they deprive their partner of a say in the matter. Another reason those with anxiety delay resolving problems is the emotional baggage or drama that comes with it. Anxious people find it difficult to communicate their emotions and thus avoid anything involving emotional turmoil.

When Trust and Intimacy Issues Come In

It is natural for trust concerns to arise in a partnership with inadequate communication. Intimacy anxiety—the dread of being overly emotionally involved or attached to someone—is quite common. Anxious people are terrified of being judged and criticized by others, even in their relationships, and therefore they avoid becoming emotionally involved with others. Anxious people are often distrustful, and considering that relationships are built on trust, having a partner who doesn't trust you doesn't sit well with most people. Those with anxiety who have trust and intimacy issues are also more likely to be in relationships that are shallow.

Having trust issues is one of the negative effects of anxiety on a relationship. It is characterized by always assuming the worst, being suspicious about everything, distancing yourself from your partner, etc. It's very hard for an anxious individual to trust someone, especially when they've been hurt in the past; due to their tendency to overthink, they never really forget those part hurts, and then they become insecure about everything and everyone. They'd rather distance themselves from everyone because they're scared of being hurt or let down, or of not being good enough.

The Need for Emotional Resilience

Emotional resilience can be defined as the ability to cope with difficult situations, adversity, and trauma. In this harsh modern-day world where making someone cry helps you win points on social media and emotionally assaulting someone implies you're an "alpha male," it's critical to develop emotional resilience. This helps us shrug off cruel remarks, backstabbing, and many other emotional assaults. We have no control over what happens to us, so being emotionally resilient will help us adapt, shrug it off, and bounce back to a state of wellbeing.

Nelson Mandela once said, "The greatest glory in living lies not in never falling, but in rising every time we fall." To rise after adversity and trauma does not imply that we do not feel anything; it simply means that we have a thicker skin or recover faster when we fall. It means that we recognize that we have been harmed and broken, yet we do not lose our strength and instead continue on. Being emotionally resilient will help you survive even the most ferocious storms.

Stress is a key cause of anxiety, and being emotionally resilient will help those with anxiety develop positive coping strategies for stressful events, lowering their likelihood of becoming unwell as a result of the stress and overthinking. Overthinking is stressful on the human body and has a number of negative consequences, but having a coping method for whatever life throws our way can help us bounce back and keep going—and the more we do this, the easier it is to bounce back and recover from terrible circumstances. Individuals with anxiety who develop emotional resilience begin to think differently and more positively rather than worrying over the past (which I'm sure, in many cases, we'd like to forget). It enables us to progress and heal, and it shapes us into better versions of ourselves.

To do this, we must acknowledge that our ideas influence our actions, which is the first step in developing emotional resilience. Following acceptance, the next step is to find balance by focusing on the positive aspects of life rather than the negative.

Reasons we need to be emotionally resilient:

1. Reduced anxiety: Being emotionally resilient enables us, especially those who struggle with anxiety, to focus on the positive aspects of life rather than linger on the negative. It transforms our mode of thinking and helps us uncover our willpower. Overcoming adversity boosts self-esteem and confidence, which reduces worry. It allows us to put aside our continual worrying and focus on methods to improve ourselves.

2. Risk of physical sickness is reduced: Stress weakens the human body, making it more prone to illness and infection; being resilient in stressful situations considerably reduces this risk. Stress aggravates preexisting medical issues, and emotional resilience helps us relax and find constructive answers to unpleasant situations.

3. Longer-lasting and healthier relationships: Being emotionally resilient benefits everyone, not just anxious people, because the ability to accept that not everything in life will go our way, and that we have to bounce back, shrug it off, and get back into the ring, leads to healthier and stronger relationships. Having a partner who supports you increases your chances of success. When both partners are resilient, they may be able to concentrate on the positives while learning from the negatives. It also prevents people struggling with anxiety and overthinking from isolating themselves from those who love them when they face difficulties; instead, it improves their thinking and communication skills and helps them form stronger bonds.

MAIN IDEAS

Let's return to Daniel's situation as discussed at the beginning of this chapter. As Daniel's worry and overthinking intensified, his relationship with Lauren began to suffer. His constant preoccupation with small details and worst-case scenarios left little room for spontaneity, joy, and connection. While he was initially admired for his responsible nature, his excessive worry started to overshadow his positive qualities. Instead of being present and enjoying the moment with Lauren, his mind was consumed by overanalyzing every aspect of their relationship.

As time went on, Daniel's inability to switch off his worries created a growing distance between him and Lauren. Despite her attempts to reassure him and offer support, his mind remained fixated on imaginary problems and potential pitfalls. The lack of peace and relaxation within Daniel's mind made it challenging for him to truly appreciate and cherish the love they shared. Ultimately, the strain caused by his constant worrying became too much for their relationship to bear, leading to their breakup.

Daniel's experience highlights the destructive nature of excessive worry and overthinking in relationships. It serves as a reminder that finding a balance between responsibility and letting go of unnecessary anxiety is crucial for fostering healthy connections with others.

Anxiety and overthinking can have a negative impact on the dynamics of a relationship, affecting both persons involved. Anxiety frequently causes a state of perpetual tension, prompting romantic partners to doubt themselves, each other, and the stability of their connection. This can lead them to excessively examine every element of their interactions, resulting in hypersensitivity to perceived threats and a lack of trust. As a result, communication may become strained, intimacy may suffer, and tensions may flare up. The negative cycle of anxiety and overthinking can create a poisonous environment, weakening the relationship's basis of trust and emotional connection.

Furthermore, anxiety and overthinking can have a negative impact on a person's wellbeing, self-esteem, and mental health in a relationship. Constant worrying and ruminating can result in increased stress, sleep difficulties, and even medical problems. Individuals may become fixated on negative ideas and worst-case scenarios, making it difficult to appreciate the current moment or adopt a cheerful attitude. This self-centered attitude can also lead to greater demands for reassurance and affirmation from their partner, putting further strain on the relationship. If not addressed and managed successfully, anxiety and overthinking can contribute to a cycle of unhappiness, insecurity, and instability, damaging the relationship's general health and durability.

WORKBOOK THREE

Section 1: Self-Reflection

1. Describe your own experience with anxiety and overthinking in relationships. How does it manifest for you?

2. Reflect on how anxiety and overthinking have affected your past and current relationships. What negative patterns or challenges have you noticed?

3. Explore the possible underlying causes of your anxiety and overthinking in relationships. Are there any past experiences or personal beliefs that contribute to these patterns?

4. Section 2: Identifying the Impact

5. How do anxiety and overthinking affect your communication with your partner? Do you tend to overanalyze their words or actions? How does this impact the quality of your conversations?

6. Reflect on the level of trust in your relationship. Have anxiety and overthinking affected your ability to trust your partner fully? How does this impact your overall connection?

7. Consider the impact of anxiety and overthinking on intimacy and vulnerability. Do you find it difficult to be open and emotionally available due to these patterns? How does it affect your ability to connect on a deeper level?

Section 3: Communication and Conflict Resolution

8. Practice active listening exercises to improve your communication skills. This can include paraphrasing, summarizing, and asking open-ended questions.

Section 4: Self-Care and Anxiety Management

9. Identify self-care activities that help alleviate anxiety and promote emotional wellbeing. This could include exercise, journaling, or engaging in hobbies.

10. Seek professional help if needed. Research therapists or counselors specializing in anxiety and relationship issues. Consider reaching out for support and guidance.

Section 5: Building Trust and Nurturing the Relationship

11. Reflect on your partner's perspective and practice empathy. Put yourself in their shoes and consider how your anxiety and overthinking may affect them. Discuss your findings with your partner.

Conclusion:

Reflect on the insights gained from this workbook. Consider the changes you want to make in your approach to anxiety and overthinking in your relationship.

PART TWO

Connect More to Love More

In this second part, you'll be introduced to strategies by which you can prevent relationship anxiety and overthinking from ruining your relationship. This part consists of discussions on the following topics:

- Loosening the anxiety thread loop

- Deepening your connections

- Building healthy habits

You'll find valuable resources and guidance to overcome the challenges of relationship anxiety and overthinking. In focusing on loosening the anxiety thread loop, you'll learn techniques to interrupt negative thought patterns and cultivate a more balanced perspective. Additionally, you'll explore strategies for deepening your connection with your partner, fostering trust, and enhancing emotional intimacy. Through building healthy habits, you'll discover actionable steps to create a solid foundation for a thriving relationship.

Embrace this opportunity to empower yourself with the knowledge and skills to navigate relationship challenges with resilience and create a more harmonious and fulfilling partnership. Enjoy!

CHAPTER FOUR

LOOSENING THE ANXIETY THREAD LOOP

"Cast your burden on the Lord, And He shall sustain you; He shall never permit the righteous to be moved."

—Proverbs 55:22

"Anxiety is a whispering thread that tries to suffocate our dreams. Don't let it silence your potential. Gather the courage to break free and weave a tapestry of fulfillment."

—Roy T. Bennett

In the bustling city of New York, there was a man named Matt. He was a diligent and ambitious individual, but his drive for success often came at the cost of his peace of mind. In his relationships, Matt had a tendency to overanalyze every interaction, constantly second-guessing both himself and his partner and fearing rejection.

One day, Matt met Lily, a free-spirited artist with a radiant smile that could melt his worries away. As they embarked on their journey of love and companionship, Matt's anxiety began to tighten its grip, threatening to suffocate their connection and ruin their relationship. Sensitive to his distress, Lily, with her compassionate nature, decided to address the issue. She took Matt's hands and whispered, "Matt, I see the beauty in your heart, and I believe in us. Let's break free from the chains of anxiety and overthinking together. Trust in our love, trust in me." They began to work on exercises that could help Matt with his anxiety and also help Lily to become more patient and understanding.

Anxiety is a mental health problem that affects people all over the world. It is characterized by dread and agitation, which can seriously disrupt our daily life and general wellbeing. Academics and mental health specialists are constantly investigating methods to alleviate anxiety symptoms and make patients feel better. One intriguing concept that is gaining traction is known as "loosening the anxiety thread loop." The goal of this strategy is to figure out how to stop the cycle of anxious thoughts and behaviors that keeps us in a state of anxiety.

Neuroplasticity: It's Possible to Rewire Your Anxious Brain

Neuroplasticity is a fancy term that basically means our brains can change and adapt throughout our lives; it's "the brain's ability to rewire itself by paving new neural pathways when it feels the need to adapt" (Sharma, 2022). While it's true that the brain is "a beautiful thing" and "a complex learning machine to help you navigate life's many challenges" (Lebow, 2021), it also serves the role of protecting us from danger, and as a result it can become "confused, and to keep us safe, it can make us feel more anxious and alert" (Sharma, 2022). There is good news, though: "Your brain has the ability to rewire itself, making new connections between neurons and remapping the information you've gathered so far" (Lebow, 2021).

"By paving new neural pathways and creating new connections between neurons, we can train our brains to reduce anxiety and response" (Sharma, 2022). For example, if someone suffers a brain injury or a stroke and loses their motor skills, physical therapy can potentially help that person to regain those skills. This is due to neuroplasticity. And guess what? This doesn't only apply to physical skills; we can also "train [our] brain to promote positive thinking that can help improve [our] mental health" (Sharma, 2022).

It was once believed that the structure and function of the brain were fixed and unchanging after a certain age. However, new research has shown that the brain is pliable and capable of rewiring itself even in maturity. This notion of neuroplasticity offers hope for those who suffer from anxiety since it implies that it is feasible to rewire an anxious brain and lessen the impact of worry on one's life.

So, how does neuroplasticity work? Well, our brain's neurons can form new connections and adjust themselves based on our experiences and the things happening around us. If we keep activating certain neural pathways, those connections get stronger. On the other hand, if we stop using certain pathways, they weaken. For people with anxiety, this means that patterns of anxious thoughts and behaviors become deeply ingrained in the brain, making it harder to break free of the anxiety.

Identifying Negative Thought Patterns

Negative thinking happens at an unconscious level and is often the root cause of some of our negative behavior (Swaby, 2019). Negative thought patterns can also be referred to as cognitive distortions. By becoming aware of these patterns, we can challenge and reframe them, ultimately reducing anxiety and promoting healthier relationship dynamics. Types of cognitive distortions include:

1. Catastrophizing: This involves exaggerating the significance of events, such as when you make a mistake (Stress & Development Lab, Harvard University). For example, someone might catastrophize by believing that a minor disagreement with their partner will inevitably lead to the end of the relationship. Essentially, catastrophizing is

taking in the situation and coming to the (inaccurate) conclusion that "the worst outcome is going to happen to us" (Roncero, 2021).

2. Selective abstraction: This is "when we pay attention to a certain piece of information and ignore the rest of the information and context" (Roncero, 2021). Similar to catastrophizing, it involves magnifying certain negative elements and discounting positive or neutral aspects, leading to distorted perceptions and increased anxiety. In the context of a relationship, selective abstraction could manifest as fixating on a negative comment from your partner while disregarding the overall positive aspects of the partnership.

3. Personalization: This involves assuming excessive responsibility for negative events or outcomes, even when they are beyond one's control. In the context of a relationship, personalization can manifest as taking on the full burden of a problem, believing that you are solely responsible for the difficulties your partner is experiencing. For instance, someone may blame themselves entirely for a relationship conflict, disregarding external factors or the other person's role.

Identifying negative thought patterns is a crucial step in reducing anxiety and overthinking in your relationship. By recognizing cognitive distortions such as catastrophizing, selective abstraction, and personalization, you can challenge these negative patterns and cultivate more balanced and realistic thinking.

Challenging Your Negative Thoughts: What Works

Negative thoughts, or cognitive distortions, are "a form of unhealthy self-talk" and "can quickly consume all of our thoughts" (High Focus Treatment

Centers, 2021). So what can we do about it? "The key to changing your negative thoughts is to understand how you think now (and the problems that result), then use strategies to change these thoughts or make them have less of an effect" (Cuncic, 2023).

Negative thoughts have a way of sneaking in, messing with our heads, and making us doubt everyone—including our partner, the person we're meant to trust wholeheartedly. They really do have a way of throwing us off-balance, especially when it comes to relationships. But breathe a sigh of relief: we are more than able to challenge those thoughts and regain control *through Christ Who strengthens us.* By finding effective methods and strategies to tackle our negative thinking, we can break free from the grip of anxiety and build healthier, more beautiful relationships.

So, what really works when it comes to challenging negative thoughts?

1. Identifying and understanding: The first and most crucial step is to identify the negative thought pattern(s) you tend to experience. There are multiple patterns, including personalization, catastrophizing, selective abstraction, and black-and-white thinking, among many others. It is crucial to identify and understand these thought patterns. Read about them and about the kinds of emotions they bring up, as well as what triggers them.

2. Acceptance: I am sure this sounds confusing, doesn't it? *Robert, you just said we should and are more than able to challenge these negative thought patterns. Why then are you telling me to accept them?* Because you are accepting the thoughts for what they are: thoughts, and not facts. A negative thought is just something your mind has made up and not your reality.

3. Give yourself a break: It's so very easy to blame ourselves for anything that goes wrong. This thought pattern is called personalization and, as explained earlier, it involves assuming excessive responsibility for negative events or outcomes, even when they're beyond your control. In your relationship, it could manifest as taking responsibility for disagreements, or assuming any problem in your relationship is all your fault. This not only tears you down as a person, it could make you unnecessarily willing to stay in a wrong relationship, or could make your partner feel suffocated and manipulated. Giving yourself a break does not relieve you of all responsibility, but it involves accepting the fact that you are human, and that everyone makes mistakes (including you and your partner). Giving yourself a break can be both physical and mental. Physically, it may involve taking time off from work, engaging in leisure activities, or simply allowing yourself to rest and recover. Mentally, it entails giving your mind a break from constant thinking and worrying. It can also involve practicing self-care, disconnecting from the world for a while, and asking for help.

4. Mindfulness: "Mindfulness is the practice of gently focusing your awareness on the present moment over and over again" (Hoshaw, 2020). The mind is like a child with a sugar rush, always running wild. Mindfulness involves taking control over your mind, rather than letting it run roughshod over you. You can practice mindfulness by carrying out simple daily exercises like cooking or gardening and informing your mind about what you're doing at that particular moment. This helps you to focus on the present moment rather than being carried away by thoughts that most likely do not relate to that moment. You could also start a thought journal; writing down your thoughts (especially the ones that seem overwhelming) can be a

great way to release the tension and stress that typically come with the negativity. Why not add Bible verses to your thoughts as you write them down? This is a great way to counter the negative thinking, and it could help you to focus on what God says rather than what your mind says.

5. Gratitude: Yes, gratitude. Gratitude can be a great way of challenging your negative thoughts. Gratitude generally provides a countereffect to overthinking and negative thinking. Thinking about what you do have and being grateful to God can help you overcome those negative and ungrateful thoughts. Likewise, in your relationship, being grateful for your partner and reminiscing on the beautiful moments you've had together can help you overcome negative thoughts, doubts, and fears.*

*Click HERE to get these worksheets to practice some self-care and self-compassion techniques.

Practicing Positive Self-Talk

Self-talk can be defined as "the internal dialogue a person has with themselves" and "is a natural cognitive process" (Richards, 2022). Everyone naturally engages in self-talk throughout the day (Morris, 2016), but it's up to you whether that self-talk is positive and encouraging or negative and discouraging (Holland, 2020). Negative self-talk is an extremely damaging way of talking to yourself. It affects your emotions, leading to even more damaging self-talk and behavior. Essentially, it is a prominent component of the vicious anxiety cycle. For example, you may repeatedly tell yourself that you can't pass a difficult exam—and then, when you do fail, you say, "I knew it." And on it goes.

Now, please note that "positive self-talk doesn't mean ignoring the negative or unpleasant aspects of life. Instead, it's flipping the narrative so that you can approach these issues in a more positive and productive way" (DPS Staff, 2021). It involves creating "an internal dialogue that makes a person feel good about themselves" (Richards, 2022). If you cultivate positive self-talk, it can help you develop effective ways of coping with and letting go of your anxiety and overthinking. Methods by which you can practice positive self-talk include:

1. Recognize negative thinking: The first and most crucial step is to identify and recognize your negative thinking. As explained earlier, there are three major types of negative thought patterns:

   - Personalization—taking absolute responsibility for any negative event that occurs

   - Catastrophizing—exaggerating issues and imagining the worst possible outcome

   - Selective abstraction—paying attention to negative aspects of an issue and ignoring other factors

Recognizing your negative thinking can make it easier to turn your thoughts into positive ones. For example, if you begin to have wild thoughts about your partner cheating on you just because they weren't able to pick up your call, recognizing your negative thinking at that moment can help you convert "*Is she cheating on me?*" into "*She's probably busy. She'll call back as soon as she can.*"

2. Treat yourself the way you would treat a friend: If your friend were to come to you with unfounded and irrational suspicions about their partner cheating, wouldn't you speak sense to them calmly but

sternly? This is what I mean by treating yourself the way you would treat a dear friend. Kindly but sternly, talk to and treat yourself better.

3. Make self-care a priority: This is an essential step in practicing positive self-talk. Taking care of your physical, emotional, and mental wellbeing can greatly influence your internal dialogue. Make sure you're getting enough sleep, take breaks when needed, and engage in activities that can help you unwind and recharge. Learn to say no when necessary, and prioritize activities that can help you and your partner relax together and bond with each other. Draw boundaries as well if you feel they are needed.

4. Limit your exposure to negativity: It could be a friend, it could be social media. Whatever you feel is contributing to your negative thoughts concerning yourself and your relationship should be removed from your life. Deleting certain social media apps from your phone, or ghosting that particular person who never has anything positive to say, is not too great a sacrifice to make for the sake of your mental wellbeing and relationship.

5. Change your vocabulary: Self-talk is your inner dialogue, right? So what words do you tend to use when speaking to yourself? Changing your vocabulary involves being watchful and cautious with your words, and consciously using positive words and sentences rather than negative ones.

6. Practice positive affirmations: Posting positive affirmations and Bible verses about yourself around your room or in visible places around your space can be a great way to challenge negative self-talk.

7. Laugh: Learn to find the humor in situations around you. I'm not saying you should never take things seriously, but learn to let certain

things roll off your back and just laugh. Laugh at yourself, at funny situations, and with your partner.

Reversing the 4 Stages of Anxiety

The stages of anxiety are described by numerous theories and frameworks. The "anxiety cycle" described by Clark and Beck (2010) is a widely used model that describes four stages: trigger, assessment, physical response, and behavioral response. These stages help in developing an understanding of the progression and manifestation of anxiety symptoms.

The trigger is the starting point of the anxiety cycle. External occurrences or internal thoughts, memories, or feelings that cause anxiety are examples of triggers. Triggers can differ greatly amongst people and can include specific situations, social interactions, perceived threats, or even anticipatory anxiety. A trigger could be a word your partner says or their ignoring a call in your presence, for example. Triggers start the assessment process, which leads to the second stage of anxiety.

The trigger is mentally assessed in the second stage. This stage involves interpreting the trigger in regard to personal significance, threat, or danger. Cognitive assessments include beliefs, thoughts, and perceptions regarding the trigger, oneself, and one's ability to deal.

The third stage of the anxiety cycle involves the physical response. This stage encompasses the physiological reactions that accompany anxiety, such as increased heart rate, rapid breathing, muscle tension, sweating, and heightened alertness (Clark & Beck, 2010).

These physical symptoms are caused by the body's natural stress reaction, often known as the "fight-or-flight" response, which prepares a person to deal with perceived threats or hazards.

The behavioral response is the final stage of the anxiety cycle. This stage includes the anxiety-related avoidance behaviors that people participate in. Our behavioral responses to anxiety can differ depending on the nature of the anxiety. To relieve anxiety, some people engage in behaviors such as avoiding social situations or specific triggers, while others participate in safety-seeking activities or rituals. These activities are intended to regulate or relieve anxiety symptoms, but they can also reinforce and extend the anxiety cycle over time.

It is important to note that the stages of anxiety described above are not necessarily linear or isolated. They can interact and influence each other, creating a cyclic pattern (i.e., the anxiety cycle). For example, behavioral responses (such as avoidance) may reinforce cognitive assessments (such as confirming the perceived threat) and prolong the anxiety cycle (Clark & Beck, 2010).

Now, how do we reverse or counteract the effects of these stages? While reversing the four stages of anxiety may be difficult, there are methods that can assist us in managing and reducing anxiety symptoms. These strategies address each stage of the cycle, with the goal of breaking the pattern and encouraging a more adaptive response to triggers.

To address the trigger stage, individuals can benefit from identifying and understanding their specific triggers. Keeping a trigger diary or participating in self-reflection might help you identify thoughts and events that can cause anxiety. Cognitive restructuring approaches, such as challenging irrational thoughts or beliefs related to triggers, might assist in reframing negative interpretations and reducing perceived threats (Hofmann, 2011).

Individuals might concentrate on improving their cognitive assessments of triggers throughout the assessment stage. CBT (cognitive behavioral therapy) is a well-established strategy that focuses on recognizing and addressing erroneous thoughts and beliefs that lead to anxiety (Beck, 2011). Examining evidence for and against anxious beliefs, establishing more balanced ideas, and producing alternative explanations for triggers can all be part of this process. Acceptance-based therapies, such as Acceptance and Commitment Therapy (ACT), can also assist individuals in developing acceptance and willingness to feel anxiety while aligning their actions with their beliefs (Hayes et al., 2012).

Managing the physiological symptoms linked with anxiety is part of addressing the physical reaction stage. Regular exercise and relaxing activities like meditation can help control the body's stress response and promote general well-being (Rosenbaum et al., 2014).

In the behavioral response stage, individuals can work on gradually confronting and approaching feared situations through exposure-based techniques. Gradual exposure therapy allows individuals to confront anxiety-provoking situations in a controlled and systematic manner, gradually reducing avoidance behaviors (Choy et al., 2007). This can be accomplished by either imaginal exposure (mentally imagining the feared situation) or in vivo exposure (actually participating in the feared situation). With time, patience, and practice, individuals can gain confidence and minimize anxiety-related avoidance behaviors.

It is essential that I point out that reversing the anxiety stages will require relentless work, patience, and support. Working with a skilled mental health practitioner, such as a psychologist or therapist specializing in anxiety disorders, can provide greater help and support in applying these strategies to your life.

The 4 Rs That Work

Psychologist Jeffrey Schwartz created 4 Rs to assist in reducing anxiety (Pinnacle Recovery, 2019). They offer a way by which you can distance yourself from "an anxiety spiral" (Shea, 2021), acting as a framework for managing and overcoming anxiety. The 4 Rs are Relabel, Reattribute, Refocus, and Revalue. Let's explore each of these in more detail:

1. Relabel: The first step is to label what you're dealing with (Shea, 2021). Recognize that what you're experiencing is a manifestation of your anxiety (Burns, 1999). Labeling the issue can "put some of the power back in your hands, turning a rogue wave into something a little more manageable, or at least identifiable" (Shea, 2021). This allows you to separate yourself from the overwhelming emotions and gain a sense of control.

2. Reattribute: Next up, it's important to challenge and reframe the negative thoughts and beliefs that accompany your anxiety. Instead of attributing the feelings to personal failures or weaknesses, it's crucial to recognize that they are primarily driven by anxiety itself. You can detach your identity from the anxiety and acquire a more realistic perspective by reattributing the feelings to anxiety. While there might be other contributors to your anxiety, you need to realize that your current anxiety is due to those factors and not to your flaws as a person.

3. Refocus: Refocusing your mind involves consciously directing your thoughts away from your anxiety to something more positive and productive. It could involve engaging in activities you enjoy, calling a friend for a quick chitchat, or focusing on the present moment.

Refocusing helps break the cycle of overthinking and excessive worry associated with anxiety.

4. Revalue: It's now time to revalue. Ask yourself questions about what could have happened if you had given in to your anxiety. By challenging negative beliefs and assumptions associated with anxiety, you can reduce its influence over your thoughts and actions. Recognize that anxiety does not define you as a person and that you have the power to revalue its importance.

Implementing the four Rs is a continuous process that requires patience. Although progress is not always straightforward, you will be able to gradually let go of anxiety and overthinking by relabeling, reattributing, refocusing, and revaluing these patterns, thereby creating a healthy relationship built on trust, communication, and emotional wellbeing.

The Role of Self-Awareness

Self-awareness "gives us the power to influence outcomes"; it "helps us become better decision-makers and gives us more self-confidence" (Aronov-Jacoby, 2022). In the words of psychologists Shelley Duval and Robert Wicklund, it is "the ability to focus on yourself and how your actions, thoughts, or emotions do or don't align with your internal standards. If you're highly self-aware, you can objectively evaluate yourself, manage your emotions, align your behavior with your values, and understand correctly how others perceive you" (cited in Betz, 2022). Simply put, "Self-awareness is knowing yourself. It is understanding your feelings, motives, goals, and biases" (Soken-Huberty, 2023).

Self-awareness is essential for letting go of anxiety and overthinking in your relationships. It's all about developing a deep awareness of your own ideas, feelings, and habits, allowing you to gain crucial insights into what causes your anxiety and how it shows up in your relationships, allowing you to address and manage it better.

Being able to recognize and examine your anxious thoughts is a crucial element of self-awareness. When anxiety begins to seep in, simply noticing and being aware of these feelings and thoughts allows you to separate from them and restore control.

Self-awareness also assists you in recognizing how your anxiety affects your relationships. It enables you to observe how it influences your communication, emotional availability, and capacity to trust and connect with your spouse or partner. This awareness is effective because it allows you to differentiate between what is genuine and the distorted impressions caused by anxiety.

It takes time and effort to develop self-awareness. It entails paying attention to your thoughts, feelings, and behaviors in various settings, particularly during difficult times in your relationships. Self-reflection activities, writing, and counseling may all be extremely beneficial in increasing your self-awareness and developing the skills you need to handle anxiety and overthinking in your relationships.

Cognitive Restructuring for Negative Thoughts

Cognitive restructuring is a cornerstone of cognitive behavioral therapy (Stanborough, 2020). It is a technique mostly used to change our thought patterns. It can be used to replace negative thoughts with more positive and balanced ones that do not lead to anxiety.

The first thing to do is identify your negative thoughts: are you catastrophizing, personalizing, or thinking in terms of selective abstraction? After recognizing these patterns, the next thing to do is to examine the root factors. Rationally and calmly, identify the triggers. This leads to the next step, which involves examining whether there's any truth to your thoughts. After this, consciously and purposefully replace these thoughts with more balanced ones that relate to the situation but do not cause panic or anxiety.

How CBT Works

According to the UK's National Health Service (2022), "Cognitive behavioural therapy (CBT) is a talking therapy that can help you manage your problems by changing the way you think and behave." This technique is highly effective in allowing us to change our thought patterns in order to change our behavior (Davis, 2023).

The recognition that our thoughts, feelings, and behaviors are all interconnected is a core principle of CBT. Our thoughts have the ability to influence how we feel and act, and vice versa. Individuals suffering from anxiety and overthinking are prone to erroneous thinking patterns defined by negative assumptions, catastrophic interpretations, or excessive worry about future outcomes.

CBT helps people become aware of their incorrect thoughts and challenge the veracity of those thoughts. The therapist helps the client to discover and assess their automatic thoughts, looking at the evidence for and against them, followed by replacing irrational or negative thoughts with more balanced and realistic ones (Beck, 2011).

For example, if a person suffering from anxiety has the automatic thought, "My partner will leave me if I make a mistake," the therapist will assist them in analyzing the evidence for this assumption. They could talk about previous experiences, the partner's actions, and alternative theories. The client begins to reframe their thinking as a result of this process, seeing that their anxiety-driven beliefs are not supported by reliable evidence.

CBT focuses on changing behaviors that lead to anxiety and overthinking in addition to addressing thoughts. Individuals are encouraged to conduct behavioral experiments and put new coping techniques into practice in real-life settings.

CBT also acknowledges the impact of environmental and interpersonal factors on anxiety and overthinking. The therapist may explore relationship dynamics, communication patterns, and social support networks with the client in order to identify areas that require growth. This technique teaches people how their connections can both contribute to and ease anxiety and overthinking.

It's important to remember that CBT is a therapy in which the therapist and the client work together, and it is also short-term and time-bound. The client must participate actively in the therapy process, working with their therapist to develop goals and practice new skills. Treatment approaches and strategies are then applied in real life, helping the client apply what they have learned and continue improvement outside of treatment sessions.

Employing Graded Exposure

Graded exposure therapy focuses on breaking the link between your anxiety trigger and your brain's reaction that causes the physiological anxiety response (Hutchinson, 2022). As its name suggests, it involves gradually exposing yourself to feared situations and/or stimuli. A hierarchy is created, and you start by facing the smaller fears, slowly working up to the larger ones. It's quite different from flooding, which is another exposure technique that involves exposing yourself to the feared situations and/or stimuli all at once. Flooding is not often used, as it's difficult for most individuals to manage that level of exposure.

During the graded exposure process, the client is encouraged to apply the coping techniques and strategies already learned. Continuous exposure in this form helps the client to slowly but surely overcome their fears and anxiety-causing thoughts.

Using gradual exposure requires patience and perseverance. It is typical to feel some discomfort and worry during the process, but with each successful exposure, you can build resilience and acquire more control over your anxious thoughts and actions, including the ones that show up in your relationship.

Remember that the purpose of graded exposure therapy is to build a healthier relationship with anxiety rather than to eradicate all anxious thoughts. It is about learning to accept and regulate your anxiety while remaining involved in meaningful and happy relationships.

Neuroplasticity Exercises That Work

Neuroplasticity is our brain's ability "to change and adapt," and research shows that it's "a fundamental part of keeping cognitively fit" (Sugden, 2022). Your brain is like a muscle: the more you exercise it, the stronger it gets. When your brain processes new information, neurons fire, new pathways form, and the malleable brain alters its shape and structure (Thompson, 2022); isn't that incredible? For many years, it was believed that we were born with a finite number of neurons, and that as we grew older, these cells died—however, recent research has brought to light the beautiful realization that our brains can continue to change and develop throughout our adult years. Picture your brain as an interconnected interplay of neurons and pathways. These neurons and pathways light up as you use them; for example, thinking about the word "book" puts to work every neuron and pathway connected with the word "book." If you begin to learn a new language, new pathways are formed, and when you then think about the word "book," the new pathways connecting "book" to the new language are activated.

Improving your neuroplasticity has also been shown to reduce the incidence of age-related cognitive illnesses, so it's incredibly beneficial to engage in neuroplasticity exercises (Sugden, 2022).

Examples of neuroplasticity exercises include:

1. Learning a new language: As we discussed in the example above, studying a language is a fantastic opportunity to develop your neuroplasticity; "every word is an opportunity for a new neural connection to be created in the brain" (Sugden, 2022).

2. Learning how to play a musical instrument: Acquiring a new skill with a musical instrument "may increase connectivity between brain regions and help form new neural networks" (Ackerman, 2018). Additionally, studies show that learning a musical instrument lowers our risk of cognitive impairment later in life (Sugden, 2022).

3. Learning a physical skill: Working on a new physical skill, such as juggling, is a great way to increase your brain's neuroplasticity as you create new pathways related to the connection between vision and movement (Sugden, 2022).

4. Playing stimulating games like chess: A mentally stimulating game, such as chess, "has endless potential for neuroplasticity" (Thompson, 2022).

5. Exercise: Of course, we all know that exercise is good for us on a physical level, and it can reduce anxiety and overthinking in its own right, but guess what? It can also increase neuroplasticity because it actually changes the structure of the brain (Sugden, 2022).

6. Non-dominant hand exercises: Practicing skills with your non-dominant hand also helps your brain to form new connections (Ackerman, 2018). For example, you could attempt to write a sentence or brush your teeth with your non-dominant hand. One expert suggests doing these exercises "while balancing on one leg for a double neuroplasticity bonus" (Thompson, 2022).

By actively engaging in neuroplasticity exercises such as these, you can reshape your neural pathways and reduce your tendency to be anxious and overthink about your relationship.

Cognitive Restructuring Worksheets

The following worksheets are designed to help you practice cognitive restructuring techniques and loosen the anxiety thread loop in your relationship. By challenging and reframing your negative thoughts, you can gain a more balanced perspective and reduce anxiety and overthinking. Take your time to work through each exercise, and feel free to add any additional insights or reflections as you progress. Remember, this is a process of self-discovery and growth. Let's begin!

Worksheet 1: Identifying Negative Thought Patterns

Instructions:

- Reflect on your recent experiences in relationships.

- Write down any recurring negative thoughts or beliefs that come to mind.

- Consider the specific situations or triggers that tend to activate these negative thoughts.

- Take note of the emotions associated with these thoughts.

Example:

- Negative Thought: "I'm not good enough for my partner."

- Triggering Situation: When my partner spends time with their friends without me.

- Emotions: Inadequacy, insecurity, jealousy

Worksheet 2: Cognitive Restructuring

Instructions:

- Choose one negative thought identified in Worksheet 1 to work with.

- Write down the evidence that supports this negative thought.

- Now, challenge the negative thought by finding alternative evidence or perspectives that contradict it.

- Generate a more balanced and realistic thought or belief based on the evidence you have gathered.

- Write down the new thought or belief and consider how it might affect your feelings and behaviors in your relationship.

Example:

- Negative Thought: "I'm not good enough for my partner."

- Supporting Evidence: Sometimes I make mistakes and feel insecure.

- Challenging Evidence: My partner tells me they love and appreciate me. I have qualities that they admire.

- New Thought: "I have my own unique strengths and qualities that make me worthy of love and affection."

- Impact on Feelings and Behaviors: This new belief boosts my self-esteem and allows me to feel more secure in my relationship.

Worksheet 3: Applying Cognitive Restructuring

Instructions:

- Recall a recent situation in which you experienced anxiety or overthinking in your relationship.

- Write down the negative thoughts that emerged from that situation.

- Apply the cognitive restructuring process by challenging the negative thought with alternative evidence and generating a more balanced thought.

- Reflect on how this new thought might have influenced your emotions and behaviors in that situation.

By practicing these exercises regularly, you can develop a more balanced and realistic perspective, promoting greater emotional wellbeing and healthier connections. Remember, change takes time and effort, so be patient with yourself.

CBT Worksheets

Worksheet 1: Recognizing Negative Thoughts

Instructions:

- Reflect on your recent experiences in your relationship(s).

- Write down any negative thoughts or beliefs that have contributed to your anxiety and overthinking.

- Identify the triggers or specific situations that tend to activate these negative thoughts.

- Note the emotions or physical sensations associated with these thoughts.

Worksheet 2: Challenging the Thoughts

Instructions:

- Choose one negative thought identified in Worksheet 1 to focus on.

- Write down the evidence that supports this negative thought.

- Now, challenge the negative thought by examining the evidence against it.

- Generate a more realistic and balanced thought based on the evidence you have gathered.

- Write down the new thought and consider how it might influence your emotions and behaviors in your relationship.

Worksheet 3: Behavior Experiment

Instructions:

- Identify a specific anxiety-provoking situation in your relationship.

- Write down the negative thought associated with that situation.

- Create a behavioral experiment to test the validity of the negative thought.

- Plan and carry out the experiment, noting any observations or new insights gained.

- Reflect on the results and consider how they challenge or reshape the negative thought.

Remember to practice these techniques consistently and be patient with yourself as you navigate the journey towards a healthier relationship.

MAIN IDEAS

Let's return to Matt and Lily from the opening of this chapter. Through their shared commitment and support for one another, the couple embarked on a journey of growth and healing. They recognized that overcoming anxiety and overthinking required both individual effort and a strong bond between them. They challenged their negative thoughts by engaging in cognitive restructuring, encouraging one another to replace self-doubt with self-compassion and realistic perspectives. Additionally, they embraced graded exposure therapy, gradually facing their fears and insecurities as a team and celebrating each small victory along the way. As they navigated this path together, their love and trust blossomed, and the grip of anxiety slowly loosened its hold.

When it comes to letting go of anxiety and overthinking in your relationship, loosening the anxiety thread loop is crucial. By actively incorporating strategies like cognitive restructuring, graded exposure, gratitude practice, and behavioral activation, you have the power to reshape your thoughts, face your fears step by step, stay present in the moment, cultivate positive emotions, and engage in meaningful activities with your partner. These practices work hand in hand with the brain's neuroplasticity, allowing you to rewire your thinking patterns and reduce anxiety and overthinking. Remember, it takes dedication, patience, and support, but by breaking free from the anxiety thread loop, you can nurture healthier relationships and experience better emotional wellbeing.

WORKBOOK FOUR

Section 1: Understanding Your Anxiety

- What are some common triggers for anxiety and overthinking in your relationship?

- How does anxiety impact your thoughts, emotions, and behaviors in your relationship?

- Reflect on past experiences where anxiety and overthinking have affected your relationship(s). What patterns or themes do you notice?

Section 2: Cognitive Restructuring

- Identify one negative thought or belief you commonly have about yourself or your relationship. Challenge this belief by asking yourself: What evidence supports this thought? What evidence contradicts it?

- Replace negative thoughts with more balanced and helpful alternatives. Write down affirmations or positive statements you can repeat to yourself when anxiety arises.

- How can you reframe situations in your relationship to focus on more realistic and constructive perspectives?

Section 3: Graded Exposure

- Create a fear hierarchy related to your anxiety. List situations or actions that elicit that anxiety, starting from least to most anxiety-provoking.

- Choose one situation from your fear hierarchy and plan a small step you can take to expose yourself to it. What support or resources do you need to ensure a safe and manageable exposure?

- Reflect on your experiences after engaging in graded exposure. How did you feel before, during, and after the exposure? Did your anxiety and overthinking change? What did you learn from the process?

Section 4: Building Positive Experiences

- Identify activities or hobbies that bring you joy and fulfillment. How often do you engage in these activities? How can you incorporate them into your routine more regularly?

- Practice gratitude by reflecting on and writing down three things you appreciate about your relationship each day. How does this practice influence your mindset and overall wellbeing?

- Share positive experiences and moments of growth with your partner. How does celebrating these moments contribute to a stronger connection and reduced anxiety?

Section 6: Support and Self-Care

- Who can you turn to for support when you're feeling overwhelmed by anxiety and overthinking about your relationship? How can you communicate your needs effectively to them?

- What self-care practices are essential for managing your anxiety and promoting your wellbeing? Create a self-care plan and commit to implementing it regularly.

Remember, this workbook is designed to guide you through the process of loosening the anxiety thread loop. Take your time, be kind to yourself, and embrace the journey of growth and letting go. You have the strength and resilience to cultivate healthier, more fulfilling relationships.

CHAPTER FIVE

DEEPENING YOUR CONNECTIONS

"The words of the reckless pierce like swords, but the tongue of the wise brings healing."

—Proverbs 12:18

"The most important thing in communication is hearing what isn't said."

—Peter Drucker

Malcolm had always believed that love is enough to keep a relationship going, which is why he didn't try to deepen his connection with Caroline when they got married—but it turns out he couldn't have been more wrong. As a kid, he was famed for being the cool, aloof kid who wasn't bothered by anything, but adulthood is a whole different ballgame, as he would soon come to know. Shortly after his marriage to Caroline, they began experiencing problems: he wouldn't make time to just relax and have a real conversation with her or sit on the couch with her and talk to her about things that matter (all of which build trust and intimacy in a relationship). Malcolm was as bullheaded as they come. Slowly, this led to misunderstandings which could have been resolved easily if the partners were communicating with each other. It then led to trust issues, which led to fights, and eventually a separation that left Malcolm wondering what went wrong.

So, tell me—what do you think went wrong? Hopefully, the answer is pretty clear: they didn't build a deep connection that would sustain and warm them during the cold, harsh times in life.

What does it mean to deepen your connection in a relationship? Just like it takes two to tango, it takes two partners to make the effort to be closer and more intimate with each other. Being deeply connected means being trusting and loving as well as supportive and communicating with each other about everything going on. These little "unimportant" things strengthen the bonds of a relationship and bring the partners closer as well as giving them a deeper understanding of each other.

The Role of Effective Communication

The role of effective communication in a relationship cannot be overemphasized (Smith, 2021). It is key to a healthy relationship. All couples have different modes of communication, so they have to find what works for them and stick to it. Communication helps us to understand our partner, which prevents major issues and deepens our connection (as long as we remain open and trusting enough to communicate). Communication is essential because no one is a superhuman with mind-reading powers; we actually have to say what's on our mind so we can work together with our partner to find solutions. The more we do this, the more each partner knows what the other needs, sometimes even without verbal communication.

Some of the reasons effective communication is so important are:

1. Intimacy: Intimacy can mean different things for different couples. For some, it's romantic; for some, it's the simple acts that make you feel like you are your partner's world. A simple act of intimacy could be bringing your partner who works as a teacher a cup of honey tea, knowing their voice is strained from work. These little things help show your partner that you listen to them when they talk about work or their life or the future. Effective communication is not just about

talking but also about listening and trying to see things from their point of view, which gives you a deeper understanding of who they are and what makes them tick. When there is effective communication in your relationship, intimacy is a sure result.

2. Trust: Communicating your interests, thoughts, experiences, and ideas with your partner shows them you trust them and that they can trust you with the same. This is a one-way ticket to a healthy relationship. Trust is one of the essential elements of a relationship. The presence of trust prevents unnecessary arguments that arise from assuming the worst of each other. When both partners trust each other completely, they have faith in each other, and whenever there's a problem, they can bring it up in a calm and respectful manner instead of casting blame without proof or interrogating each other because of their insecurity. When partners trust each other completely, they are emotionally connected and can weather any storm that may threaten their bond.

3. Companionship: Another important effect of communication is that it builds companionship. The sharing of interests and experiences creates a sense of comradeship between the partners, and having someone to whom you can talk about anything is the best treasure in the world.

4. Concentration on major problems: Another role of effective communication is that it helps partners focus on the major problems threatening their bond and allows them to make time to discuss and tackle these problems head-on, rather than avoiding them and getting distracted by little things.

Common Communication Pitfalls to Avoid

"If you and your partner are struggling to understand one another's point of view, it's possible you may open yourself up to common communication mistakes" (Baum, 2021). Here are some common communication pitfalls to avoid:

1. Not listening: When having conversations with your partner, you should be giving them your full attention, and that means staying off your phone and turning off the music or television so you can focus. However, some people do all of this and still don't listen to their partner. Listening to your partner involves hearing what they're saying, giving them the floor to express themselves, and not interrupting them, but also asking questions to show you're interested and engaged. Failing to listen and interrupting just to drop a rebuttal or two is rude and can lead to a whole myriad of problems, which could sink the relationship.

2. Not acknowledging your partner's point of view: Is there real communication between partners if they don't try to see things from each other's point of view? No, there isn't. Why? Because refusing to acknowledge your partner's point of view will make them feel like you don't care. Seeing things from their perspective will help you understand why they do things, why they need more assurance, why they react the way they do, etc.

3. Jumping to conclusions: Jumping to conclusions about what your partner is discussing with you because you feel you've heard something like it before or you know how it ends is just rude, but is also actually quite common. It's disastrous to constantly interrupt your partner and assume you know what they're going to say. By

doing this, you're missing the message they're trying to convey and at the same time you're making them feel unimportant.

4. Avoiding conflict: Most people would rather avoid a difficult situation than tackle it head-on. Why? Because they would rather avoid conflict than face it due to the effects it might have on their relationship. The irony here is that avoiding conflict has a greater negative effect on a relationship than facing such conflict. When partners are withholding information from each other or refusing to address problems, the relationship is sure to crumble sooner rather than later.

5. Being indirect and/or closed off: Communicating indirectly with your partner because you feel they should know what you're saying or what you want is not exactly clever. We need to understand that our partners cannot read our minds, so expecting them to know what we want when we don't express it is weird and disastrous for the relationship. There should be "no guesswork that opens you up to potential communication struggles" (Baum, 2021). Being straightforward with your partner helps prevent misunderstandings and larger problems.

The Art of Active Listening

I know you're probably thinking, "This is my thing; I'm a good listener." Well, I'm sorry to tell you that you're most likely not. Perhaps you've heard the quote, "There's a difference between listening and waiting for your turn to speak" (Grossman, 2018). There's a difference between actively listening to someone and just waiting for them to finish so you can drop your rebuttal or give a response. Many relationships have been crippled and destroyed because of the inability of the partners to actively listen to each other. When actively listening to someone, you're paying them the utmost attention, and this shows them how valuable they are to you. Active listening is an art, and like every piece of artwork, it takes time and effort to create something beautiful (which, in this case, is a healthy, long-lasting relationship).

The following are tips to help you become a better active listener:

1. Focus and pay rapt attention to the speaker: To actively listen to someone, you have to pay full attention to them and what they're talking about. Don't have your phone in your hand; put it, and any other distractions, away (Grossman, 2018). You must make eye contact in order to catch their facial expressions and deduce how they're feeling as well as read their body language and tone. All these factors will give you an idea of how they're truly feeling and the message they're trying to pass across to you. Some individuals say one thing and mean the other, so it's the attention to minor details that prevents misunderstandings and costly misinterpretations.

2. No interruptions: Being an active listener means more than just hearing what your partner has to say; it means not interrupting them even when they say something you don't agree with. Interruptions don't necessarily have to be verbal, either—you could interrupt your partner by fake coughing or making obscene gestures. The absence of interruptions in your conversations will make your partner feel valued and loved.

3. Ask clarifying questions: If you don't understand something, asking questions like, "Can you explain that more?" when your partner pauses is key to being an active listener. It shows that you're interested in the conversation at hand, that you genuinely care, and that you want to know more.

4. Don't jump to conclusions: There's a reason this was also included in our list of communication pitfalls in the previous section. When you're listening to someone, it's critical not to jump to conclusions. All of us sometimes battle with the urge to jump in and end a statement for someone or guess quite loudly how a story ends. However, this behavior can be quite disastrous for a relationship, as it is disrespectful and not part of active listening.

Other quick tips include:

- Don't impose your own opinions.
- Don't get defensive and emotional.
- Don't be judgmental.

Building Deeper Connections With Vulnerability

What does vulnerability have to do with it? Well, vulnerability is "a big part of authenticity and connection" (Iyarn, 2020). However, in today's world, vulnerability is synonymous with weakness, and to be weak means to be trampled upon by others. This is why many hide their real selves and pretend to be emotionless and cold. An example of how society has made us believe vulnerability is weak is the saying, "Men don't cry." Instead of being encouraged to express their emotions and talk about problems with someone, men are taught to "suck it up" and "man up." But what many don't know is that being vulnerable with someone shows them the real you—and by the real you, I don't mean the detached version of you, but the corny, goofy, and emotional hot mess we all are inside. Being vulnerable and expressing your emotions doesn't make you weak; it shows that you're strong and confident enough to be open about yourself.

Being vulnerable with someone builds intimacy and stronger connections, which is key to a healthy, happy relationship. When we show someone our most vulnerable self, it sends a message that we trust them, and this builds a deep connection that can weather any storm. It also creates a safe space for them to open up to you in return. Being vulnerable with someone shows them your flaws and insecurities; it reveals your imperfect and beautiful self, and this is a step towards building a relationship that will stand the test of time. Vulnerability can also lead to growth as we accept that we're not going to be perfect no matter how hard we try, but we can be the best versions of our flawed selves if we try hard enough.

Being vulnerable builds deeper and more meaningful connections and gives us the chance to be open and experience ourselves in ways we haven't dreamed of. The first step to being vulnerable is accepting that you're imperfect and beautiful just as you are, then working towards mastering your imperfections. With time, you'll become the best version of yourself.

The Role of Intimacy

Intimacy, though hard to define, is that unexplainable feeling of trust and closeness you have with your partner. It is that feeling you get when you're sitting together in silence, holding hands. Sometimes you don't even have to speak to understand what the other the person is currently feeling. Intimacy "is all about feeling alive, content, ecstatic, and at the same time, being vulnerable" (Smith, 2021).

Emotional, intellectual, spiritual, and physical intimacy are all aspects of intimacy. Emotionally speaking, sharing your feelings, concerns, dreams, and weaknesses with your partner creates a secure and supportive environment for real self-expression. Intellectual intimacy involves having meaningful talks, sharing ideas, and respecting one another's point of view. Spiritual intimacy brings you together on a deeper level, allowing you to share your values, beliefs, and purpose. It involves being able to pray with and for each other, growing together as you both learn from the Word, and work together in fulfilling purpose and enriching your lives.

Intimacy is essential for the growth and deepening of your relationship. It entails a strong emotional, physical, and psychological bond with your partner, promoting feelings of closeness, vulnerability, and trust. Anxiety and overthinking, unfortunately, frequently obstruct one's ability to completely feel and grow in intimacy.

Anxiety and overthinking can impede the formation and maintenance of intimacy in a variety of ways. First, anxiety is frequently caused by a fear of vulnerability and rejection. We may hesitate to open up emotionally or disclose our actual selves when we are apprehensive, fearing criticism or desertion. Overthinking can increase our worries by causing us to overthink every interaction, mistrust our partner's motives, or invent scenarios that may not be accurate. These behaviors can obstruct intimacy by keeping us from truly engaging and connecting with our partner.

Intimacy is a wonderful and transformational journey that involves transparency, vulnerability, and a real desire to connect with your partner. Here are some suggestions for cultivating intimacy:

1. Create a safe space: Create a non-judgmental setting in which you and your partner may express yourselves genuinely. Encourage open conversation, active listening, and respect for one another. This secure environment will promote closeness and trust.

2. Demonstrate emotional availability: Be emotionally accessible to your partner and receptive to their feelings and experiences. Demonstrate

empathy, understanding, and support. Allow your partner to connect with your inner self by openly and honestly communicating your own thoughts and feelings. Remember, intimacy requires vulnerability. Even if it's difficult, keep reminding yourself that there is strength in vulnerability and give yourself to your partner. You can also discuss the difficulties you have opening up, and together you can work on a solution or compromise that works for you both. Doing this should make you less scared of judgment or of being hurt.

3. Spend quality time together: Schedule uninterrupted time to interact with your partner. Engage in intimate activities such as going on dates, taking walks together, or simply having meaningful conversations. Take a break from serious activities once in a while and just have fun together. Do silly things like having a food fight, or playing board games and attaching prizes. Quality time establishes the foundation for emotional intimacy.

4. Explore shared interests: Participate in things that both of you enjoy and find meaningful. Discover new activities or rediscover old ones together. Shared interests and experiences strengthen bonds and provide for quality time and shared memories.

5. Practice trust and honesty: The cornerstone of intimacy is trust. Maintain open and honest communication and be trustworthy. Trust your partner and be open and vulnerable with them. Building trust lays a solid basis for intimacy to flourish.

6. Pursue continual growth: Intimacy is a lifelong adventure that requires continual growth. Be willing to learn new things about yourself and your relationship. Accept new experiences, challenges,

and opportunities for personal development. Allow your relationship to deepen and evolve through time.

Humor Also Helps

Have you ever heard the phrase, "Laughter is the best medicine"? Not only is laughter good for you, but having a sense of humor can be attractive to your partner as well (Greengross, 2018). In fact, a sense of humor often shows up near the top of people's list of desirable traits in a romantic partner (DiDenato, 2013).

Humor, while often overlooked, can play an important role in deepening your connection and promoting a sense of joy and closeness in your relationship. It has the ability to relieve stress, reduce anxiety, and generate a happy and lighthearted environment. You may find you can let go of some fear and overthinking by embracing humor, allowing for a more honest and meaningful connection with your partner.

Here are just a few of the benefits of bringing humor into your relationship:

1. Icebreaker and bonding tool: Humor is an excellent icebreaker, allowing people to feel more at ease with one another. Sharing a chuckle or a funny moment might assist in breaking down boundaries and fostering togetherness. It can be a terrific approach to start a conversation, connect with someone, and establish trust.

2. Stress reduction: Relationships can be stressful, conflicting, and challenging at times. By brightening the mood and dissipating tension, humor functions as a natural stress reliever. It provides a brief respite from the stresses of everyday life, allowing you and your partner to rest, recharge, and approach challenges with new eyes.

3. Enhanced communication: Humor can improve communication by creating a lively and open environment. It promotes active listening by allowing you and your partner to engage in clever banter, share amusing anecdotes, and laugh together. This lighthearted way to communicate fosters greater understanding, empathy, and a stronger bond between partners.

Clearly, humor in your everyday life and in your relationship can be a wonderful and gratifying experience. Here are some tips for incorporating humor into your interactions with your partner:

1. Be playful: Approach situations with a lighthearted attitude. Look for ways to add humor into regular activities, such as lively banter, witty quips, or amusing observations. Allow your imagination to run wild (not too wild, though!) and embrace your inner child.

2. Find common ground: Discover mutual hobbies and humor preferences with your partner. Together, you can watch comedy shows or movies, or read funny books. Discuss hilarious anecdotes or funny memories from your past. Developing a shared sense of humor strengthens your bond.

3. Embrace mistakes and laughter: Instead of being frustrated by errors or mishaps, learn to laugh at them. Find humor in life's imperfections and motivate your partner to do the same. Laughing together improves your bond and boosts resilience.

Keep in mind that comedy is very subjective, and what one person considers hilarious may not be entertaining to another. There is a difference between laughing at someone and laughing with them. So, even when having fun, be cautious and sensitive. Genuine humor should provide joy and connection.

Conflict Resolution Strategies You Need

"Conflict is inherently uncomfortable for most of us, in both personal and professional contexts, but learning to effectively handle conflicts in a productive, healthy way is essential" (Krakoff, n.d). Conflicts "are struggles that can arise during an active disagreement of opinions or interests, so it's important to understand how to navigate and resolve them" (Herrity, 2022). Developing the skill of conflict resolution can take many years of practice and effort, but there are some simple things you can start out with to begin improving this skill (Krakoff, n.d).

Any relationship will inevitably have conflict, but how we handle those conflicts has a big influence on just how strong and deep our bonds are. And so, it is important that we develop effective conflict resolution techniques. Here are some crucial tactics to take into account:

1. Open and respectful communication: Conflict resolution requires effective communication. Establish a private, judgment-free area where both of you feel free to communicate your ideas and emotions. Engage in active listening, make an effort to comprehend one another's viewpoints, and react with respect and empathy.

2. Focus on the issue, not your partner: When discussing the conflict, remember to keep the conversation on the specific issue at hand rather than insulting, criticizing, or demeaning your partner and what they have to say. Keep your focus on finding a solution rather than bringing up sensitive personal topics (such as past disagreements you have had, or the past mistakes of your partner) that could worsen the

problem and prevent you both from communicating effectively. You can do this by taking a deep breath or a timeout whenever you notice you are both off-topic. Waiting for your emotions to cool off is also an effective tip; however, be careful it does not reach the point of keeping malice.

3. Engage in problem-solving: Use your disagreements as a chance to work together on a resolution through cooperative problem-solving. Take into account all of your options and seek solutions that satisfy the requirements of both of you. Be adaptable and open-minded, prepared to consider your partner's opinions and thoughts.

4. Use "I" not "you": Use "I" phrases to convey your thoughts and feelings to avoid placing blame or coming across as defensive. For example, say, "I feel hurt when..." rather than, "You always..." This way, you are taking accountability rather than blaming your partner and causing them to lash out in defense .

5. Apologize and forgive: If you have offended your partner or made a mistake, accept responsibility for your actions and provide a heartfelt apology. Likewise, be willing to overlook your partner's transgressions and let go of grudges. Forgiveness and apologies are effective means of mending your relationship and strengthening your bond.

Keep in mind that conflict resolution is a continuous process that calls for patience, understanding, and a sincere desire to maintain and nurture the relationship. By using these techniques, you may improve your relationship and let go of any anxiety or overthinking that could result from unresolved problems.

Setting and Maintaining Healthy Boundaries

You may think that boundaries are only for people you're not very close with or who consistently try to hurt or offend you in some way, but they're actually necessary in romantic relationships too. In your relationship, you can "think of [boundaries] as a framework rather than rigid guidelines" (Pattemore, 2021). Setting and upholding healthy boundaries is essential for developing and fostering long-lasting, satisfying bonds. Boundaries are rules we set up to safeguard our physical, emotional, and mental health while also honoring the boundaries of others. We build a foundation of trust, encourage self-care, and lessen anxiety and overthinking by establishing and upholding boundaries.

"Without healthy boundaries, your relationships can become toxic and unsatisfying and your well-being can suffer" (Reid, 2023). Our boundaries indicate where we stop and others start. They aid in the development of our sense of self, independence, and private space. Boundaries cover a wide range of topics, including time-related, emotional, physical, and intellectual ones. Setting and upholding boundaries begin with understanding their significance.

Here are some helpful hints to help you with establishing and maintaining healthy boundaries with your partner:

1. Begin with self-reflection: Take some time to consider your own needs, values, and personal boundaries. Consider what makes you feel at ease and what makes you uncomfortable. Understanding your personal limits is vital before conveying them effectively to your partner.

2. Engage in open communication: Discuss your boundaries with your partner in an open and honest manner. Express your needs, desires,

and expectations clearly while carefully listening to their point of view. Try to talk gently but firmly as much as possible. You might even try to find the humor in the issue and joke about it once the serious talk is finished; this can soothe whatever sting your partner may have felt throughout the discussion.

3. Be specific and concrete: When establishing boundaries, be specific and provide concrete examples. Define which behaviors, activities, or situations are acceptable and which are not. This clarity helps to avoid misunderstandings and keeps you both on the same page.

4. Listen to your gut: When it comes to boundaries, pay heed to your feelings and trust your gut. Respect your intuition if something doesn't seem right or correspond with your values and principles. Trust yourself and explain your feelings to your significant other honestly.

5. Have mutual respect: Boundaries should be mutually respected. Respect your partner's boundaries as much as they should respect yours. This reciprocal respect generates an environment of understanding and equality in the relationship.

6. Do regular check-ins: Reevaluate your boundaries by regularly checking in with yourself and your partner. Boundaries may need to change or evolve as your relationship does. Continuous conversation and good boundary maintenance are made possible through open and honest communication.

Keep in mind that boundaries are an important part of both self-care and a healthy relationship, and that it's acceptable to alter your boundaries as you grow and develop and gain experience.

Effective Communication Worksheets for Couples

Instructions: Answer the following questions and complete the suggested exercises to improve your communication with your partner.

Part 1: Self-Reflection

- How would you rate your current communication skills with your partner on a scale of 1 to 10? (1 = poor, 10 = excellent) Why did you choose this rating?

- Identify one area of communication that you would like to improve in your relationship. Describe why this area is important to you.

- What are some barriers or challenges that you and your partner face when it comes to effective communication?

Part 2: Active Listening

- Describe what active listening means to you and why it is crucial for effective communication in a relationship.

- Recall a recent conversation with your partner where your active listening was lacking. What could you have done differently to improve your listening skills in that situation?

Exercise:

Choose a topic of discussion with your partner. Take turns speaking and practicing active listening skills. Afterward, reflect on the experience and discuss how it felt to be listened to attentively.

Part 3: Non-Verbal Communication

- How important is non-verbal communication in your relationship? Provide some examples of non-verbal cues that you and your partner commonly use.

- Reflect on a recent disagreement or conflict with your partner. Were there any non-verbal cues that were misinterpreted or that contributed to the misunderstanding? How could you address this in the future?

Exercise:

Engage in a role-play activity with your partner where you communicate without using words. Pay attention to each other's non-verbal cues and discuss the challenges and insights gained from this exercise.

Part 4: Expressing Needs and Emotions

- Why is it important to effectively express your needs and emotions to your partner? What impact can it have on your relationship?

- Share one specific need or emotion that you find challenging to express to your partner. What makes it difficult, and how do you think it affects your relationship?

Exercise:

Write a letter or journal entry expressing your needs or emotions to your partner. Take turns sharing and discussing the contents of your letters, focusing on understanding and support.

Part 5: Conflict Resolution

- Describe a conflict resolution style that you and your partner often adopt. How effective is this style in resolving conflicts? What improvements could be made?

- Think of a recent conflict that escalated and was not resolved satisfactorily. How could you have approached the situation differently to achieve a more positive outcome?

Exercise:

Choose a previous conflict that remains unresolved. Practice using active listening, expressing needs, and finding a compromise or resolution together. Reflect on the process and its impact on your relationship.

Conclusion:

Improving communication skills takes time and practice. Use this worksheet as a starting point for open discussions with your partner. Remember, effective communication is essential for building a strong and healthy relationship.

Vulnerability and Intimacy Exercises

As we discussed in the section on vulnerability, "vulnerability creates true, meaningful connection" (Mantell, n.d). If you can create vulnerability and intimacy within your relationship, "you share your feelings, needs, fears, successes, and failures knowing you will continue to be loved and cared for by your partner" (Madison, 2020). And although it might be extremely scary, vulnerability is interwoven with intimacy, and one cannot exist without the other.

Here are some exercises you can practice:

1. Show gratitude: Express your gratitude for and to each other. Tell your partner about specific qualities you value in them or positive parts of your connection. This activity encourages emotional intimacy and vulnerability and cultivates a positive mindset.

2. Write love letters: Express your affection, awe, and gratitude through sincere letters to one another. Spend some time thinking about how you feel about your partner. Share these letters together, letting yourself be open to receiving love and encouragement.

3. Schedule emotional check-ins: Continually update one another on your emotional health. Open-ended inquiries like, "How are you feeling today?" and, "Is there anything on your mind that you'd like to share?" are appropriate. This fosters vulnerability by giving each of you the chance to express more intense feelings and worries.

4. Share weaknesses: Talk to your partner about any anxieties or weaknesses you may have. Talk about your aspirations, worries, and insecurities. This activity fosters closeness and trust by providing a safe area for both partners to comfort and reassure one another.

5. Build trust: Take part in trust-building activities that call for transparency and require you to rely on one another. This can be trust falls, blindfolded trust walks, or other activities that foster a sense of security and strengthen your bonds of affection.

Remember that vulnerability exercises should be approached with sensitivity and respect for each other's comfort levels. It's important to create an environment where both of you will feel safe and supported. There is bound to be some discomfort or fear, as vulnerability and intimacy can be scary to some; however, since these exercises are to foster intimacy, you should try as much as possible to ignore your fears and allow yourself to be vulnerable.

MAIN IDEAS

Think back to Malcolm's situation. In the wake of his separation from his wife, Caroline, Malcolm underwent a period of self-reflection and soul-searching. He realized that his belief in the power of love alone was misguided, and that sustaining a healthy relationship requires active effort and a willingness to deepen emotional connections. Through this painful experience, Malcolm learned the importance of effective communication, vulnerability, and being present for his partner. He vowed to make changes in his approach to his relationship, committing to being more attentive, empathetic, and open. He and Caroline eventually got back together—but not after a lot of hard work, patience, and soul-baring exercises and questions.

Deepening your connection with your partner is a wonderful journey that can assist you in letting go of anxiety and overthinking in your relationship. By practicing self-awareness, embracing vulnerability, and employing effective strategies such as effective communication, setting healthy boundaries, humor, and engaging in intimacy exercises, we can create a solid foundation for a meaningful and fulfilling relationship. It is through these practices that we can cultivate trust, intimacy, and emotional connection, ultimately allowing us to experience deeper levels of love and fulfillment in our relationship.

WORKBOOK FIVE

Section 1: Understanding Anxiety and Overthinking in Your Relationship

1.1 Reflective Questions:

- How do anxiety and overthinking impact your relationships?

- What are the common triggers or situations that provoke anxiety or overthinking for you?

- How do anxiety and overthinking affect your ability to connect with your partner?

1.2 Exercise: Identifying Anxiety and Overthinking Patterns

- Keep a journal of your anxious thoughts and overthinking episodes in your relationship.

- Reflect on the underlying fears, doubts, or insecurities that drive these patterns.

- Identify any recurring themes or patterns that emerge from your observations.

Section 2: Effective Communication for Deeper Connections

2.1 Reflective Questions:

- How do you currently communicate with your partner during challenging or emotional moments?

- What barriers or obstacles do you face when trying to express your needs and emotions?

- How can you improve your communication to foster a deeper emotional connection?

2.2 Exercise: Active Listening and Empathy

- Practice active listening skills by fully focusing on your partner's words, non-verbal cues, and emotions.

- Reflect on your partner's perspective and validate their feelings.

- Engage in empathy exercises to better understand and connect with your partner's experiences.

Section 3: Cultivating Emotional Connection

3.1 Reflective Questions:

- How would you describe the current level of emotional connection in your relationship?

- What activities or experiences deepen your emotional connection with your partner?

- Are there any barriers preventing you from cultivating a deeper emotional connection?

3.2 Exercise: Quality Time and Shared Experiences

- Set aside dedicated quality time with your partner, free from distractions and technology.

- Engage in activities that promote shared experiences and emotional connection, such as going on dates, taking walks, or pursuing mutual interests.

- Reflect on the impact of these activities on your emotional connection and discuss with your partner.

CHAPTER SIX

BUILDING HEALTHY HABITS

"Above all else, guard your heart, for everything you do flows from it."

—Proverbs 4:23

"A healthy relationship keeps the doors and windows wide open. Plenty of air is circulating and no one feels trapped. Relationships thrive in this environment. Keep your doors and windows open. If the person is meant to be in your life, all the open doors and windows in the world will not make them leave. Trust the truth."

—Anonymous.

Hailey and Justin's relationship blossomed amidst the vibrant backdrop of a bustling city. Drawn to each other's charismatic personalities and shared interests, they embarked on a passionate romance. However, beneath the surface, their bond was marred by a lack of trust and mutual respect.

As time passed, insecurities took hold. They engaged in a destructive cycle of mind games, testing the limits of each other's loyalty and commitment. Communication became a minefield filled with passive-aggressive remarks and suppressed emotions.

Their toxic dynamic eroded the foundation of their love, leaving them emotionally drained and disconnected.

Navigating the intricacies of love while tackling life's challenges can be quite the balancing act. Falling in love might be a walk in the park, but keeping that flame burning amidst the daily grind requires some effort.

For those with an inclination to overthink and a touch of anxiety, prioritizing their relationship can feel like a daunting task. Balancing work pressures, financial responsibilities, parenting duties, and an ever-growing to-do list can amplify their worries, making it harder to be fully present for their partner. The constant cycle of thoughts and analysis can become overwhelming, leaving little room to nurture the relationship amidst the chaos of everyday life.

However, recognizing the impact of anxiety and overthinking is the first step towards finding a healthier equilibrium. By acknowledging these challenges and taking proactive steps, like practicing self-care and open communication, individuals can create space for their relationship to thrive. It's about finding that delicate balance between addressing life's demands and cherishing the emotional bond that brought you and your partner together.

Remember, love doesn't have to be perfect, but it's the little moments of togetherness that make it all worthwhile.

Why Your Relationship Needs Healthy Habits

Maintaining healthy habits while in a relationship can contribute significantly to one's happiness and life satisfaction. Those with healthy habits are less prone to encountering physical and mental health issues. Extensive research has explored and revealed the numerous benefits that healthy relationships can have on our overall wellbeing, encompassing both our habits and our mental health.

Let us further explore the profound positive impacts that cultivating healthy habits in your relationship can bring to your lives.

1. Decreased stress: "Having someone to talk to, rely on, and share the load can have a significant impact on how we perceive the problem" (Smith, 2021). The act of sharing our thoughts, concerns, and burdens with another person can provide us with emotional support, a fresh perspective, and a sense of shared responsibility. It is vital to nurture a meaningful connection with your partner, as they can greatly contribute to your overall wellbeing and resilience in the face of life's challenges.

2. Added meaning to life: A healthy relationship "can give a person a sense of purpose and fulfillment" (Acenda Integrated Health, n.d.). Knowing that you are genuinely loved and cared for by another person can infuse your life with a sense of purpose and meaning due to the support, progress, and shared dreams that partners foster together in a romantic relationship. Being in a loving relationship helps people to support each other's dreams and work together to achieve common goals. As both partners contribute to each other's personal development and journey, this combined effort fosters a strong sense of unity and shared purpose.

3. Encouragement of healthy behaviors: If you're in a loving relationship, it's likely that your partner "encourage[s] [you] to exercise, eat healthy, and follow up with medical problems" (Phelps, 2020). They often serve as a source of encouragement and support, motivating us to prioritize our physical and mental wellbeing. Whether it's through gentle reminders, joint participation in activities, or offering guidance, our romantic partner can encourage us to exercise

regularly, make healthier food choices, and address medical issues quickly.

4. Increased happiness: It's true; being in a healthy relationship can actually make you happier (Salaky, 2017). A healthy relationship provides a strong emotional foundation. It offers a safe space to express your emotions, share your joys and sorrows, and feel understood and validated. Having a supportive partner who listens, empathizes, and offers comfort can significantly enhance your emotional wellbeing and overall happiness.

5. Enhanced communication: By actively listening, expressing thoughts and emotions clearly, and resolving conflicts constructively, you can improve your understanding of each other, minimize misunderstandings, and foster a deeper connection.

6. Increased trust and intimacy: When partners consistently prioritize their wellbeing and maintain healthy habits, it establishes a sense of reliability and trust. They can rely on each other to prioritize their health and make choices that support their overall wellbeing, which strengthens the foundation of trust in the relationship.

A Happy Couple Is a Healthy Couple

When we think of a happy couple, certain individuals we know may come to mind. These couples are often characterized by their visible happiness and inseparable bond. We observe the genuine smiles exchanged between the wife and husband, as well as their constant laughter and playful interactions. The wife's affectionate way of speaking to her husband and the husband's gestures of physical closeness, like placing his arm around her or resting his hand on her back, leave a lasting impression.

In the presence of such couples, we can sense the sparkle in their eyes and witness the effortless way they engage with each other. Stepping into their home, we immediately notice the absence of tension and the abundance of comfort and tranquility.

Those couples who exude happiness and love seem to possess a secret or knowledge that eludes us. It's as if they have discovered a transformative key that could potentially revive even the most lackluster or damaged relationships.

So, what does a happy couple look like specifically?

1. They are happy individuals: And by happiness, we don't mean "superficial emotions" (Los Angeles Christian Counseling, 2020). The Bible tells us that "*a happy heart is good medicine and a joyful mind causes healing, but a broken heart dries up the bones*" (Proverbs 17:22). In relationships, true happiness involves emotional wellbeing, compatibility, effective communication, mutual support, quality time, and intimacy. When these aspects are nurtured, they contribute to a deeper sense of fulfillment and satisfaction within the partnership. True happiness in relationships encompasses a lasting and genuine sense of joy and contentment.

2. They have fun together: Happy couples find joy in spending time together and prioritize having fun in their relationship. They actively seek out activities and experiences that bring them pleasure and create positive memories. By engaging in shared interests, exploring new adventures, or simply enjoying each other's company, they create a vibrant and enjoyable dynamic.

3. They pray together: Prayer increases marital satisfaction and decreases the chances of infidelity (Los Angeles Christian Counseling,

2020). 1 Thessalonians 5:16-18 says, *"Rejoice always, pray without ceasing, give thanks in all circumstances; for this is the will of God in Christ Jesus for you."* These practices of rejoicing, praying, and giving thanks together create a foundation of positivity, spirituality, and appreciation, enhancing the happiness and fulfillment a couple finds in their relationship.

4. They forgive easily: The ability to forgive easily is a key characteristic that contributes to a happy couple's overall wellbeing and relationship satisfaction. Forgiveness allows partners to let go of past hurts, conflicts, and mistakes, promoting emotional healing and growth within the relationship. By forgiving easily, couples create a climate of understanding, empathy, and compassion, fostering a sense of trust and emotional safety. It prevents the accumulation of negative emotions and resentment, allowing the couple to move forward and maintain a positive and harmonious connection. This willingness to forgive promotes effective communication, conflict resolution, and the ability to work through challenges together.

5. They don't forget the things that initially drew them together: It is common for happy couples to hold on to the memories and qualities that initially attracted them to each other. They cherish and remember the things that brought them together and sparked their connection. This includes the shared interests, values, and experiences that formed the foundation of their relationship. By not forgetting these initial aspects, happy couples keep their bond strong and maintain a sense of appreciation for one another. They actively nurture and celebrate the qualities and moments that made them fall in love. This practice helps to sustain their positive feelings and attraction, allowing the relationship to thrive over time. By holding on

to the essence of what drew them together, happy couples continue to find joy, fulfillment, and a deep sense of connection in their partnership.

Setting Smart Goals for Your Relationship

Relationship goals serve as a guiding mission statement for couples, tailored to their unique dynamic. They can range in complexity, depending on the preferences of each couple. The essence of a well-crafted relationship goal lies in its ability to align with the core values of both partners. Furthermore, these goals should possess a quality of flexibility and adaptability, enabling them to evolve alongside the changing stages of the partners' lives. These smart goals include, but are not limited to:

1. Financial independence: When working on financial independence as a couple, you can establish smart goals such as saving a specific amount of money each month, creating a joint budget, reducing unnecessary expenses, or seeking additional sources of income. By setting these goals, you can approach your financial journey with clarity, focus, and a higher chance of success.

2. Making time for each other: You don't necessarily have to schedule one-on-one time in your calendar, but you should spend time together that doesn't involve being on your phones (Davis, 2022). If you're aiming for a satisfying relationship, it's crucial to make quality time a top priority. Taking the time to connect and bond with your partner is essential for nurturing your emotional connection. Whether it's going on dates, enjoying hobbies together, or simply having meaningful conversations, allocating quality time is a fundamental aspect of building a happy and healthy relationship.

3. Gratitude: Another important goal within your relationship should be expressing gratitude. This is all about recognizing and appreciating your partner's efforts, qualities, and actions. By actively showing gratitude, you can create a positive and supportive atmosphere in your relationship. Express appreciation for both the big and small gestures, acknowledge each other's contributions, and regularly say thank you. Gratitude reinforces a sense of value, love, and respect in your relationship. When you make a conscious effort to show gratitude, you strengthen your bond and cultivate a more fulfilling and harmonious partnership.

4. "Me" time: Making room for personal solitude is essential in any relationship. You should intentionally set aside periods where each of you can have uninterrupted alone time. This goal recognizes the importance of individuality and self-care within your partnership. By dedicating specific moments to personal solitude, you create space for self-reflection, relaxation, and pursuing individual interests. This time allows each partner to recharge, rejuvenate, and maintain a healthy sense of self. It also fosters personal growth, independence, and self-awareness, which all contribute to a stronger and more balanced relationship.

5. Maintaining a healthy lifestyle: Setting up healthy eating and exercise habits as you age is important, and having a partner who shares the same goals can really help you stick with your health commitments (Davis, 2022). This helps to improve the health and wellbeing of both you and your partner.

Introducing New Routines

We all have habits that become ingrained in our daily routine, such as brushing our teeth, making the bed, or unwinding with a drink after a long day. These activities become second nature as we perform them without much thought.

When it comes to relationships, routines are often associated with mundane tasks necessary for a smoothly functioning life. However, routines can be more than that. They can serve as valuable tools in maintaining a strong and stable relationship, especially during stressful or transitional periods.

Positive rituals within a relationship can offer significant benefits. They have the power to enhance communication and connection between partners, leading to a greater sense of security and reducing any doubts or uncertainties that may arise.

These rituals can be simple acts of love and affection, such as sharing a daily hug, having a regular date night, or exchanging notes of appreciation. By incorporating these rituals into the relationship, you can strengthen your bond as a couple and navigate challenges more effectively.

Healthy Habits to Prioritize in Your Relationship

While no relationship is without its challenges, it is evident that some couples thrive while others struggle. So, what sets them apart? The reality is that happiness in a relationship is not a matter of chance. In fact, the healthiest and happiest couples are intentional in their efforts to build and sustain their love.

The healthy habits to prioritize are:

1. Making your spiritual wellbeing a priority: Prioritizing spiritual wellbeing in your relationship includes praying together, going to church and worship concerts together, and studying the Word together (Walters, 2022). As a couple, prioritizing your spiritual wellbeing involves jointly nurturing and cultivating your spiritual connection and growth.

2. Communicating: By now, we are pretty familiar with the idea that communication is key for a healthy relationship (Hall, 2020). It involves the ability to convey thoughts, feelings, and needs clearly and to actively listen to one another. It also allows partners to understand each other on a deeper level. For more specific tips, you can revisit Chapter 5.

3. Asking rather than assuming: In any relationship, one crucial habit to prioritize is avoiding assumptions and instead practicing open communication by asking questions. Assuming can lead to misunderstandings, misinterpretations, and unnecessary conflicts. By taking the time to ask questions (asking gently and politely, not interrogating like a drill sergeant) and seek clarification, you create an atmosphere of understanding, empathy, and trust.

4. Sharing household responsibilities: This entails actively participating in the various tasks and chores required to maintain a functional and comfortable living environment. By sharing these responsibilities, couples foster a sense of teamwork, equality, and mutual support. It helps prevent feelings of burden or resentment that can arise when one person feels overwhelmed with all the household duties.

5. This also promotes fairness and balance in the relationship, as both partners contribute their time and effort to maintain the home they

share. Moreover, it allows for better time management and reduces individual stress levels, freeing up quality time to spend together or pursue personal interests. Effective communication and cooperation are key to successfully sharing household responsibilities, ensuring that you both feel heard, understood, and valued. By prioritizing this habit, you can create a harmonious and supportive environment where the workload is shared, leading to a stronger and more balanced relationship.

6. Trusting each other: Trust is a fundamental habit to prioritize in your relationship. It serves as the cornerstone for a strong and healthy connection. Trust is built on honesty, integrity, and reliability. It means having confidence in your partner's character and intentions. Prioritizing trust entails open and honest communication in which both partners feel free to share their opinions and emotions. It also includes honoring commitments and being reliable. Building trust takes time and consistency to demonstrate dependability and commitment.

Practicing Gratitude and Affection

Expressing gratitude and affection to your partner offers numerous benefits. However, consistently finding meaningful ways to do so might be challenging. To help you cultivate gratitude and affection in your relationship, here are some helpful tips.

1. Give compliments: "Have you ever caught yourself thinking something nice about your partner, such as admiring the way they look, or how they interact with you and others? Instead of keeping that thought to yourself, say it out loud" (Howard, 2021). Take a

moment to specifically acknowledge and communicate what you appreciated in that particular moment.

2. Express appreciation via notes, texts, or letters: Another way to show gratitude to your partner is by writing a heartfelt note, text, or letter. Taking the time to put your thoughts into writing allows you to convey your feelings in a sincere and lasting way.

3. Pitch in and give your partner a break: An additional way to show gratitude to your partner is by offering to help and giving them a break. Take initiative in sharing responsibilities and tasks, allowing your partner some much-needed rest or time for themselves. This act of support and consideration demonstrates your appreciation for their efforts and can strengthen your bond.

Physical Activity Together

Engaging in physical activity has a direct influence on our mood, which in turn affects various aspects of our lives, including our relationships. Therefore, it is logical to believe that exercising together can strengthen your bond with your partner.

Physical activities as a couple provide a unique and shared experience. There are several ways to include fitness in your daily routine, whether you prefer to go for walks, bike rides, or hikes, or go swimming together.

Exercising together not only provides physical stimulation, but it also helps to bolster mental wellbeing. Working out with someone else provides mutual support and motivation, fostering a sense of solidarity and teamwork. Furthermore, physical exercise produces endorphins in the brain, which are natural mood-enhancing substances that can aid in reducing depression and stress. Here are a few more reasons why engaging in physical activity can improve your relationship:

1. Support and encouragement: Exercising together allows you to support and encourage each other, creating a positive and motivating environment.

2. Quality time: Engaging in physical activities provides dedicated time for you and your partner to bond and connect on a deeper level, strengthening your relationship.

3. Health benefits: Regular exercise has several health advantages, including greater fitness, improved cardiovascular health, increased energy levels, and general wellbeing, which can benefit both you and your partner.

4. Enhanced mood: Endorphins are released during physical exercise, which enhance mood and generate a sensation of enjoyment and fulfillment.

Forgiveness Is Key

You've probably heard about how important forgiveness is when it comes to relationships. Why? Well, "let's face it, people are not perfect" (Firestone, 2020). Finding a soulmate doesn't erase our individual differences, and sooner or later every couple is bound to have disagreements and points of contention. Striving to find a "perfect" partner will definitely lead to continuous disappointment. We all have a past and have done things we're not proud of. Rather than trying to do what only the blood of Jesus can do (washing others of their sins), we should accept our partner's different opinions, shortcomings, and flaws while cultivating forgiveness for a lasting relationship.

Forgiveness Worksheets

Reflection on Forgiveness:

a. Reflect on a recent situation where you felt hurt or wronged by your partner. What emotions did it evoke in you?

b. How did you respond to the situation? Did you express your feelings to your partner or hold them back?

c. How did the unresolved issue impact your relationship? Did it create distance, tension, or resentment?

d. Did you keep malice? Did you do something that you felt your partner deserved for hurting you?

Understanding the Importance of Forgiveness:

a. What does forgiveness mean to you in the context of your relationship?

b. Why do you think forgiveness is important for building a healthy and strong relationship?

c. How can practicing forgiveness positively impact both you and your partner?

d. What does the Bible say about forgiveness?

Communication and Empathy:

a. Have an open and honest conversation with your partner about forgiveness. Share your reflections from the previous exercises and ask for their perspective.

b. How does your partner perceive forgiveness? Are there any differences or similarities in your understanding?

c. How can you enhance your communication and empathy when discussing forgiveness in your relationship?

Setting Forgiveness Goals:

a. Identify specific situations or patterns where forgiveness is needed in your relationship.

b. Discuss and establish guidelines for expressing remorse and seeking forgiveness when one of you has caused hurt or harm.

c. What steps can you both take to foster forgiveness (such as active listening, empathetic understanding, and offering sincere apologies)?

d. Turn to God. Pray together with your partner on the issue of forgiveness. Search for Bible verses on forgiveness and ruminate on them daily.

Practicing Forgiveness:

a. Recall a past situation where you forgave your partner. How did it affect your relationship and personal wellbeing?

b. Are there any ongoing forgiveness challenges in your relationship that you need to address? If yes, discuss strategies to overcome them.

c. Commit to practicing forgiveness regularly and monitor the positive impact it has on your relationship.

Self-Reflection:

   a. Reflect on your own ability to forgive. Are there any personal barriers or past experiences that make forgiveness difficult for you?

   b. How can you work on overcoming these barriers and cultivating a mindset of forgiveness?

   c. What self-care practices can you engage in to maintain emotional wellbeing and support the forgiveness process?

Remember, building healthy habits of forgiveness takes time and effort. Be patient with yourself and your partner as you navigate through these challenges and work on building forgiveness in your relationship.

MAIN IDEAS

Let's return to Hailey and Justin's story. The two of them recognized the need for positive changes in their relationship, as they noticed that their lack of trust and mutual respect was slowly eroding the foundation they had once built. To rebuild their connection, they consciously prioritized spending quality time together. They dedicated specific moments to reconnecting and understanding each other on a deeper level, aiming to reignite the fading spark in their relationship. Engaging in activities that promoted open communication and shared experiences became their way of rebuilding their emotional bond and rediscovering their passion.

In addition, Hailey and Justin embraced the transformative power of forgiveness. They actively chose to let go of past hurts and made an effort to understand each other's perspectives. By practicing forgiveness, they broke free from their destructive cycle of behavior and created a safe space for understanding and personal growth within their relationship. With each positive step they took, their commitment to building healthier habits grew stronger, leading them toward a more profound and fulfilling connection.

Healthy relationship habits are essential for cultivating meaningful and strong relationships. Prioritizing quality time, expressing gratitude, and practicing forgiveness are all examples of these habits. You and your partner can strengthen your bond and build a deeper emotional connection by setting out devoted moments for each other, away from distractions. Activities that promote open communication and shared experiences increase closeness and lead to a joyful and balanced relationship. Furthermore, expressing gratitude for one another creates a pleasant and supportive environment, reaffirming your mutual love and respect. Finally, practicing forgiveness allows you to move on while overcoming problems, providing a place of understanding and personal progress. By actively incorporating these healthy habits into your relationship, you can foster a stronger and more harmonious partnership that stands the test of time.

WORKBOOK SIX

Section 1: Reflecting on Your Relationship

1.1 Relationship Assessment:

- Rate the overall satisfaction and fulfillment in your relationship on a scale of 1 to 10.

- Identify the key areas that you feel need improvement in your relationship.

- Reflect on the current habits and patterns that contribute to both the beauty and the challenges in your relationship.

1.2 Identifying Healthy Habits:

- List three healthy habits that you believe are important for building a strong relationship.

- Describe how each of these habits contributes to a positive and fulfilling partnership.

- Reflect on whether you and your partner currently practice these habits consistently.

Section 2: Communication and Emotional Connection

2.1 Quality Time:

- Reflect on how much dedicated quality time you and your partner currently spend together.

- Identify any barriers or distractions that prevent you from having meaningful time together.

- Set a goal for increasing the amount and quality of your shared time. List specific activities or routines you can implement to achieve this goal.

2.2 Effective Communication:

- Assess the current state of communication in your relationship.

- Identify any communication patterns or behaviors that hinder open and effective communication.

- List three strategies or techniques that can improve your communication with your partner.

Section 3: Gratitude and Appreciation

3.1 Expressing Gratitude:

- Reflect on how frequently you express gratitude towards your partner.

- Identify specific qualities, actions, or efforts of your partner that you appreciate.

- Set a goal for expressing gratitude more consistently. List ways you can actively show appreciation to your partner on a regular basis.

3.2 Gratitude Reflection:

- Take turns with your partner to share three things you are grateful for about each other.

- Discuss how expressing and receiving gratitude positively impacts your relationship.

- Explore ways to integrate gratitude into your daily routine as a couple.

Section 4: Forgiveness

4.1 Cultivating Forgiveness:

- Reflect on your personal ability to forgive and let go of past hurts.

- Discuss with your partner the importance of forgiveness in your relationship.

- Set goals for cultivating forgiveness, both towards your partner and within yourself. List specific actions or practices you can undertake to promote forgiveness.

Remember, building healthy habits in your relationship is an ongoing process. Revisit this workbook periodically to assess your progress, refine your goals, and continue nurturing a strong and fulfilling partnership. Don't forget to pray!

PART THREE

Coping with Anxiety for Long-Lasting Happiness in Your Relationship

In the first and second parts of this book, you gained an understanding of what anxiety and overthinking are (especially relationship anxiety); you were also introduced to strategies by which you can manage anxiety and overthinking and prevent it from damaging your relationship. In this third part, you'll be introduced to how you can cope with your anxiety and overthinking in order to achieve long-lasting happiness. This part includes:

- Decluttering your way to happiness

- Coping strategies that work

First, we'll look at the ability of decluttering to create a more peaceful and fulfilling environment, both externally and internally. Then, we will give you tried-and-true coping skills for dealing with anxiety and overthinking, helping you to create a happier and better relationship. Prepare to embark on the road to lasting happiness!

CHAPTER SEVEN

DECLUTTERING YOUR WAY TO HAPPINESS

"To everything there is a season, A time for every purpose under heaven."
—Ecclesiastes 3:1

Alayna had always been a meticulous person, obsessing over every detail in her life, especially in her romantic relationships. Her mind was cluttered with worries, doubts, and endless overthinking about her partner's actions and intentions. It took a toll on her happiness and strained the connection she had with her partner. One day, while tidying up her apartment, she stumbled upon a book about decluttering both physical spaces and the mind. Intrigued, she decided to give it a try.

In today's fast-paced and jam-packed world, our lives are often loaded with an overwhelming quantity of information, possessions, and duties. And while we struggle to make sense of our chaotic reality, we may discover that we have neglected both our thoughts and our physical spaces, causing them to become crowded with irrelevant thoughts, ideas, and trinkets. The effects of this clutter, though, may go well beyond our physical surroundings; it can seep into our relationships, causing anxiety and overthinking that puts unnecessary strain on the connection.

Clutter in our lives may take many forms, ranging from physical clutter in our houses to mental clutter that hampers our thoughts and emotions.

This is when the habit of decluttering comes in handy. Decluttering is more than just cleaning up our physical environment; it is a transforming process that involves letting go of the unwanted baggage we carry in our minds. By actively decluttering our minds and spaces, we may find it easier to create space for joy, calm, and true connections in our relationships and to manage the anxiety and overthinking that weigh us down.

Understanding Mental Clutter

We have become used to regarding the stressed-out, overwhelmed, and negative feelings we sometimes get as part of life. Despite its effect on our lives and mental state, we just shrug and go on with our day thinking it's quite normal. But it isn't—it is a damaging state of being that lessens productivity and affects the way we live and interact with others. This is known as mental clutter.

Just as physical clutter in our home can make us feel overwhelmed "mental clutter is anything that makes our minds feel like they're on overdrive" (Daisy, 2020). So, what is mental clutter? It's "the excess thoughts and ideas that crowd your mind and prevent you from thinking clearly or focusing on your tasks at hand" (Jenna, 2023). It can show up as a never-ending stream of negative self-talk, racing thoughts, and/or a heightened sensation of uncertainty and fear. Mental clutter can have a negative impact on our emotional wellbeing, capacity to communicate effectively, and overall relationship satisfaction.

Mental clutter sometimes appears as anxiety and overthinking in the context of relationships. It can cause uncertainty, insecurity, and an insatiable need for acceptance. This mental state can damage relationships by producing misunderstandings, disagreements, and a lack of trust.

Mental clutter can occur in a variety of ways, and the way it shows up varies from person to person. Here are some common manifestations of mental clutter:

a. Racing thoughts: Your mind may be continually bombarded with a barrage of thoughts, making it difficult to focus or maintain mental stillness. These ideas could be repetitive, invasive, or unfavorable.

b. Overthinking: Overanalyzing and ruminating on past or current events, or what might happen in the future, is a common source of mental clutter. This can result in a loop of rumination and an inability to make solid decisions.

c. Anxiety and worry: Mental clutter may contribute to increased worry and anxiety. You may become anxious about numerous areas of your relationship, such as the partnership's stability, your partner's feelings, or possible conflicts.

d. Negative self-talk: Negative internal talk is a part of having mental clutter. You may criticize yourself, doubt your own worth, or constantly question your actions and intentions in the relationship.

e. Catastrophic thinking: Mental clutter can lead to a tendency to imagine worst-case scenarios or to overanalyze circumstances. This may worsen anxiety and create a sense of unease and uncertainty in the relationship.

Decluttering Is Self-Care

When we think of self-care, activities such as relaxing by a pool, going to the spa, and engaging in hobbies often come to mind. While these are all great forms of taking care of yourself, you need to remember to take care of your mental wellbeing, too (Poplin, 2022). Decluttering may not be an exciting process—after all, nobody wants to tackle that overflowing sock drawer, and nobody wants to have to face what's going on in their head—but still, it is an essential part of self-care. Self-care activities should nurture both your physical and your emotional health (Colino, 2022).

Physical decluttering, therefore, is a deliberate act of self-care that may have a significant influence on your mental and emotional health. Here are a few ways that decluttering might benefit you:

a. Improved mental clarity: Crowded surroundings can lead to a cluttered mind. It might be difficult to concentrate and think clearly when your physical environment is unorganized and chaotic. You can create a more beneficial atmosphere for mental clarity and productivity by cleaning and arranging your space. When that overflowing sock drawer is eventually sorted out, your mind won't keep on going back to it when you're supposed to be working (especially if you're working from home where it can be easily seen).

b. Reduced tension: Clutter can be a substantial cause of tension. It overwhelms our senses, intensifies visual distractions, and causes mental and emotional heaviness. Decluttering helps you to recover control and order in your daily activities, lowering stress and encouraging a better sense of quiet and serenity.

c. Increased productivity and efficiency: Physical and mental clutter alike may make it difficult to be productive and effective. We can reduce distractions, better utilize our resources, and create a more efficient and structured workflow by decluttering. This frees up mental energy and makes room for more intense and productive tasks.

Benefits of Decluttering for Your Mental Health

Why do we need to declutter? "If the physical space around us feels scattered, it's likely our mental space will feel the same" (Beckwith &

Parkhurst, 2022). Decluttering can have significant benefits for your mental health, particularly in relation to anxiety and overthinking. Here are some key benefits of decluttering:

a. Increased self-esteem and confidence: Decluttering might help you feel better about yourself. You will feel more accomplished and empowered as you take charge of your environment and regulate your thoughts more efficiently. This can lead to higher self-esteem and confidence in other aspects of your life, such as your relationships.

b. Emotional wellbeing: Clutter can elicit negative feelings and memories connected with prior experiences or unsolved problems. Decluttering allows you to let go of physical belongings as well as mental baggage, making room for pleasant emotions and a stronger sense of emotional wellbeing. It allows you to concentrate on the current moment and build a more cheerful and happy attitude.

c. Improved sleep quality: Sleep can be disrupted by an overactive mind packed with clutter and racing thoughts. Decluttering contributes to a more tranquil and serene bedroom atmosphere, which promotes relaxation and good sleep. You can wake up feeling more refreshed and invigorated by eliminating physical and mental clutter before bed.

d. Improved relationship: Mental clutter can cause tension and strain in relationships. Decluttering creates a more harmonic and serene environment, which promotes greater communication and understanding. Furthermore, reducing overthinking and worry allows you to be more present and attentive to your partner's demands, boosting the quality of your interactions.

Decluttering Your Mind: A How-To Guide

Your mind has an enormous influence over your daily experiences. However, it can easily get overwhelmed by the sheer volume of information and thoughts it processes at times. In such cases, your cognitive capacity may deteriorate, making it harder to think clearly, make informed decisions, and retain productivity. Furthermore, negativity can impair your mental and emotional wellbeing. To be honest, finding effective strategies to clean and restore mental clarity can be a difficult task—but not to worry, here are some simple ways to start decluttering your mind:

a. Set priorities: Making a list of priorities allows you to "take all those thoughts and decisions and put them into action" (Solvere Living, 2023). Prioritization is a necessary discipline for decluttering the mind, enabling you to effectively filter out distractions and focus on tasks that align with your goals because you're keeping in mind what genuinely matters and merits your attention. It allows you to intelligently manage your limited mental resources, make informed decisions, boost your productivity, and retain clear thinking. Setting priorities is a useful tool for navigating life's difficulties and ensuring that your efforts are focused on what is truly important.

b. Exercise regularly: Regular exercise is an effective approach to cleansing your mind. Physical activity relieves stress and tension by increasing endorphin levels and generating a happy mental state. Thisimproves mental clarity and provides an outlet for any pent-up emotions. It also improves overall mental wellbeing, focus, and concentration, and creates calmer and more balanced thinking. The physical and mental relaxation caused by exercise will allow you to tackle challenging tasks and situations with renewed vigor and clarity.

c. Transfer your thoughts to paper: Writing down the jumble of thoughts in your mind can be a very helpful way to mentally declutter (Eisler, 2019). Writing down your problems, for example, allows you to externalize them and acquire clarity. It assists in processing emotions, reflecting on experiences, and organizing your thoughts. Writing your thoughts in a diary provides a secure and private space to offload your mental burdens, reducing overwhelm and encouraging mental order. Journaling on a regular basis allows you to gain insights, detect trends in your behavior, and develop a better self-understanding.

d. Learn to let go: "Accept yourself, love yourself, and keep moving forward" (Nazish, 2017). Accepting yourself, including your shortcomings and flaws, frees you from the burden of self-judgment and comparison. Adopting self-love allows you to cultivate inner serenity. Furthermore, by letting go of the past and focusing on the future, you divert your attention away from past mistakes or unfavorable experiences and towards personal development and self-improvement. This approach motivates you to establish objectives, learn from setbacks, and strive for constant improvement.

e. Seek support: Seeking help is another effective approach to clearing your mind. You can create a safe space for free dialogue and emotional expression by reaching out to trustworthy individuals such as friends, family members, or a therapist. Sharing your feelings and thoughts with others can help you gain perspective, validate your experiences, and let go of any pent-up stress or anxiety. When you seek help, you allow understanding and empathy into your life, which relieves the stress of having to handle everything on your own. Engaging in meaningful conversations with people and receiving direction or advice from them can give clarity and fresh insights. It also increases your sense of connection and creates a support network on which you may rely in difficult times.

Decluttering Your Space

Are you envious of the spotless, clutter-free houses featured on home décor blogs and websites? Minimalist spaces and the promise of decluttering tactics can be appealing. I'm sure it's no surprise to you by now that decluttering can have a major influence not only on your physical space but also on your general wellbeing—but is simplicity genuinely livable? The answer is yes, if you make the required effort.

Decluttering extends beyond simply cleaning up your physical surroundings. It entails deliberately organizing and removing unneeded stuff in order to create a more practical and harmonious living environment. It frees up physical space, making it easier to access the items you need. This increases efficiency while decreasing the time and stress associated with looking for misplaced things. Furthermore, a clutter-free environment can boost productivity and focus, allowing you to complete activities with greater ease and concentration.

Decluttering also offers emotional benefits. It can be freeing to let go of belongings that no longer serve a purpose or have sentimental value. It allows you to make room for new experiences and memories, as well as promotes a sense of rejuvenation and growth. To declutter your space:

- Consider dividing objects into categories such as "keep," "donate," or "toss" to efficiently declutter your home.

- Consider the benefits of living with less and what genuinely brings worth to your life.

- Simplify your storage methods, create routines for keeping things organized, and fight the need to amass unnecessary objects in the future.

Taking Digital Detoxes

What is a digital detox?

One definition of a digital detox is "to take a break from using electronic devices or certain media for a period of time, from a few days to several months" (Cleveland Clinic, 2021). Here are some things to avoid while on a digital detox:

- Social media
- Email and messaging apps for anything other than work
- Online recreation
- News consumption
- TV

The most common type of digital detox is a vacation from looking at or engaging in social media. Negative social media encounters can cause anxiety and despair, as well as lower self-esteem. This includes the following:

- Becoming upset or disturbed by the things you see
- Cyberbullying (verbal bullying on the internet)
- Comparisons on a social level

The Advantages of Digital Detoxes:

Digital detoxification is an important strategy in today's technology-driven environment. It involves purposefully separating yourself from the digital world in order to establish a healthier and more balanced relationship with technology, and this has multiple advantages for your mental and emotional health.

Digital detoxing has been shown to improve real-life connections and relationships. Constant digital distractions might make it difficult to engage in meaningful connections with others. You will have more time and attention to dedicate to face-to-face talks, quality time with loved ones, and indulging in things that bring you joy and fulfillment if you step away from screens.

Furthermore, digital detoxes encourage better sleep. The blue light emitted by screens has been shown to disturb our natural sleep cycles and sleep quality. By disconnecting from digital gadgets before bedtime, you create a relaxing environment and increase your chances of getting a good night's sleep.

Signs that you should put down your gadget:

Do you think you need a digital detox? If you encounter any of the following when using electronic media, then it may be time to disconnect:

- Irritability, frustration, or anger
- Feeling uneasy
- Sleep deprivation or interruption
- Comparison to others
- An obligation to consume, reply, react, or check in
- Fear of missing out

How to do a digital detox (some of the information below has been drawn from the Cleveland Clinic, 2021):

a. Decide on what you want to change: It is critical to first identify the exact behavior or habits you intend to change. This might include excessive social media use, frequently checking emails or notifications, spending too much time playing video games, or any other digital activity that you believe is affecting your wellbeing or productivity.

b. Reduce your fear of missing out: Don't worry, you're not alone in this feeling (Tuca, 2023). Training ourselves to overcome the fear of missing out (FOMO) and the sense of urgency that frequently drives our ongoing digital involvement is a key component of undergoing a digital detox. While detoxing, you may experience anxiety about missing out on something important or exciting that is happening online, whether it's a social event, a news update, or even the everyday routines of your friends and acquaintances. To solve this, it's critical to remember that disconnecting from your devices will not cause the world to stop spinning. Remind yourself that disconnecting from digital platforms does not imply missing out on life; rather, it helps you to completely engage with the current moment and concentrate on your own wellbeing and personal growth.

c. Reflect on yourself: Take regular breaks during your digital detox to reflect on your progress and how the detox is affecting your life. Take note of any changes in your mood, energy level, productivity, and general wellbeing. Self-reflection will enable you to assess the benefits of limiting digital consumption and to reaffirm your commitment to a healthier relationship with technology.

d. Find alternatives: Finding alternative activities to replace the time you would normally spend on digital devices is a critical component of a good digital detox. Look for hobbies or interests that you have ignored or would like to pursue further, such as reading, exercising, spending time in nature, pursuing creative outlets such as painting or playing a musical instrument, or simply spending quality time with loved ones. Experiment with different activities to identify those that provide joy, relaxation, or a sense of accomplishment. Engaging in these new activities will not only help divert you from digital temptations, but will also provide a rewarding and engaging experience during your detox.

Habits for Happiness in Your Relationship

There are several general habits you can adopt that may help boost your happiness and overall wellbeing (and, therefore, your relationship satisfaction as well). Here are several examples:

a. Smile: Smiling is a natural outward expression of happiness (Pietrangelo, 2023). It's also a simple and effective method of improving your mood and bringing more happiness into your life. When you're genuinely happy, you probably smile. What's remarkable is that by smiling consciously, you can actually activate emotions of happiness and improve your mood. Have you ever wondered why, when you're with friends, you laugh at things you usually wouldn't find funny? That's because smiling and laughing are contagious. When you smile at others, you almost always get a smile back, resulting in a positive social encounter and creating a sense of connection and belonging. A simple smile can strengthen your interpersonal relationships, give you an approachable demeanor, and even boost your professional relationships.

b. Practice mindfulness: Being fully present and aware of the current moment without judgment is what mindfulness is all about. You can improve your sense of peace and happiness by practicing this habit.

c. Perform acts of kindness: Being good to others might boost your own happiness. Small acts of kindness, such as assisting someone in need or expressing thanks, not only benefit others but also generate a sense of purpose and satisfaction within yourself.

d. Have optimism: Developing an optimistic mindset means focusing on the positive, keeping hope alive, and having a positive outlook on life. You can build better happiness and resilience by reframing obstacles as opportunities and adopting a growth mindset.

Practicing Happiness Worksheet

1. Gratitude Reflection:

- List three things you appreciate about your relationship.
- List another three things you appreciate specifically about your partner.
- Reflect on how expressing gratitude can help you let go of anxiety and overthinking.

2. Positive Self-Talk:

- Write down three positive affirmations about yourself and your relationship.
- How can incorporating positive self-talk contribute to reducing anxiety and promoting happiness?

3. Letting Go Exercise:

- Identify one anxiety-inducing thought or overthinking pattern related to your relationship.

- Challenge and reframe that thought with a more realistic and positive perspective.

- Talk to your partner about this thought and discuss it sincerely with them.

- Reflect on how letting go of negative thoughts can enhance your overall happiness and wellbeing.

4. Acts of Kindness:

- Brainstorm three acts of kindness you can perform for your partner.

- Take action and complete one act of kindness this week.

- Reflect on how spreading kindness enhances your relationship and contributes to your own happiness.

5. Joyful Moments Journal:

- Set aside a few minutes each day to write down moments of joy or happiness in your relationship.

- Describe the situation, your feelings, and why it brought you happiness.

- Review your journal regularly to remind yourself of the positive aspects of your relationship.

6. Self-Care Plan:

- Create a self-care plan that is specifically tailored to reducing anxiety and promoting happiness in your relationship.

- List activities or practices that bring you joy, relaxation, and rejuvenation.

- Schedule regular self-care practices and commit to implementing them.

- Try carrying out these exercises with your partner and reflect on how this affects you both.

Remember, the purpose of this worksheet is to assist you in actively practicing happiness and letting go of worry and overthinking in your relationship. Take the time to complete each activity carefully and reflect on how it affects your wellbeing.

MAIN IDEAS

Let's return to Alayna. Inspired by a great book she had read, Alayna embarked on a journey of self-reflection and letting go. She started by acknowledging her anxious thoughts and their impact on her romantic relationship. Gradually, she learned to recognize when her mind was spiraling into overthinking mode. With patience and practice, she began detaching herself from unnecessary worries, releasing the grip of anxiety that had held her captive for so long. As she let go of cluttered thoughts, her connection with her partner blossomed. She embraced vulnerability, communicated more openly, and allowed herself to trust and be fully present in the relationship. With each step, Alayna discovered that decluttering her mind was the key to unlocking happiness and fostering a deeper, more fulfilling bond with her loved ones.

To declutter your way to happiness, you must simplify and organize all elements of your life in order to create a more harmonious and serene environment. Cleaning your physical space lowers tension and promotes a sense of serenity. Furthermore, giving up material goods that no longer serve a function can provide a sense of release and make room for new experiences.

In addition to physical clutter, decluttering your mental and emotional space is essential. Let go of negative thinking, poisonous relationships, and bad behaviors. By decluttering, you make room for more clarity, focus, and, eventually, happiness.

WORKBOOK SEVEN

Part 1: Mind Decluttering

1. Identify Mental Clutter:

- Take a moment to reflect on any recurring negative thoughts, worries, or mental distractions that contribute to clutter in your mind.

- Write down three specific examples of mental clutter that you would like to address.

2. Challenge Negative Thoughts:

- Choose one negative thought related to your relationship from your list.

- Write down evidence that supports and contradicts this thought.

- Create a more balanced and realistic perspective by considering the evidence against the negative thought.

3. Journaling:

- Start a journal to unload your thoughts and emotions.

- Write freely, without judgment or expectation.

- Use the journal as a tool to declutter your mind and gain clarity.

4. Practice Self-Compassion:

- Write down three affirmations or positive statements about yourself and your relationship.

- Repeat these affirmations daily as a reminder to be kind to yourself and let go of self-criticism.

Part 2: Space Decluttering

1. Assess Your Environment:

- Look around your living space and identify areas that feel cluttered and overwhelming.

- Write down three specific areas or items that you want to declutter.

2. Decluttering Plan:

- Develop a plan of action to tackle each area or item.

- Break it down into smaller tasks and set a timeline for completion.

- Consider enlisting the help of your partner for support.

3. Sorting and Organizing:

- Start decluttering one area at a time.

- Sort items into categories: keep, donate/sell, or discard.

- Find proper storage solutions for the items you decide to keep.

4. Simplify Your Space:

- Embrace minimalism by removing unnecessary items and keeping only what brings you joy or serves a purpose.

- Create a peaceful and organized space that promotes relaxation and clarity.

5. Maintenance:

- Develop habits to maintain a clutter-free environment.

- Set a regular schedule for decluttering and tidying up your space.

Remember, decluttering your mind and space is an ongoing process. Be patient with yourself and celebrate small victories along the way. As you declutter, you create space for more peace, clarity, and positive energy in your life.

CHAPTER EIGHT

COPING STRATEGIES THAT WORK

"Look at the birds of the air, for they neither sow nor reap nor gather into barns; yet your heavenly Father feeds them. Are you not of more value than they?"

—Matthew 6:26

"Focus on what you can control and let go of what is beyond your control. Release the need to fix everything and trust in the process of life and relationships."

—Eckhart Tolle

Ariana had always been a worrier, often finding it difficult to let go of her worries and fully immerse herself in her relationships. This negatively affected not only her mental health, but also her relationships. One day, Ariana attended a personal development workshop and was immediately impressed by one of the speakers, Jane. Drawn to Jane's calm demeanor and the way she seemed to have insight into Ariana's inner thoughts, Ariana mustered the courage to approach her after the session. She poured her heart out, sharing her struggles with anxiety and the impact it had on her relationships.

Jane listened attentively, empathizing with Ariana's journey. Drawing from her own experience, she shared the coping strategies that had transformed his life and relationships. Jane emphasized the power of self-compassion, urging Ariana to be kind to herself and challenge her self-critical thoughts.

She encouraged her to engage in activities that brought her joy, fostering a sense of balance and fulfillment.

Anxiety may easily take hold of our lives in today's demanding society, hurting not just our personal wellbeing but also our relationships with others. Constant anxiety, self-doubt, and overthinking may block true connections, leaving us craving efficient coping skills that might bring us closer to inner peace and deepen our relationships. This is when the effectiveness of coping mechanisms comes into play.

Coping strategies are techniques and methods that assist us in navigating the difficulties of anxiety and cultivating healthy relationships. They give us the ability to release ourselves from anxiety's grip, allowing us to be completely present in our relationships and create stronger connections. These strategies do not aim to avoid or suppress our emotions, but rather to build up resilience and self-awareness in order to navigate them with grace and authenticity.

Safety Behaviors Are Unhealthy

It is critical to realize the impact of safety habits when it comes to managing anxiety and developing healthy relationships. We all develop these behaviors to cope with our anxieties and uncertainties, seeking control and relief. Basically, "safety behaviors are used in an attempt to prevent fears from coming true and to feel more comfortable in fearful situations" (Qhek, 2022). However, it is critical to recognize that relying on safety habits can be detrimental in the long term, both for ourselves and for our relationships (Peterson, 2018).

Safety habits, you see, may briefly ease our anxiety and provide us with a temporary feeling of control, but they prevent us from confronting and overcoming our worries over time. They reinforce our belief that the things we are afraid of are genuinely dangerous, keeping us in an anxiety loop. Furthermore, safety behaviors can strain our relationships by instilling in us an unhealthy dependence on reassurance-seeking or by limiting our ability to fully participate in shared events.

Recognizing and addressing these safety habits is critical for breaking free from the hold of anxiety and fostering healthy relationships. It requires bravery to question the assumptions that underpin them and progressively diminish our reliance on them. Seeking professional treatment, such as therapy or counseling, may be extremely beneficial in creating alternative coping methods that promote emotional wellbeing and encourage confronting our concerns.

By letting go of safety habits, we create a deeper feeling of self-trust and resilience, making room for personal development and the chance to meet life's obstacles with bravery. We develop open communication, vulnerability, and trust in our relationships by letting go of incessant reassurance-seeking and adopting a healthy perspective. Here are the most common types of safety behaviors to look out for.

1. Avoidance: Avoidance refers to purposefully avoiding circumstances, locations, or people that cause uneasiness. To alleviate discomfort, for example, someone suffering from social anxiety may shun social outings or opportunities for public speaking. While avoidance may bring short respite, it promotes the notion that the dreaded scenario is genuinely harmful, making long-term anxiety management challenging.

2. Dependency on reassurance: Individuals may seek excessive reassurance from others in order to reduce their uneasiness. They

may continuously want affirmation, comfort, or confirmation that everything is fine. While seeking support is a natural aspect of every relationship, relying on reassurance excessively can strain your relationship and foster dependency by reinforcing the need for external validation to handle your anxiety.

3. Checking habits: Checking habits entail continuously examining and rechecking items to ensure safety or prevent injury—for example, repeatedly inspecting locks, appliances, or personal possessions to ensure their security.

4. Rituals and compulsions: Another sort of safety behavior is engaging in rituals or obsessive actions. These rituals may consist of precise action sequences or repetitive behaviors targeted at alleviating anxiety. Excessive handwashing, organizing items in a precise order, or repeating certain phrases are examples.

Healthy vs. Unhealthy Coping Skills

Coping skills are methods by which we can better deal with stress, anxiety, and uncomfortable emotions. Healthy coping skills play an essential role in your relationship to help you overcome challenges, develop resilience, and maintain emotional wellbeing. However, it is crucial to distinguish between healthy and unhealthy coping skills, as the latter can worsen anxiety and overthinking rather than alleviate it. Let's take a closer look:

1. Healthy coping skills: Healthy coping skills promote emotional wellbeing and contribute to the general health of your relationship. They are adaptable, constructive, and efficient in dealing with stress and worry. Here are a few examples:

a. Self-care: Exercise, getting adequate sleep, eating healthy meals, consciously taking proper care of yourself, and practicing relaxation methods are all examples of self-care activities that can help reduce anxiety and positively affect the state of your health and relationship. Taking care of your physical and mental health is essential for having a positive attitude in your relationship.

b. Communication: Healthy relationships require open and honest communication. Communication can make or break a relationship. Expressing your opinions, thoughts, and feelings in a transparent and polite manner promotes efficient problem-solving and mutual understanding. Active listening and assertiveness are two communication skills that can help minimize misunderstandings and lessen anxiety in relationships.

c. Setting boundaries: Maintaining a balanced and respectful dynamic in your relationship requires the establishment of appropriate boundaries—emphasis on *appropriate*! Be aware that it is possible to use boundaries the wrong way and turn them into a safety strategy, one that enables you to push your loved ones away. Appropriate boundary-setting entails identifying your personal boundaries and conveying them to your partner. This protects your wellbeing and ensures that both parties feel at ease, protected, and appreciated.

2. Unhealthy coping techniques: On the other side, unhealthy coping techniques may offer momentary solace but ultimately worsen anxiety and overanalyzing in relationships. They are regressive and may be detrimental to emotional health. Here are a few examples:

a. Precautions: It is possible to experience a momentary reprieve from tension or conflict by avoiding or repressing emotions and trying circumstances. But ignoring issues rather than dealing with them head-on might eventually result in unsolved problems, animosity, and elevated anxiety.

b. Substance abuse: Using alcohol or other drugs to deal with stress or worry is a bad coping strategy. Abuse of substances can exacerbate mental health conditions, lead to new issues, and damage relationships.

c. Excessive control: Excessive control can result from anxiety and insecurity, as can the need to manage every element of a relationship or a partner's ongoing need for affirmation. This excessive need for control undermines emotional intimacy and trust while also causing overthinking and anxiety.

It's important to recognize that everyone may exhibit both healthy and unhealthy coping skills at different times. However, the goal is to cultivate self-awareness and actively work towards replacing unhealthy coping mechanisms with healthier alternatives.

Self-Soothing Exercises

Self-soothing "is an emotional regulation strategy used to regain equilibrium after an upsetting event" (Nash, 2022). It should be noted that the overuse or improper use of self-soothing strategies can lead to emotional avoidance, disruption of intimate relationships, or unhealthy safety behaviors, as discussed earlier (Schwartz, 2022; Nash, 2022). These strategies "are meant to be short-term, temporary tools to allow a person to overcome difficult situations and negative emotions" (Schwartz, 2022).

Self-soothing has numerous benefits. First, it "activates the parasympathetic nervous [system], helping to decrease symptoms of anxiety, stress, and panic," thereby reducing impulsivity and helping you to pay attention to what's happening in the moment (Schwartz, 2022).

You can foster a better relationship with both yourself and your partner and improve your general wellbeing by implementing self-soothing exercises into your daily routine. Let's dive deeper into a few self-calming exercises:

1. Breathing techniques: Practice deep breathing by paying attention to your breath for a while. Exercises that include deep breathing are really easy to do but effective at promoting calm. Get into a comfortable posture and take a slow, deep breath through your nose, letting your belly expand. Release any tension or stress by exhaling slowly through your mouth. Do this for several minutes while feeling the peaceful rhythm of your breath. You may quickly and effectively reduce anxiety by practicing deep breathing anywhere, at any time.

2. Progressive muscle relaxation: When you experience stress in your body, progressive muscle relaxation can help you release it. Begin by tensing a specific muscle area, such as your shoulders, for a few seconds, and then deliberately release the tension while focusing on the sense of relaxation and relief it brings. Do the same for different muscle groups. This helps you to relax as you become more aware of your body.

3. Guided imagination: Allow your mind to transport you to a serene place—somewhere that brings you a sense of calm and tranquility. It could be a peaceful and warm beach with the ocean breeze all around

you, a breathtaking garden, or a quaint cottage in the mountains. It can be a place you've been to, a place that you link with relaxation, maybe that place you visited on a vacation and had a great time. Think about the feelings you experienced while you were there, the person or people you were with, and the sense of relaxation and camaraderie that was present. Engage all your senses in this visualization, noticing the sights, sounds, smells, and textures around you. Allow yourself to be fully present in this soothing mental image, letting go of any anxieties that may be weighing on your mind.

Breathing Exercises

Breathing exercises are powerful tools that can help us manage anxiety and overthinking in various aspects of life, including relationships. When we feel overwhelmed or anxious, our breathing often becomes shallow and rapid, contributing to a cycle of stress and negative thinking. Engaging in specific breathing exercises can help break this cycle by activating the body's relaxation response and promoting a sense of calm and emotional balance.

Anxiety causes us "to take rapid, shallow breaths that come directly from the chest" (Ankrom, 2023). This "causes an upset in the body's oxygen and carbon dioxide levels, resulting in increased heart rate, dizziness, muscle tension, and other physical sensations," which may even lead to panic attacks (Ankrom, 2023).

Diaphragmatic or deep breathing, on the other hand, allows you to calm yourself when you're in a scary or anxiety-inducing situation (Ankrom, 2023). Breathe deeply into your abdomen, not shallowly into your chest. Find a quiet and comfortable area to sit or lie down to do this breathing exercise. Place one hand on your stomach and the other on your chest. Allow your stomach to rise as you take a deep breath. Hold for a few seconds, then exhale through your lips, allowing your stomach to return to its regular position. Repeat many times, focusing on how your breath enters and exits your body.

Deep belly breathing like this can assist in calming your nervous system and activating your body's relaxation response. By doing this on purpose, we communicate to our brain that we are safe and in charge. Because it reduces the physiological response associated with stress, it can help ease feelings of anxiety.

Another beneficial breathing technique is "4-7-8" breathing. This method was developed by Dr. Andrew Weil to help manage breathing and promote a sensation of serenity. To practice this, close your eyes and sit comfortably. Count to four while inhaling deeply through your nose. For seven counts, hold your breath. Then, for eight counts, slowly exhale through your lips.

Another effective breathing technique is called "equal breathing." This exercise involves inhaling and exhaling for an equal count, promoting a sense of equilibrium and inner calm. To practice this technique, find a comfortable position and begin by taking a slow, deep breath in through your nose, counting to four. Then, exhale slowly through your nose for the same count of four. Continue this rhythmic breathing pattern for several minutes, focusing on the gentle rise and fall of your breath.

Equal breathing aids in the regulation of the autonomic nerve system, which regulates our body's stress reaction. We engage the parasympathetic nerve system by actively coordinating our breathing and exhalation, which counteracts the "fight or flight" reaction and produces calm. This technique may be especially helpful in relationships during difficult or uncomfortable situations because it helps us to answer from a position of calm and clarity rather than reacting impulsively out of fear.

Practicing Journaling

If you have been paying attention, you will have noticed that I've mentioned journaling several times in this book. There's a reason why. There is something especially soothing and relaxing about putting your thoughts and emotions to paper. It helps us look at and assess our thoughts differently than when they're only in our heads. It's also "the cheapest form of therapy because it is so therapeutic to perform a brain-dump" (Vidakovic, 2023). It offers the opportunity to problem-solve as you sort through various worries and to let go of what you can't control (Feyoh, 2023).

However, these benefits don't occur automatically or immediately. There comes first a sense of temporary relief, the kind that comes with letting go of something huge or burdening. However, over time, as you read what you've written over again, you'll begin to assess those words differently and eventually have different thoughts and come up with alternative viewpoints.

Journal Prompts

A journal "is a record of significant experiences and [is] used to explore ideas that take shape" (Vidakovic, 2023). Journaling can help you avoid "drowning in [your] own fearful thoughts" (Feyoh, 2023). Below are some useful journaling prompts you can use in managing your anxiety and overthinking, especially when it comes to your relationship (some prompts are taken from Feyoh, 2023; Vidakovic, 2023):

1. What three things scare you the most and why? When you face the things that scare you, you take from them the ability to cause anxiety

and/or overthinking in you. You give them less power over your life and relationship.

2. List your current worries in life.

3. Reflect on a recent situation where anxiety or overthinking affected your relationship. What were the triggers that intensified these feelings? How did they manifest in your thoughts, emotions, and behaviors?

4. Describe a specific fear or worry you often experience in your relationship. What evidence do you have to support this fear? Are there any alternative perspectives or explanations that you can consider?

5. Explore the patterns of overthinking that tend to emerge in your relationship. What repetitive thoughts or scenarios occupy your mind? How do they impact your overall wellbeing and the dynamics of your relationship?

6. Identify three negative beliefs or self-limiting thoughts that contribute to anxiety or overthinking in your relationship. Where do these beliefs originate from, and how do they affect your perception of yourself and your partner?

7. Consider the role of self-compassion in letting go of anxiety and overthinking. How can you cultivate a more compassionate and understanding attitude towards yourself in moments of relationship-related stress or uncertainty?

8. Write a letter to yourself, offering words of encouragement and support as you navigate your relationship challenges. What advice

would you give to yourself to promote self-growth, resilience, and inner peace?

9. Explore the concept of acceptance in relationships. What aspects of your relationship do you struggle to accept? How might embracing acceptance contribute to reducing anxiety and overthinking?

10. Reflect on the impact of setting healthy boundaries in your relationship. Are there any specific boundaries you need to establish or reinforce? How can these boundaries create a sense of safety and reduce anxiety and overthinking?

Remember, journaling is personal and requires deep thinking. Use these journal prompts as a way of managing your anxiety. Ensure that you are honest with yourself, making your journal a safe space—one that isn't used as a crutch.

MAIN IDEAS

Remember Ariana from the start of this chapter? As she embarked on her path of letting go of anxiety and nurturing her relationships, she embraced the coping strategies that Jane had shared. She began practicing mindfulness, allowing herself to fully experience each moment without judgment. Ariana also incorporated self-care rituals into her daily routine, such as engaging in creative pursuits and spending time in nature. Over time, she noticed a profound shift within herself. The grip of anxiety loosened, allowing her to be more present and attuned to her loved ones.

She learned to communicate her feelings and needs with authenticity, cultivating deeper connections built on trust and understanding. Ariana's relationships flourished, enriched by her newfound sense of inner peace and resilience. Through her journey, she realized that coping strategies that work are not a one-size-fits-all solution but a personalized exploration of self-discovery and growth. By embracing these strategies and letting go of anxiety, Ariana found herself on a transformative path towards vibrant relationships and a life filled with joy and fulfillment.

Developing effective coping strategies to let go of anxiety and overthinking in your relationship is a crucial step towards improving your mental health and building a healthier connection with your partner. It is also important that you're able to recognize and let go of the unhealthy safety behaviors that aggravate your anxiety. By consciously choosing self-soothing exercises such as deep breathing and journaling, you can find moments of peace and self-reflection amidst relationship challenges. Developing a personalized coping plan, assessing your progress, and adjusting your strategies along the way will enable you to fine-tune your approach and continue growing.

WORKBOOK EIGHT

Instructions: This is to help you create coping strategies that will allow you to build a relationship free from anxiety and overthinking. Answer each question truthfully, because this workbook is for your benefit.

Part 1: Understanding Your Triggers

a. What are some common situations or events that trigger anxiety or overthinking in your relationship?

b. How do these triggers affect your thoughts, emotions, and behaviors?

Part 2: Healthy Coping Strategies

a. Self-Care and Stress Management:

- List three self-care activities that help you relax and recharge.

- How often do you currently engage in these activities? Are there any additional self-care practices you would like to incorporate?

b. Effective Communication Techniques:

- Reflect on a recent situation where communication caused anxiety or overthinking. How could you have approached the situation differently to promote better communication and reduce anxiety?

- Identify two communication techniques you can practice to enhance your ability to express your thoughts and emotions effectively in your relationship.

c. Establishing Boundaries:

- In what areas of your relationship do you struggle with setting boundaries?

- Identify one boundary you would like to establish or reinforce. How will this boundary contribute to reducing anxiety and overthinking in your relationship?

    d. Seeking Support:

- Who are the individuals in your life whom you trust and feel comfortable seeking support from when facing relationship-related anxieties or overthinking?

- Reflect on the importance of seeking professional support when needed. Are there any barriers or concerns preventing you from seeking professional help if necessary?

Part 3: Developing a Personalized Coping Plan

a. Unhealthy Safety Behaviors:

- Reflect on any unhealthy safety behaviors or coping mechanisms that you tend to rely on when experiencing anxiety or overthinking in your relationship.

- Identify three unhealthy safety behaviors you would like to let go of.

- Why do you believe these behaviors are detrimental to your wellbeing and relationship?

b. Deep Breathing Techniques:

- Practice a deep breathing exercise for a few minutes. Focus on inhaling deeply through your nose and exhaling slowly through your mouth.

- How do you feel after engaging in this exercise?

c. Self-Soothing Exercises:

- Choose one self-soothing exercise from this chapter or elsewhere that resonates with you. Describe the exercise and how it promotes relaxation and peace of mind.

d. Journaling:

- Reflect on the benefits of journaling as a self-soothing and self-reflective practice. Have you tried journaling before? If yes, how has it helped you? If not, are you open to giving it a try?

- Commit to incorporating journaling into your routine. Determine a frequency (daily, weekly, etc.) and set aside a specific time for journaling.

- What topics or prompts will you explore in your journal entries?

e. Assessing Current Coping Strategies:

- Reflect on your current coping strategies for anxiety and overthinking in your relationship. Which strategies have been effective? Which ones have been less helpful?

f. Choosing Effective Coping Techniques:

- Select two or three coping strategies from this chapter or elsewhere that resonate with you. Explain why you believe they will be effective in helping you let go of anxiety and overthinking in your relationship.

g. Creating a Daily Coping Routine:

- Outline a daily routine that incorporates your chosen coping strategies. Be specific about when and how you plan to engage in these activities.

- Consider setting reminders or establishing a schedule to help you stay consistent.

h. Tracking Progress and Adjusting Strategies:

- Describe how you will track your progress and evaluate the effectiveness of your coping strategies.

- How will you adjust your coping plan if you find certain strategies are not as helpful as anticipated?

CONCLUSION

Remember Ariana from the previous chapter? Well, she met a guy named Dan and, employing all they had learned about letting go of anxiety and overthinking in their relationship, they were both able to overcome these challenges and build a beautiful relationship. They eventually had a beautiful wedding, and the lovely Jane was Ariana's maid of honor.

In wrapping up this journey of letting go of anxiety and overthinking in your relationships, it's important to remember that this process is deeply personal and transformative for each of us. Throughout our exploration of coping strategies, we've gained valuable insights into how to navigate and overcome these challenges, and I commend you for your commitment to your wellbeing and that of your relationships.

As we've discovered, self-care and stress management should be at the forefront of your efforts. Prioritizing activities that help you relax and recharge is vital in nurturing your emotional and mental wellbeing. By taking care of yourself, you create a solid foundation from which healthier relationships can grow.

Effective communication techniques are another powerful tool in our journey. Learning to express yourself authentically and openly can reduce misunderstandings and alleviate anxiety. It may take time and practice, but remember that every step you take toward improving your communication skills brings you closer to building more fulfilling connections.

Establishing and reinforcing boundaries is an essential aspect of cultivating healthier relationships. Recognize the areas where you struggle with setting boundaries, and consider the impact it has on your wellbeing. By clearly defining and asserting your boundaries, you create a safe and respectful space for yourself and others.

In the process of decluttering, you embark on a journey to create a more organized and harmonious living space. By letting go of unnecessary belongings, you can create room for clarity and peace in your environment. Decluttering offers an opportunity to assess your possessions and prioritize what truly adds value to your life. As you engage in this process, you will find that decluttering is not just about physical objects but also about letting go of the emotional attachments and mental clutter that can weigh you down.

Throughout this process, don't underestimate the power of seeking support. Trusted individuals who understand and care about you can provide invaluable insights and encouragement. Additionally, remember that professional help is always available if needed. Seeking guidance from therapists or counselors can offer a fresh perspective and support you in your journey of growth.

As you let go of unhealthy safety behaviors, such as excessive worrying or seeking constant reassurance, embrace self-soothing exercises like deep breathing and journaling. These practices allow you to find moments of tranquility and self-reflection, nurturing a deeper understanding of yourself and your emotions.

In conclusion, I want to emphasize that this journey is unique to you. Be patient with yourself and approach it with self-compassion. Commit to incorporating these coping strategies into your life and adapt them to suit your needs. By doing so, you open the door to a more harmonious relationship and personal growth that will be beautiful to see.

I'm thrilled you've completed Book #1 and grateful you chose my book from the many options available. Your journey through its pages means a lot to me.

I have a small favor to ask. **Please take a moment to share your insights on Amazon**.

Your review is more than feedback—it's a source of light for others seeking guidance in their relationships. What stood out to you? How has the book influenced your perspective?

Your thoughts will not only guide others but also inspire the journey ahead. Your honest review will enrich our community.

I can't wait to read your reflections on Amazon. Thank you for being a pivotal part of this journey.

>> Leave a review on Amazon US <<

>> Leave a review on Amazon UK <<

BOOK #2

Overcome Overthinking and Anxiety in Your Relationship

A Practical Guide to Improve Communication, Solve Conflicts and Build a Healthy Marriage

By Robert J. Charles, Ph.D., D.Min

Introduction

Marriage is never going out of style. It will never become old news. I know, I know, that's a pretty bold declaration, but I can be sure of this because humans are social animals, and we can never deny one of our most crucial needs: the need for companionship.

Intimate relationships are great, but nothing brings a man and woman as close as marriage. Yes, marriage comes with many benefits; however, it also involves many responsibilities. It's sort of like owning a private jet. There are a whole lot of perks that come with it, but if you look beyond the cushioned seats and open bar, you'll see that you've got to keep that baby running, and that is only possible when you're able to take responsibility.

Communication is the oil that marriage relies on to function. Without effective communication in a marriage, the moving parts of the relationship begin to experience wear and tear. Over time, there'll be so much rust that the whole thing will fail altogether. Overthinking, which is the main focus of this book, is the enemy of effective communication in a marriage. If you're an overthinker and you've been worried sick about how this habit is affecting your relationship with your significant other, you're in the right place. This is where you're going to deal with it once and for all. I won't sugar-coat facts in this book, because I believe you're here for the truth.

Overthinking and anxiety are a problem for so many people. I've seen them ruin relationships–romantic and platonic alike. What happens is almost like something out of a book or movie: someone thinks something is real when it isn't. They spend time believing the lie and working themselves up until they're soaked in a big, murky bowl of unreal thoughts. Their thoughts then affect their perception and their behavior. Things begin to get out of hand if the thoughts go unchecked.

Divorce is ramping up in our society. Many new marriages will end in divorce. I wrote this book to help you not be part of these statistics.

When you go into a relationship, you lay down a part of yourself in the inevitable exchange of vulnerability. Because you expect the other person to trust you and have faith in you, you must do the same. Anyone who has come to this point in a relationship expects to be treated well, and it only makes sense if they flinch when things don't seem to be going as planned.

You're permitted to flinch. But you should not permit yourself to overthink. Especially as a habit.

When you've found the one you love and care about, the least you can do is honor them and focus on real thoughts instead of mirages. Wondering if they're happy with you? Ask. Ask instead of imagining they're not. Ask instead of overthinking whether they honestly need some alone time or they just don't want to talk to you.

I just punched you with the power of communication over imagination. I've got more punching where that came from. The goal is simple: to equip you with these truths that'll help you to overcome this nasty habit that's ruining your relationship.

Maybe you're looking out for yourself too much.

Looking out for yourself isn't bad, and I can't say you should feel guilty for doing that. But when does it become too much for comfort? Simple. When you begin to get paranoid doing it. It's very easy for an overthinker to become paranoid because the thoughts just go from one level of negativity to another in a spiral of doom and gloom. I get that becoming vulnerable comes with some fear of being betrayed, but your fear can make overthinking worse and ultimately cause a breakdown in the relationship you cherish.

You've got this.

By and large, I'm very sure that you're going to be fine. Yes, it will take some work, a mental shift or two, redefining a couple of things, and some healthy actions to back it all up. It'll take work and determination, but I'm sure you've got those, and I'll be really glad to walk you through this journey. I will also be presenting to you a biblical perspective on some aspects of overthinking, especially as it pertains to your relationship with your spouse. I hope you'll enjoy the read and the journey. Get ready for an eye-opening ride.

PART 1

Becoming Aware of Your Overthinking Issues

The other day, I watched my dog sit on her mat in the corner and chew on a bone I got for her. Every time I turned my head to look at her, she'd stop chewing, lick her lips, and sniff in my direction as if trying to detect a silent command. She'd wait for as long as I held her gaze, blink rapidly, and if I still said nothing, she'd whine a bit. Eventually, she'd pick up her bone and continue chewing, but a few seconds later she'd turn to look at me again and find me still staring at her. Rinse and repeat. I always chuckled to myself after each episode of this. But more than finding amusement in my dog's behavior, I was bewildered by her level of awareness.

—Grace

Awareness is a powerful concept. Oftentimes, humans seem to have trouble being aware. It's almost as if someone else has to point out to us what we're doing right or wrong (especially wrong!) before we even realize that we're doing it.

The first part of this book deals with awareness because that's the first step to solving any issue. You need awareness that you have a problem, as well as an understanding of the nature of that problem. This is what opens the door to the possibility of a solution.

So, let's become aware of what overthinking is exactly. Let's see how overthinking might be affecting our relationship with our spouse. Let's go gain some perspective.

While you're going through this book, I want to ask you for one small favor. Could you please consider writing a review on the platform? Posting a review is the best and easiest way to spread the word about this book and support healthy relationships in the lives of so many couples.

CHAPTER 1

OVERTHINKING: A SWORD IN RELATIONSHIPS

"Overthinking, also best known as creating problems that are never there."

–David Sikhosana

Whose mind goes on tours when they're alone at any time of the day? Yours. Whose mind takes the express train through lands, seas, and mountains? Yours. If you've identified yourself in both of these scenarios— sweet! You definitely qualify for this ride.

We've all been there at some point, trapped in the overthinking spiral; some are still in it (no shame there). Downslopes in relationships are at the heart of many hurts that we go through as individuals. But what's at the heart of those downslopes? Suspiciousness? Insecurities?

It's human to have thoughts. It's expected and even healthy. You aren't a robot. You need thoughts to make your day-to-day decisions. And it's normal to act on your thoughts. The thought of a certain special someone may pop up now and then in your mind like a phone notification, except this notification is not bothersome or a thorn in the flesh of your focus; you revel in how sweet and special this person is to you. You daydream about the present and about the beautiful future of togetherness that awaits you...

...until the missiles of "what-ifs" and "maybes" attack your blissful ride. Thinking is good. Imagining is good. Yes, even getting lost in your thoughts is okay from time to time. The dicey part involves one thing and one thing only: the content and quality of your thinking.

What's overthinking all about?

Everyone who has a soul is able to think. In fact, thinking is crucial to being humane and rational. But—and here's the big but—there are times your thinking oversteps its bounds. One minute you thought your partner was the best person in the world; the next minute, you think she or he is a villain of some sort. Soon, you both are trying to fix broken parts of your relationship because of some thought that popped into your mind. Pretty miserable, isn't it?

Have you ever caught yourself creating some *masterpiece* of anxious thoughts in your mind that revolves solely around a change in the tone of a person's voice, their attitude, or the words they use? Like, involving no real facts, just your perception of the situation. Well, have you? Sure you have! I mean, why else would you be reading this book? Bingo.

For example, you might wonder why someone's voice seems lower than normal, leading you to think about why he or she didn't add your name to a morning greeting like other times... Yikes! What torment! You then begin to read between the lines, investigating things that should have been allowed to just die a quick, natural death. But no. You dwell far too long on your suspicions and assumptions, get moody and cranky, and start seeing unreal realities.

Patterns like these are all too common with people who are letting overthinking ruin their relationships. With time, a feeling of resentment that you never intended to have begins to build up inside you towards your loved one, and accusations eventually set in. Depending on how far your mind has traveled on that non-issue, overthinking has the capability to ruin things for you completely. You'd be shocked.

When you start to sense that your thoughts are beginning to spiral out of control and you're obsessing over little things, whether they were done or not done, said or not said, it's indeed time to rein in your brain.

Understandably, overthinking can be born out of past experiences. Maybe you were ghosted by someone in the past, and it was only later you began to realize all the signs that were playing out right before your eyes. That might have contributed to your becoming someone who finds it difficult to take anyone at face value. In other words, it's hard to ever trust again. It might be that you often replay conversations in your head, then beat yourself up every second for not giving the perfect retort to that bully at work. Yeah, the list seems endless.

It would be unfair to ignore the fact that past experiences can mold your identity and perspective. Past experiences can affect your interactions with others. It gets really bad if you're a victim of abuse. I empathize with you, I really do. It's not your fault that your views about life and certain groups of people have been distorted by an experience that left your heart and mind scarred. Trust me, I know it's frustrating when you can't help but see the worst in a situation or person, even when that person has good intentions. If you see how your overthinking can affect your relationship, leaving you with more hurt, you can take that huge step towards changing the pattern of your thoughts.

How Overthinking and Anxiety Affect Your Relationship

Overthinking and anxiety can have devastating effects on relationships that start out with so much promise. Overanalyzing can wreck mental health and leave you and your partner hurt. Your partner will feel grossly distrusted when you see everything wrong in every single little thing they do or say— or don't say.

Real quick, let's move straight to the non-negotiable things that happen to your relationship when you overthink. You probably already know these, but it makes sense to list them out here at this point, just in case you actually don't know how rapidly overthinking can make your relationship into a huge mess.

1. Lost trust

No one enjoys being mounted with heaps of accusations. Your pessimism and paranoia will definitely wreck the heck out of your communication level. When communication is lost, loopholes are created for mistrust to grow. Simple.

2. Mental exhaustion

Your significant other is liable to become exhausted when they have to explain and re-explain everything to you. They will, no doubt, become exasperated about the conclusions and assumptions that you come up with perpetually. This is the point where they begin to avoid having conversations with you or even avoid you completely. No one enjoys being subjected to constant interrogation about whatever accusations your mind has concocted. And if you continue doing this, you'll end up feeling exhausted yourself.

3. Constant conflict

Constant confrontations and overanalyzing make you come across as a cranky, unhappy person who's looking to pick a fight. If the other person isn't comfortable with your accusations, a counter-confrontation is bound to occur, leading to deeper conflict. Words that you never meant to say can be forced out of your mouth in that state of anger.

4. Inability to live in the moment

Your "what-ifs" and "maybes" are keeping you from creating beautiful memories with your spouse. You'll often end up ruining the present that promises to lead to a beautiful future. The moment you start second-guessing everything, you won't enjoy your relationship anymore. A relationship that's meant to make you happy can become the reason for constant bouts of anxiety, all thanks to your overactive mind.

5. Reliving past traumas

As a victim of trauma, it can be difficult to accept the beauty and goodness that's in front of you. It can seem too good to be true that your life is going well. Give overthinking free rein, and pretty soon it'll seem reasonable to start self-sabotaging. Your emotional well-being (and that of others) is affected when you replay your trauma in your head and use that old brush to paint those who want the best for you—especially if it's your spouse. As they say, "hurt people hurt people." Don't allow past trauma to become your current reality.

6. Frustration and constant fights

When you find yourself picking fights about the minutest of things, you have most likely become sad and anxious. At some point, you might even loathe your present self and begin to wonder how you got to that state. From self-loathing, depression sets in. Of course, the resulting breakdown in your relationship will leave you even more frustrated.

7. Health problems

Are you the type who never vents or lets out some steam? If all you do is keep mute and allow those poisonous thoughts to eat you up, guess what'll follow shortly thereafter? Yep, health issues. When anxiety sets in, the body often responds with increased heart rate, nausea, decreased immune function, low sex drive, chronic exhaustion, and so on. You can't enjoy your relationship if you aren't healthy yourself. Your body responds to what your mind tells it.

Clearly, overthinking does more harm than good. Scratch that! Overthinking does NO good. This is not to remind you of or make you feel regret about your past relationships that did not work out (possibly due to overthinking). This is just a step in the right direction–identifying the problem and the havoc it has caused and seeking a way out. That's exactly why you're reading this book.

Signs That You're Hyper-Analyzing Specific Parts of Your Relationship

Hyper-analyzing your relationship is one sure way to demolish all the bricks of trust and harmony you've built together. You use the poisonous "what-ifs," "maybes," "shouldas," and "wouldas" to dissect everything that might be wrong in your relationship. (You could win first place in a math competition if you considered applying that hyper-calculative part of your mind to a more useful pursuit, you know.) Here are some signs that you're hyper-analyzing your relationship:

You see "no" as a total rejection

This attitude screams "six-year-old who doesn't take no for an answer." You've probably seen or heard of a kid who cries and whines about not getting the answer they want. If you're acting like this (but the grownup version), you've got to change your mindset. Life won't always give you what you demand, and neither will the person you're married to.

Before you take offense, ask yourself, "Do I say yes to everyone, always? And when I say yes, do I sometimes wish I had said no?" There are times you say yes and realize it's to your own detriment, right? Now, where am I going with this?

1. A "no" could be because what you're asking is not convenient for your partner. Respect that and remember the times they've come through for you. Don't allow your selfishness to ruin your relationship simply because your partner is unable to agree to your needs at a certain point in time.

2. It could mean your request triggered your partner the wrong way, and they'd rather maintain whatever boundaries they've set. If your partner feels uncomfortable, let it go.

A peaceful relationship is a bad sign for you

Were you raised in a toxic environment, ridden with conflict? You might have grown to believe that a relationship must be dramatic. This is a wrong perspective about love. Love doesn't have to be tough; it doesn't have to be nasty and dirty. It might come with challenges, but the goal is to recognize that the enemy is the challenge itself, not each other.

You apologize too much

Yes, there's such a thing as apologizing too much. Apologies happen because you did something wrong, right? If you're always making the wrong moves, you'll always have to apologize, and that can be a wake-up call to examine your thinking patterns since actions are controlled by thoughts.

Sometimes, however, it's not that you're actually doing all the wrong things; it's just that you think that you are. If you have a string of failed relationships, anxiety might develop at the beginning of a new one. You might then overthink your actions and feel you must be doing something wrong. This might a result of emotional abuse you experienced at some point in your life where someone degraded you verbally. They may have told you that you never do anything right, for example, making you jittery and full of apologies for things you shouldn't have to apologize for.

You're afraid your partner might leave you

Fear of abandonment and rejection become engraved in our heart right from childhood. If you begin to see every challenge in your relationship as a threat that they'll leave you, it might be a sign that you're overthinking certain aspects of your relationship.

You overthink every irregularity

Relationships and marriages sometimes hit the rocks because one partner reads a trivial situation wrong. If you're someone who believes that life runs on the principle of one-size-fits-all, you're in for a rude awakening. But that doesn't have to be a bad thing. Instead of assuming the worst, flip the thoughts to the positive: What if this is the perfect person for you? What if your partner isn't playing you like others have in the past? What if your spouse's silence doesn't mean they're holding a grudge?

Gaining Awareness of Your Overthinking

If you want to get out of your own head, you need to acknowledge that being stuck in there is a real problem you need to deal with. Recognize that you can be a stumbling block in the path of your happiness through your thoughts. Don't spray the garden of your life with diesel fuel when there's a freshwater stream nearby. Being aware of your thoughts by paying attention to them is a journey you must be willing to take.

Take a deep breath. Inhale slowly, then exhale slowly. Done? Now, stop thinking about the process of doing that breathing exercise. You're overthinking again. Take a deep breath. Great! See, that wasn't difficult. Here's how to gain awareness of your overthinking in general.

Pay attention to the trail of your thoughts

Being aware of how your thoughts begin and end can be a great reawakening for you. If you notice that you're replaying events or conversations between you and your partner, that's dangerous ground. You might end up exaggerating unimportant situations or building resentments that weren't there initially because you have a habit of rehashing events, replaying the day, and reconsidering every single word your partner said.

A soldier needs to know the wiles of an enemy before making a move. Right now, get into "studying yourself" mode. See yourself as a fighter who's bent on winning a battle. Your mind informs most of the decisions that control your life. Now, it's time to fight.

Do you have negative thoughts when you're stressed out? Do you find yourself feeling unworthy when you scroll through feeds on Instagram or nice pictures of your friends having fun on their WhatsApp stories? At what time of the day do negative thoughts come to you? Does loneliness contribute to the back-and-forth your mind takes? These are ways to study and analyze how your thoughts come together in order to fight them.

Acknowledge that you're exaggerating

Recognize that your "what-ifs" are preventing you from being kind to yourself. Instead of thinking about the worst-case scenario, acknowledge that you just might be feeding your mind with too many negatives. Overthinking is like bringing a bull into a china shop; it's taking too much potential damage and ruining the things that are more important to you. Are you thinking you might lose your husband if you don't scroll through his phone? Or that your wife must no longer love you because she's not answering your text? These are negative thoughts that can make your spouse feel suffocated and untrusted if they find out what you think of them. Love should be liberating, not suffocating.

Take action to solve the problem

If there's a problem, the most reasonable thing to do is to fix it. The central purpose of this book is to show you how to go about fixing the problem. When you keep fixating on the bad thing that happened, you won't solve anything. You might even end up compounding the struggle with your overactive mind. Instead of constantly ruminating over the way your spouse responded to you at breakfast, have you considered talking to them about how it made you feel? Have you considered telling them how you'd like to be spoken to? Have you discussed with your partner your triggers? Do they know your boundaries? You'll save yourself a lot of headaches if you can be open to fixing a misunderstanding instead of rehashing it in your head.

Practically Speaking

Now that you're beginning to realize why and how your thoughts keep hovering like an uncontrollable drone, you need to schedule moments for private reflection.

Reflections are the opposite of rehashing. With reflections, you'll begin to see things more objectively. You'll see that other people aren't necessarily the problem, but you. Unlike rumination, which can lead you into a dark hole of self-sabotage, when you reflect, your eyes are opened to how you can handle matters differently.

You can set a timeframe (say 30 minutes) for worrying, ruminating, and rehashing. Allow yourself to mourn and grieve over the plans that didn't go well. Once that period is over, dust yourself off and get into something more productive. The moment you discover that overthinking is taking up time you could be using for other important things, be quick to remind yourself that you'll revisit that distressing thought later, during your next rehashing session. This method can help you get started by keeping your mind from constantly wandering.

The popular saying that an idle mind is the devil's workshop isn't far from the truth. This saying makes me imagine a creature with horns, holding a pitchfork and standing behind someone who just wants to sit and brood. Whichever way you choose to see it, when you create a vacuum, an empty space in your mind, something must occupy it. If you're engaged in projects that are worthwhile or hobbies that hold promise, negative thoughts will have no space to perch. You'll feel more relaxed and energized to take on whatever comes your way. So, get busy! We're not talking about merely distracting yourself, mind you—it's about *living*. Start living.

Let's Back Up a Bit

Is overthinking all bad? Hmm. Actually, the answer a straightforward yes, but the problem lies in folks confusing overthinking with critical thinking. They're two different things.

An analytical mind is, I daresay, an intelligent one. I once had the privilege of watching my friend interview candidates for hire in his outsourcing company. He wanted to hire an HR professional, and he had "brainy" as one of the qualifications for the ideal candidate. I chuckled when I saw his notes on this. Without flinching, he said, "Only a brainy one can hire brainy ones." But of course! When I dug further, he explained that what he was really looking for was a person with a highly analytical mind. "That sort of person," he said, "will be able to understand whatever problem we have and is the exact kind of person to look out for to fill the role."

Well, true. Having an analytical mind helps you do the high-level thinking involved in reviewing a problem and finding the solution. Analytical thinking is, as the name implies, done for analysis with a view toward finding a positive outcome. Overthinking, on the other hand, is thinking without a purpose or direction. It's thinking in scattered ways that open doors for stress and anxiety. Overthinking is just thinking and thinking, making mountains out of molehills and still arriving nowhere—basically, going around in circles.

Reasons Why You're Overthinking

I won't indulge you by helping you lie to yourself. You weren't born an overthinker. As a child, you took more risks, you were daring, and you thought you could conquer anything. Once you set your mind to achieving something, you went all-out for it. Little wonder you had no cares in the world. You thought the best of everything; you held no record of wrongs done to you by your friends; you laughed more and loved more. Great times, huh?

You see, something changed you. Let's take a look at how you got here, and the reasons why you might be overthinking.

- You were hurt by someone who betrayed your trust.
- You were abused as a child, leading to insecurities and doubts.
- You were constantly put down by people who should have lifted you up, leading to low self-esteem.
- You're a perfectionist.

- You love to attract sympathy from others.

- You're procrastinating and avoiding responsibilities.

- You overgeneralize and create stereotypes.

- You're afraid of conflict.

- You don't dare to live with uncertainty.

- You don't feel comfortable not being in control.

Do these descriptions sound like you? A couple of them, right? Life changes us in the most unexpected ways, and unfortunately, sometimes that means we have to live with some negative consequences. But there's hope.

Stress, Anxiety, and Overthinking: The Terrible Triplets

Your everyday life is bound to come with stressors, whether it's a fight with your spouse, a job that drains the heck out of you, raising a troubled kid, or so many other factors that come with living in this world. You can get stressed when your body, feelings, and thoughts respond to these external events. Dr. Melanie Greenberg, a clinical psychologist who wrote *The Stress-Proof Brain*, defines stress as "a reaction to environmental changes or forces that exceed individual resources." From this definition, there are circumstances beyond our control that might leave us disturbed and helpless, leading us down a toxic thought-rollercoaster. You might feel drained and your stress levels might increase.

Some symptoms that you experience while you're under stress include rapid heart rate and shallow breathing. When it gets chronic, the body becomes overactive in this state of stress, potentially leading to life-threatening outcomes like heart disease, high blood pressure, or a breakdown of the immune system.

Stress encourages anxiety. Other effects of stress on your mood are restlessness, lack of motivation and focus, feeling overwhelmed, irritability and sudden outbursts, insomnia, depression, and, of course, overthinking.

How does overthinking come into the picture, exactly? According to Amy Maclin, when something unfortunate or stressful happens, we tend to immediately think back to other times they felt horrible or stressful, leading to a pileup of toxic thoughts—a factor that "sets the stage" for an overthinker to keep roaming until she or he reaches a slippery slope.

Like stress, anxiety is also a response to a threat—but it's a response to a threat that does not exist, a story you've created in your head, an idea that's not real. For example, say you're asked to present a business proposal at a board meeting. You've prepared all the slides that you need, yet your heart is pounding so fast, and you wish it would stop; your palms are sweaty and you feel hot even in an air-conditioned room. These are symptoms of anxiety.

Guess who the threat is here? Nobody but the voice in your head. You've created a narrative in your head that's making you think that you might flop. You're thinking they might not like it. You've concluded that your proposal is crap. You're beginning to mourn its rejection before the actual presentation. This narrative that has been created as a result of your overthinking has triggered fear (anxiety) in you.

When anxiety steps in, it interferes with your sleep, relationships, productivity, and other aspects of life. Stress and anxiety are intertwined with overthinking. When there are issues beyond your control, you tend to stress over them and overthink them, leading to chronic worry and anxiety. Both anxiety and stress cause overthinking and are amplified by overthinking. These damaging triplets are interwoven. To break the cycle, you have to discover what informs your thoughts. Could they be coming from a place of stress or anxiety?

Wrapping Up

The bottom line is that overthinking isn't in any way healthy for your relationship. The sad fact is that it tends to go along with a lot of other unsavory habits, like stonewalling. Have you heard of stonewalling? If you haven't, don't worry; we'll talk about it in the next chapter. I'm pretty sure it's something you might have done before, or perhaps you do it often.

In the next chapter, we'll take a look at the difference healthy communication makes in a partnership compared to overthinking. You might not be aware of how damaging your habit is to your relationship, and that's what I'm about to show you.

Your Quick Workbook

What reasons have you identified for your overthinking?

_____

_____

_____

_____

_____

_____

_____

_____

In what two instances has overthinking ruined a nice day, outing, or relationship of yours?

_____

_____

_____

_____

_____

_____

_____

_____

_____

Do you have a past trauma that you haven't dealt with which might be making you overthink?

_____

_____

_____

_____

_____

_____

_____

_____

Which would you regard as the main fuel for your overthinking: stress or anxiety? Why?

_____

_____

_____

_____

_____

_____

_____

_____

_____

_____

_____

_____

CHAPTER 2

OVERTHINKING VS. HEALTHY COMMUNICATION

"Most misunderstandings in the world could be avoided if people would simply take the time to ask, 'What else could this mean?'"

—Shannon L. Alder

I remember one night when I was exhausted from work, I lay down on my bed to catch my breath as my mind wandered to my boyfriend of three years. He was the one person I needed to rant to about my day. Since he wasn't picking up his phone, I scrolled through my WhatsApp to see if he was possibly online.

"He's probably getting tired of my calls," I thought as I rolled my eyes. I turned this thought over in my mind, even when I knew he always picked up and returned my calls the moment he saw them.

"I'm sure he's online." My mind came up with another conclusion. And what do you know—I was right! I got irritated. So chatting with his friends on WhatsApp was more important than picking up my calls? I shot him a message and expected a near-instant reply. I didn't get one. I was fuming. I flung my phone on my bed, stood up, and started pacing, still fuming. The clock was ticking, and he still hadn't replied. I returned to his DM. He was still online! I highlighted the text I'd sent to him and deleted it. Of course, WhatsApp helped me shout it from the rooftops that I'd deleted a message. I wanted him to see that I knew he was ignoring me. After 10 minutes that felt like 10 years, the customized ringtone I had set solely for him buzzed into the silence of my small room. Even though I was happy to hear from him, I wouldn't let the voice in my head go. I accused him of ignoring me.

We ended up in a heated argument following my rants. After I calmed down, my boyfriend explained he'd been on a family group call, so he could neither pick up my calls nor respond to my message. That misunderstanding separated us for a while.

I stressed myself and my boyfriend out for nothing that evening. I was in too much of a hurry to accuse him of something that had not been confirmed. I was not polite in my approach to him. I allowed my emotions to get the better of me. If I'd waited to listen to his explanation, I wouldn't have found myself in that mess of a conflict.

—Leah

While we mentioned earlier that overthinking harms communication, this is not something that should be addressed just in passing. Communication is germane to the smooth running of any form of relationship, be it platonic or romantic.

The older you get, the more you realize how much you need someone to be in your corner, to be there for you in the good times and the bad. You always want to be able to converse with the people you love and care about. They're the ones you call when something happens to you, no matter how irrelevant or minute it might seem. Since they love you, it's not a bother to them. When there's a communication breakdown, however, unresolved conflicts fester. This not only ruins your relationships, but it also clogs the wheels of your peace of mind. I've yet to find someone who rejoices when they're no longer in touch with a lover they cared about, especially when the terms of separation weren't healthy.

But where does this breakdown begin? Most likely in that moment you begin to imagine the worst possible scenarios, when you speak your mind in the most unacceptable ways, when words you never meant come spewing out of your mouth. Later, you may wish you'd been quick to listen and slow to speak, but by then the damage is done. Your relationship will become a theater of constant conflict when you continue to let the issues you create in your head to fester and flourish. It's high time you killed them off.

Stonewalling: The Abuse That Ruins Communication

I sat in my office once and received a couple. The man had eyebags and was dressed in a rumpled t-shirt with baggy jeans. He looked like he badly needed a shave. His wife had her hair done in a ponytail but didn't look anywhere near as put-together as she could have. They literally dragged themselves into my office and sank into the chairs. My first instinct was that they were having marriage problems because of some mismanaged grief. Perhaps they'd lost a kid, I thought. I stood to welcome them, but what I heard nearly knocked me off balance.

"I want a divorce!" the man said.

For a moment, I debated with myself whether to point out to him that I wasn't a divorce lawyer or to just sit down and let him speak. I sat down and chose to ask him why.

"She's an expert at stonewalling. She deserves a medal!"

The woman looked hurt but didn't say anything in her defense. It was a welcome change because I usually have to calm yelling spouses during sessions.

—Benjamin

Stonewalling is simply the act of ending a conversation abruptly or refusing to discuss something that needs to be discussed. Think about the silent treatment and completely ignoring your partner. Think about avoidance of an argument and total dismissal of your partner's concerns. Yeah, that's all stonewalling. It's not good. It's abusive. It eats marriages for breakfast. Don't do it.

If you find yourself constantly falling into the habit of stonewalling, you can learn to overcome it. The antidote is communicating. Rather than avoid or dismiss a conversation that should be had, choose to talk about it.

When you stonewall, you leave room for assumptions. You also leave many questions unanswered, and your partner ends up feeling unheard. Inflicting the silent treatment on your partner might make them think you're punishing or manipulating them. Are you punishing your partner? Are you trying to manipulate them? No? Then don't stonewall.

How to Communicate Properly If You're Overthinking

Let's imagine the story of Nina, a German monkey known for staying at the gate of her cage whenever tourists come by. For some weird reason, Nina never ate the bananas that were handed over to her. Whenever she was offered bananas by tourists, she always turned her face away in disdain.

One day, a young boy came by and, after getting the same reaction from Nina, decided to take her home. After offering her a lot of fruit and trying to get her to eat something, he gave up and left her alone for a while.

But fortunately for Nina, she stumbled across a piece of bread one day, and she ravaged it so much that the whole household was surprised! Apparently, it was bread Nina had wanted all along, but because she didn't (more specifically, couldn't) *say* so, she was never offered any and so had to starve.

The power of being able to communicate!

Communicating will save you a lot of pain in your relationship. You'll do yourself and your partner a lot of good if you communicate how you feel about something instead of jumping to conclusions or completely avoiding the discussion. When you learn to give your significant other the benefit of the doubt, conflicts are easily avoided. Try to gather facts rather than hovering around motives.

Communicating when you're dealing with overthinking is easier said than done. But if you and your partner have built a healthy foundation for your relationship, it'll be easy to discuss anything, including your overthinking problems. Whichever place you're at in your relationship or marriage, there's always a good place to start talking from. Let's look at a few useful tips to help you get started.

1. Be intentional

Healthy communication is something you have to make up your mind to do. Just like you can hardly get good grades by accident, it's impossible for your communication as a couple to "just work out." It won't. You have to be the one to make it work. You have to decide that you will do your part to keep the lines of communication open, even when you're tempted to stonewall.

2. Ask for a conversation politely

When you need to talk to your partner, asking for their attention nicely will help them to approach the conversation in a more relaxed manner. Instead of starting up abruptly or aggressively and risking them becoming defensive even before the conversation has started, it's smarter to ask nicely.

3. Discuss the problem when you're both relaxed

Discussions are best saved for a time when you're both relaxed. When blood pressure is running high, maybe you can politely ask for some time to mull things over and then return to the conversation when you're both calmer. This way, you'll actually get somewhere with your discussion.

4. Try writing it

A great way to communicate with your significant other is by writing to them. The blank page gives you a lot of room to express yourself, and it's neat because you can really express yourself there. Plus, it's therapeutic for you and your partner. This is where you give yourself the chance to say the things that might be difficult to express face to face, and you can go as deeply as you need to.

5. Prepare notes for a face-to-face talk

If you prefer the good old face-to-face kitchen table hash-it-out method, it can help to come with notes highlighting all the things you want to talk about. That way, you'll feel more confident when you do start the discussion and will be able to stay on track rather than get distracted by unnecessary tangents.

6. If you ask for their help, respect their feelings

Your partner isn't responsible for dealing with your overthinking, but they can help you by understanding and supporting your desire to work on it. When you're asking for their support, it's important that they know that they have a choice and that you'll respect their decision.

Examples of Conversation Starters to Overcome Stonewalling and Improve Communication

Trying to beat the tendency to stonewall your partner can be hard. The first few words are usually the most difficult, almost like you've got a piece of bone stuck in your throat. Having good conversation starters handy can help. You can try any of these:

1. It's really hard to talk right now, but we need to.

2. Can we talk?

3. Can we go for a walk together? You don't have to say anything.

4. I know you're angry, and that's okay.

5. Tell me why you're angry and I'll listen.

6. I'm sorry. (This is a good old classic conversation starter after a fight)

Some Conversation Starters That Don't Involve Talking

1. Leave a note in a conspicuous place for your partner to find. Here's a sample of what you could put in the note:

    Hey, babe. I'm sorry our conversation ended in a fight. Gosh, we fight a lot these days, don't we? Are you up for a talk? Should we go out to that restaurant/park you love and grab something simple that we both love? I'm craving my favorite juice. What would you like?

    OR

Hey babe. I feel so angry right now I don't know where to begin. I just want you to know that I have a few things I need to get off my chest. Please, can we talk?

2. Ask your partner to help you with something. Just ask. They might still be upset, but ask politely.

3. Buy them a tasty treat and write "peace offering" on a small piece of paper.

4. Send a text.

When trying to apologize or start a conversation with your partner after an argument, NEVER attempt to replace actual words or an apology or an in-depth discussion with a gift or even an act of kindness. If you buy them something they like or do something for them, it should be a means to an end: to defuse the tension and help the two of you start talking, not to erase the wrongs or make them go away. Ignoring the issues in your marriage is a mistake. Whatever issues you ignore are likely to come back to bite you...like a half-killed serpent.

Since this is such an important point, let me reiterate: Gifts and acts of kindness don't replace having an in-depth conversation about the problem or offering an apology for what you've done wrong.

Communicating with Your Partner is Key

Saying that communication is vital in a relationship is an understatement. Many relationships hit the rocks when one person stops talking for whatever reason. This means that keeping communication lines open is a matter of life and death for your relationship. You have to do it. If you're still passionate about making the relationship or marriage work, that is.

It's through communication that you'll come to understand each other's views on different issues. Your relationship will strengthen when you freely share your joys, hurts, opinions, fears, expectations, disappointments, and even boundaries. Think of the fulfillment and happiness that will spring up when you're able to freely converse with your partner on any topic. Of course, there will be moments of silence, but when good communication is a routine, that silence will never be awkward.

However, you need to know that not all forms of communication are effective. Effective communication requires putting yourself in the other person's shoes—in other words, having empathy. It's not just about exchanging words; it's about understanding the emotion and motives behind the thoughts you're trying to get across, and the thoughts your partner is communicating. Apart from this, you also need to listen to truly understand what's been said, which will make the other person feel heard and understood.

Why is effective communication important? Here goes!

1. It keeps your relationship fresh

Greg and Hannah were just about to be married when Hannah began to complain about no longer feeling a spark. Greg was so angry about this that he refused to work things out between them and left Hannah to go ahead with the breakup. It all happened so fast that none of their friends could comprehend what had happened.

Do you know what happened to them? I'll give you two guesses. Nope, nothing to do with disappearing butterflies. Yep, everything to do with communication. Somewhere along the line, they stopped sharing their hearts. They stopped talking. The result was inevitable.

Remember how your love journey started with that special someone and you always wanted to please them? You were always conscious of your attitude towards them. You would adjust the smallest strand of hair just to look perfect for them and take ages to decide on what to wear to a dinner date. Now that the mushy rollercoaster seems to have ceased and familiarity has set in, you need to get intentional.

You can't always depend on how you feel to do the right thing, you know. The desire to have things "feel right" explains why breakups and divorces happen: the end of the emotional tingling means an end to love for most people. But it doesn't have to be this way for you.

You don't have to be dependent on that emotional reaction that seems to lead you by the hand for every thought, word, and action. Take control and love hard. Be honest with your partner about your feelings. In doing this, it'll be easier to remember why you fell in love with each other in the first place. You're able to remind one another about what attracted you to each other.

If you keep talking, you'll always have stuff to talk about. The key: keep talking.

2. You'll understand each other better

It takes a lifetime to get to know a person. If people knew the implication and real meaning of "I want to get to know you," they wouldn't be in a rush to say it. You must understand that people evolve every second, every day, and every year, including you. Yep! You're not the same person you were yesterday. Understanding this will help you see the need to communicate your needs to your partner and ask questions. Constantly speaking about your needs will give you a comfortable space to know and understand not just yourself, but also that special person in your corner.

3. It helps clear things up

I remember feeling stupid after my boyfriend explained to me that the reason he couldn't pick up my calls was because he'd been in a group call with his family. I beat myself up that night for jumping to conclusions. If I had simply taken a chill pill and waited to hear him out or asked questions, we wouldn't have had a huge fight.

—Leah

When you allow little things like assumptions to become the truth you feed on, you ruin things. Here are three ways you can avoid making assumptions: ask questions, ask questions, and ask questions. Yeah, that's all. It's that simple. What happens as a result? You get an answer. Instead of overthinking whether the person could by lying, enjoy the moment and trust your partner. Your relationship will work out as long as you're with someone who is honest. Just breathe. Keep the lines of communication open always. Not once in a while—always!

4. It builds trust

When both parties are eager to communicate their thoughts and open up, there's room for vulnerability. One person doesn't feel left out of the other's life. You'll become one another's safe place—and isn't that the dream?

Leaving No Room for Assumptions

I expected my partner to always know how I felt. I wanted her to go all-out for me without me having to say a word. But my expectations were the root cause of most of the issues we were having. I disliked the fact that she wasn't aware of my feelings, and she absolutely hated the fact that I always pointed this out and made her feel bad about it.

—James

Unfortunately, mind-reading is not a gift we're born with. You'd think that in this world where effective communication is being phased out and couples are more often on their phones than in each other's arms, the ability to read minds would come in handy for us all, but sadly that's not an option.

In light of that, you simply must learn to talk to your partner to avoid assumptions. The following are what I call communication nuggets for overthinkers:

Your partner is not the enemy.

One of the major reasons communication isn't effective is that we tend to take the offensive, leaving the other person with no choice but to be defensive.

It's a trap to think that you'll be able to get your point across by blaming or nagging your partner. Yes, your partner might have contributed in some way to your anxiety or stress, but at the end of the day, your priority should be making your relationship work, not playing blame games. In your communication, you must emphasize that whatever you're facing, you know you can get through it together.

Be completely honest and be prepared to hear what you don't want to hear.

Okay, I know this is a tough one, but the truth is, your partner might not completely understand. Nobody understands overthinking as much as overthinkers. The most important thing is that you stay honest with each other, and make sure you're on the same page as far as your relationship is concerned and there are no secrets or hidden bitterness between you.

Focus on finding a solution TOGETHER.

You shouldn't expect your partner to change overnight because of you. True, a relationship is about compromise, but it's also about understanding. What I want you to focus on is finding a balance that works for you both.

Let's say one of the triggers for your overthinking is your partner not replying to your texts right away. Try to consider their side first. You should be able to understand that it might not always be easy for them to instantly respond to your texts, and likewise, they should understand that this is very important to you and put in the extra effort. When having the conversation, try to find a balance. Don't be selfish and make demands that will be hard on your partner.

Tell your partner everything.

Hiding things can make your communication futile. You've got to lay it all out without exception—your greatest fears, your past hurts, the things that make you anxious and second-guess the relationship, everything. Take your time, but know that it's worth the effort.

You can't lose with communication. Yes, being honest about your feelings is hard and painful, but if the relationship is important to you, know that there's no way it can thrive without you both talking about your struggles. Y'all signed up for summer, winter, and everything in between.

Wrapping Up

Now that we've identified the problem and we've talked about how communication is key, we still need to tackle overthinking as a whole. A lot of people who are overthinkers feel like they are doomed to be that way forever. They say things like, "That's just how I am. I can't change it."

What if I told you that it's possible to control that tendency to ruminate? Yep. It totally is, and that's what we'll be looking at in the next chapter. Let's jump in!

Your Quick Workbook

If your partner was the person overthinking, would you want them to communicate this problem to you, or would you prefer they kept it to themselves?

_____

_____

_____

_____

_____

_____

_____

_____

_____

How difficult is it for you to communicate with your partner when you're overthinking?

_____

_____

_____

_____

_____

_____

_____

Why do you think it's hard to express yourself when you're overthinking?

_____

_____

_____

_____

_____

_____

_____

_____

Based on this chapter, what will communication help you with in your relationship?

_____

_____

_____

_____

_____

_____

_____

_____

_____

_____

_____

_____

PART 2

Attending to the Problem

Have you ever thought about what it would be like if you didn't overthink so much? Have you tried to imagine how things would improve if that wasn't a problem anymore?

Maybe you and your spouse could actually work things out for once. Maybe you'd stop crying so much. Maybe you'd stop feeling like you need to break free from your head every day. Maybe you'd even be happier?

I invite you to take a moment or two to think about it. You know you have a problem with overthinking; you've seen the damage it causes. Think about how different things can actually be. This section will show you how to achieve this dream. The best part is that you can start applying these steps right away!

CHAPTER 3

STEPS TO OVERCOME OVERTHINKING AND ANXIETY ISSUES IN YOUR RELATIONSHIP

"To think too much is a disease."

—Fyodor Dostoyevsky

Your alarm clock wakes you up at 7 a.m. sharp. You roll over to turn it off and run a hand down your face. It took you forever to actually fall asleep because your mind wouldn't stop racing. As soon as you try to get out of bed, you remember that your partner didn't come to bed last night. Probably because of the argument you had two days ago. Now you wonder if they're avoiding you. Or if they don't love you anymore. Maybe you should get a divorce. But you know you still love them. But you can't trust them anymore. Or can you? Maybe you shouldn't have snooped through their phone and accused them of lying to you and falling in love with someone else. But...but then they should know by now the kind of person you are. Why would they be okay with getting that kind of message from someone of the opposite sex? They're probably cheating... Right?

You head downstairs for breakfast and discover that your partner already left. You sigh, tired of the awkwardness and stiff silences. You start to wonder if you should call, but then you decide they probably don't want to hear from you. You head to work and you're not able to focus much because you're thinking about your home situation.

A part of you wants to drop by their workplace to surprise them with lunch, but you know you'll see that person who sent them that text. You'd rather not disturb their idyllic workplace romance. Resentment starts to build as you think of all the other times your partner has acted in a suspicious way this past month—coming home late, not eating dinner at home, going to bed earlier than you.

The stressful thoughts in your mind take a toll on your work, and you find yourself snapping at your nice coworker. Great. Now she probably hates you too. You're relieved to leave work, and you head home again to fix dinner. You don't call your partner as you usually would on your way home. They probably don't want to hear from you.

You get home to find the dinner table already set up and your partner waiting for you with a smile on their face and open arms. You're surprised, but immediately your brain goes into overdrive: *Aha! I knew it! This is obviously an action fueled by guilt. They're obviously cheating on me. Why else would they do this?* You tell your partner you're too tired to eat at the table and take your food upstairs to eat in bed. You only manage to get two forkfuls down your throat before your thoughts make you restless and take away your appetite.

You start to imagine what life would be like as a divorcee. Everyone would whisper about how your spouse cheated on you because you weren't good enough. You'd have to find a new place to stay. You'd have to change your friend group. You'd obviously never go back to the same church again... Your thoughts whirl around your mind as you sink into a fitful sleep. You're probably going to wake up tired again tomorrow.

Hey!

Does this sound familiar? Overthinking can create so many problems where there were none to begin with, making your life bleak and joyless when it could be so much better.

Opening Up to Your Partner About Your Struggles with Overthinking

What's the best thing about being in a relationship? I've been privileged to talk to several people who are in happy relationships, and they unanimously agree that having a safe space to be themselves is the best thing for them.

I agree. Being in a trusting, healthy relationship gives you the space to be yourself to the fullest, without fear of judgment or desertion. However, being an overthinker can make it hard for you to communicate with your partner for so many reasons. For example, you might feel jealous of your spouse and doubt everything they say. You might have even considered following them whenever they go out or paying a surprise visit to their workplace just to make sure they're not lying. It's even possible that you've thought of hiring a private investigator to follow them just so you can breathe easy. Does that sound familiar? It's not unusual to overthink from time to time, but it could become a very serious problem if it's not taken care of quickly.

I think the worst thing about being an overthinker and having doubts about your partner or your relationship is loneliness. It can be pretty easy to feel isolated because you can't talk to anyone about what you're thinking. Most overthinkers try to deal with the intrusive thoughts by themselves, either by trying to ignore them or stifling them so that they don't sound irrational to other people. If you're in these very uncomfortable shoes, you need to do something about it. Having someone you can talk to anytime and share your deepest thoughts with will go a long way in helping you conquer overthinking.

You need to be able to speak to your partner and reclaim your safe space. You need to fight for the right to feel seen, loved, and understood in your relationship. You've gone without it long enough.

I can almost feel you rolling your eyes and thinking, "Wow, Captain Obvious much?" Stay with me here. Communicating with your partner as an overthinker goes beyond just saying whatever's on your mind at that time. Effective communication is something that sounds simple but can be very hard to achieve, especially when you keep trying and failing at it.

Before we talk more about opening up to your partner, you need to examine yourself and your relationship. Go back to what you wanted when you first started this beautiful journey you're on right now. Remind yourself of the love, promise, and excitement you felt when it all started. Remember how much your partner loves you. Recall that your partner is someone you trust. This means you can be sure that they always want the best for you and that they are reliable. Allow yourself to understand that your partner just wants to connect with you on the deepest level possible, and keeping them in the dark just robs them of that opportunity.

Another important thing to do before speaking to your significant other is to identify the source of your thoughts. What is at the root of your fear? For example, if you're worried that your husband is paying too much attention to his female coworker all of a sudden, it's possible that you're really just afraid your husband doesn't find you desirable anymore because of the weight you've put on. Identifying the source of your worries gives you and your partner enough ammunition to tackle your fears once and for all.

Now that we've laid the groundwork, here are some guidelines to help you communicate effectively with your significant other:

Have a face-to-face conversation.

Conversations via text may cause confusion, as messages may be taken out of context and tone is difficult to decipher in writing. Keep in mind that you need to have an open and honest conversation with them.

Try to ignore your fear of rejection.

This is the hardest step for some people. I understand that it's not easy to just ignore such a powerful fear, but giving yourself a mental timeout helps. Also, some techniques like meditation and distraction work here too.

Discuss your worries.

Explain what you've been thinking and why. If you know the root cause of your fears, this would be a good time to discuss it. Ask your partner for space to talk and use statements that begin with "I." Avoid accusatory statements; instead, focus on your own feelings while reminding yourself that you value your relationship. Don't be afraid to ask for what you need, and remember to be as honest as possible.

Take regular timeouts.

If the conversation gets off track or you can see signs that an argument is brewing, calmly ask for a timeout and pause. Evaluate the conversation to see how that could have happened. It's easy to fall back into old patterns of communication here, but taking as many timeouts as needed helps.

Be vulnerable.

C. S. Lewis said, "To love at all is to be vulnerable," and I completely agree. Don't revert to defensive tactics to cover up emotions like anger, jealousy, shame, and anxiety. Instead, remind yourself that you are worthy of being loved. Loving yourself first helps you accept love from others. Involve your partner in your thought process as much as possible. Knowing that you have a companion to support you will help you feel less isolated and even improve your relationship.

Give yourself permission to receive the love and support your partner is bound to offer. If you're finding it hard to implement the guidelines above because your thoughts keep getting away from you, don't worry; the tactics we'll discuss in the next part will show you how to control your thoughts. Use these steps to guide you, especially when you're communicating with your partner.

How to Control Your Thoughts (A Step-by-Step Guide)

"Finally, brethren, whatsoever things are true, whatsoever things are honest, whatsoever things are just, whatsoever things are pure, whatsoever things are lovely, whatsoever things are of good report; if there be any virtue, and if there be any praise, think on these things."

Philippians 4:8

The ocean is really remarkable. It can be calm enough to let us frolic in its waters under the sun during summertime; it can also be cold and menacing, destroying entire countries and changing people's lives with a few tall waves. It can be docile enough to let us cruise all over it on its placid surface, and it can be powerful enough to submerge us without warning. But the danger doesn't mean people avoid the ocean or stop sailing. Instead, they've learned to control it, and many live successful lives on the sea.

Your thoughts are similar to the ocean: they can overwhelm and drown you, or you can choose to master them. Everyone should gain mastery over their thoughts, but for an overthinker, controlling your thoughts is an absolutely necessary life skill. When you control your thoughts, you can take charge of your life and position yourself for better outcomes all around. This step-by-step guide for doing just that is straightforward, practical, and it works. All you have to do is commit yourself to the process, remind yourself that you're deserving of love at every point, and watch yourself thrive.

1. Understand that thoughts are not reality

One mistake people make over and over again is believing everything they think. True freedom comes from the realization that our thoughts are just thoughts; they aren't reality unless we give them that power.

Thinking negative thoughts leads to having negative emotions, which leads to more negative thoughts and, in turn, negative emotions, and before you know it, you're stuck in a vicious cycle. These thoughts then become self-limiting beliefs, and you'll find yourself looking for evidence to back up those beliefs. Instead, distance yourself from your thoughts.

2. Observe your thoughts

Now that we've established that you're not your thoughts, you can observe them objectively. It might be difficult to categorize your thoughts when your mind is going at warp speed, but deliberately slowing down to observe helps. As you practice this often, you'll start to notice a pattern.

As you notice each thought, label it and let it pass. Labeling your thoughts will help you shed light on thought patterns and even handle your thoughts better. Using labels like "fear," "anxiety," and "jealousy" will help you understand how you're feeling. At this point, don't try to push away the thoughts or explore them further; just let them float along.

3. Fish out your negative thoughts and find the story

Now that you have an idea of the pattern your thoughts run in, identify the negative ones and start to tackle them one by one. These introspections may lead you to blame yourself, compare yourself to others, or even make you feel hopeless. Dealing with one at a time will allow you to focus on the process and help you avoid being overwhelmed.

For each negative thought, ask yourself these questions:

- What is the trigger for this thought? Is it a certain person, place, or situation?
- Why do I think this? Is there any evidence supporting it?
- What's the root cause of this?
- How do I feel when I think about this? How would I label this thought?
- How do I react to this idea? Do I have a physical reaction to this thought?
- How do I behave as a result of this belief?

4. Take charge of your story

The best way to handle negative thoughts is to treat them like a science experiment—observe them from an objective point of view, be curious, and ask questions. Once you've identified a negative thought and labeled it, don't let it keep going. Instead, bring it back, ask more questions, and gently challenge it.

Is it a rational thought? Is there any evidence to support the thought? Why should you believe it? Asking these questions helps to break the cycle; answering them rationally helps to positively reframe those thoughts. It is important to repeat this process as often as possible.

5. Step out of your mind

You've done a great job so far in controlling the thoughts in your head. It's time to take the fight outside your mind. Here are some practices to help in the battle to overcome your thoughts:

- **Stress management:** Stress can lead you to think negatively more frequently. Being intentional about managing your stress creates a level playing ground.

- **Practice self-care:** Self-care has a lot of benefits, not least of which is arming yourself to tackle your negative thoughts every day. Self-care can look like keeping a journal, listening to your favorite music, or giving yourself a small treat. Intentionality is key here as well.

- **Practice distraction:** It's easy to get caught up in your mind. Once you notice the tempo of your thoughts getting too wild to control, distract yourself so that you have the mental space to tackle these thoughts. Great ways to distract yourself include going for a walk, spending time with loved ones, taking up a hobby, or listening to music.

These steps work. However, if you don't apply them consistently, I'm afraid you won't see sustained results. They are easy to practice but they require consistency.

Check for Mental Issues That May be Compounding the Problem

One of the reasons I advocate for clear communication for chronic overthinkers is the fact that overthinking could be pointing to an underlying issue. Being an overthinker means you most likely do not feel comfortable sharing your worries with people. It's possible that you have tried to speak to one or two people about it, but you were either shut down or your worries were trivialized by the other person.

Realizing that no one understands what you're going through may make you feel defective or broken in some fundamental way. That's far from the truth, but you may in fact be dealing with a mental health issue that's making it difficult for you to overcome overthinking on your own.

Overthinking can be a symptom of several mental health disorders, which will be explored here. It might be easy for you to trace the origin of your overthinking to a particular event or period in your life, or you might realize that you've always been like this.

Either way, finding out if your overthinking could be linked to a mental health issue is essential. Your new life depends on it. I'd like to state here that there should be no shame whatsoever associated with mental illnesses. Nobody makes you feel bad when your body is ill, so why should you feel shame if your mind is? If your overthinking is in fact a symptom of a mental health issue, treating that problem is a surefire way to manage the overthinking. You might even come to realize that other symptoms you never noticed start to get resolved as well.

Low self-esteem

Having low self-esteem shouldn't be classified as a mental health disorder (and it isn't), but it's serious enough to affect your life negatively. Overthinking can be intricately linked with low self-esteem. Having negative and critical thoughts about yourself, doubting your own strength, and shying away from challenging situations because you don't believe in yourself screams low self-esteem. This frequently spills over into your relationship with your spouse and others. The truth is, everyone around you suffers, not just you. The ironic thing is that avoiding challenging situations reinforces the idea that you're not strong or capable enough. Building your self-love and self-compassion is a good way to raise your self-esteem.

Post-traumatic stress disorder (PTSD)

Overthinking as a trauma response to PTSD deserves proper attention from a professional. Sometimes, you might not recall experiencing a traumatic event, but you might have symptoms that point to PTSD anyway.

Experiencing a traumatic event can change a lot for you. If you find yourself being hyperaware of your environment, having flashbacks about the event or related events, having trouble sleeping, and constantly ruminating about potential dangers, or the likelihood of another traumatic event, you're likely suffering from PTSD and need to seek help from a professional.

Anxiety

Anxiety disorders are mental disturbances characterized by excessive worrying. It's normal to feel anxious about important events, public speaking, and stuff like that, but when you're unable to function normally because of anxiety, it becomes a problem.

If you find yourself having extremely anxiety in reaction to certain events or emotions and you can't really control how you respond to certain situations, you might have an anxiety condition. It's nothing to be worried about—it can be managed. You're more likely to have an anxiety disorder if you've witnessed a traumatic event or you have a shy, inhibited personality type.

Anxiety disturbances can also be inherited because a family history of anxiety can increase your likelihood of getting one. Some thyroid conditions have also been associated with this disorder (Siegmann et al., 2018). Dry mouth, palpitations, difficulty in breathing, and nausea are some common symptoms.

Depression

Depression and overthinking go hand in hand. Overthinking is both a common symptom of and a major risk factor for depression (Nguyen et al., 2019; Michl et al., 2013). This means that it's entirely possible to get depressed if you're an overthinker, or to overthink because you are depressed. We can't really say which causes which, but overthinking has been associated with stress, anxiety, and depression.

Other common symptoms of depression are feeling hopeless or helpless, sleeping a lot or not being able to sleep, and unusual anger or irritability, among others. Cognitive-behavioral therapy (CBT) can help with depression. Some medications, prescribed by a psychiatrist, can also help you feel better.

Obsessive-compulsive disorder (OCD)

Overthinking as a result of OCD will look like having many uncontrollable thoughts which are the object of your obsession. These thoughts will lead to you carrying out habitual, repetitive behaviors that you feel compelled to do. People with OCD cannot control their thoughts or behaviors even when they know that they're being excessive. They also do not derive any pleasure in their compulsive behaviors, although they spend a considerable amount of time each day entertaining their thoughts and acting on their compulsions (NIMH, 2020).

Wrapping Up

Sometimes there's more to your overthinking than meets the eye. It's worthwhile getting any potential mental health issues checked out to rule out any underlying causes of your overthinking. I can feel you wondering why this seems so complex, but I can tell you that whatever's worth doing at all is worth doing well. Don't give up—you can do this.

A huge consequence of overthinking for relationships is lots of arguments, the silent treatment, and fights. What if you could sort those problems out without too much fuss? What if there was a way to argue with your spouse productively? The next chapter will tell you all about how to do that.

Your Quick Workbook

Is there anyone you can confide in when you're feeling overwhelmed by your thoughts and emotions?

_____

_____

_____

Is there a thought that keeps coming up? Have you noticed a particular pattern of thought that appears over and over again?

_____

_____

_____

Based on this chapter, what activities do you think you can engage in to distract you from these thought patterns?

_____

_____

_____

CHAPTER 4

SOLVING CONFLICTS QUICKLY: A HACK

"Whenever you're in conflict with someone, there is one factor that can make the difference between damaging your relationship and deepening it. That factor is attitude."

—William James

Conflict is an unavoidable constant in every relationship. Many people think that the presence or absence of conflict in relationships determines how long the relationship will last and if the couple is really happy. That's a common misconception people fall into, especially overthinkers. I've spoken to people who tend to devolve into intense episodes of overthinking after a disagreement with their partners. This, of course, leads to withdrawal, reduced communication, and further decay in the relationship. It's not surprising to see such relationships soon come to an end.

Interestingly, research has shown that conflict is common in intimate relationships and that the more intimate the relationship is, the higher the tendency to disagree. However, the health of a relationship is better judged by the method of conflict resolution (Moland, 2011).

Truth be told, discord can be stressful. Studies show that it's associated with increased stress, anger, and the flight/fight response. This naturally leads to an increase in blood pressure. Repeated conflict can also lead to apprehension and anxiety in both partners. As you can probably surmise, conflict makes overthinking worse, which, along with anxiety, can lead to depression. On the whole, conflict can affect the stability of the relationship and leave both partners feeling isolated (Laursen, 2010).

On the flip side, conflict can also be good—even healthy—because it helps the two of you learn how to settle differences and become open to contrasting points of view. You'll also learn to be more considerate, and you'll develop your listening and understanding skills. Disagreeing can promote constructive dialogue in your relationship, which leads to intellectual growth and improved mental health. The catch here is that both partners must be allowed to express themselves in a considerate manner during the conflict.

I guess we could say that conflict is both good and bad. So what's the truth here? It's simple. The issue is not conflict itself, but rather the manner in which conflict is approached (i.e., your attitude towards it). This is a huge determinant of its effect on the relationship. While it's possible to have both the right attitude and the wrong attitude towards conflict, your goal should be to foster the right attitude, so let's start with that.

The Right Attitude Towards Relationship Conflict

Having the right attitude towards conflict and its resolution is everything. But I'd be doing you a disservice if I jumped right into that without talking about *you* first.

Yes, you.

You see, developing the right attitude towards conflict resolution depends on your self-perception. Do you love yourself enough? Can you forgive yourself for your mistakes? What's your attitude towards yourself during your inner conflicts? Are you harsh and critical of yourself? You might get away with hiding your true feelings and reactions from other people, but it'll be next to impossible to do so with your significant other. The fact remains that your internal orientation affects your external world, even in conflict resolution.

The first step to resolving conflict begins with you. Examine yourself to find the areas you need to work on. Would you benefit from more self-compassion? Do you practice self-forgiveness? Do you believe that you're deserving of real happiness and support? Are you really in tune with your feelings, or are you avoiding them? Would you rather lash out to hurt someone before they can hurt you?

I admit that it's a lot of work and there's a great deal of self-reflection to be done. Reflecting on these questions while journaling is a great way to dig deep for self-evaluation. The good news is that you don't have to do it all in one day. You can incorporate it into your morning routine and tackle these questions bit by bit.

In the process of doing this, it's natural for more questions to come up. Answer them as best you can and discuss with your partner as well if you need to. Getting your internal mind space in order and checking in with yourself is the key to breaking the cycle of frustrating arguments that end in a deadlock. As you keep doing the internal work, you'll begin to appreciate the differences in your interactions with your partner.

However, keep in mind that adopting the right attitude for conflict resolution in your relationship shouldn't come into play only when you're having an argument. Rather, you have to be ready with the right attitude at all times. Recalibrating your attitude for conflict resolution spills over into other aspects of your relationship and will improve your partnership over time.

The following steps will help you develop the attitude you need for success:

Remember that you care about your partner and the relationship.

You're committed to resolving these issues because you care—why else would you be there?

Take a step back to look at the bigger picture.

How important is the topic you're arguing about in the grand scheme of things? Could your actions have contributed to this conflict? Instead of getting swept up in your feelings, thoughts, and reactions, consider your significant other's feelings, as well as their effort and commitment to the relationship.

Be honest at all times.

However, note that being honest doesn't call for blunt, harsh words. Instead, be tactful and consider your partner's feelings while being as honest as possible.

Swallow your pride.

Someone once said, "Pride builds walls between people while humility builds bridges." When pride creeps into your interactions with your partner, it distorts your perception of the relationship and robs you of the chance to be vulnerable with them. Apologizing first might be hard, but sometimes it's necessary. Are you holding on to pride in ways that are damaging your relationship?

Remember what the fight is really about.

The biggest mistake couples often make is to assume that conflict means they're pitted against each other. That's the farthest thing from the truth. Conflict should be about you and your partner working as a team against the issue in question. Adopting an "us vs. them" mentality is a life-changing step for your relationship. Treat your significant other with compassion at all times because they're on your team. Forgive easily and often.

Show respect.

Respecting your significant other means always being considerate of them and never demeaning them or making them feel less-than.

The Wrong Attitude Towards Relationship Conflict

I think we can both agree here that conflict is practically inevitable and can even be healthy. For the most part, when you have an argument with your partner, you're probably not doing it to end the relationship; instead, you're probably trying to express yourself and your feelings. But the sad truth is that poorly handled conflict that occurs over and over again can lead to an abrupt end to the relationship. If you find that each confrontation with your partner ends in cold silence, frustration, and distance, then you need to check your attitude towards confrontation. You might be making one of these mistakes:

You're not expressing yourself often enough.

Sometimes keeping quiet because you don't want to stir things up isn't the best way to go. In fact, I daresay it's not the way to go at all. Bottling things up because you're scared of the relationship ending or because you'd rather avoid things getting messy leads to resentment, doubt, anger, and unhappiness.

It might seem like the easy way out, but it eventually becomes stressful when you finally let your feelings out. And make no mistake, these feelings will come out, one way or another. So if you're reading this and thinking, "Well, thank goodness I don't argue much with my partner, and I'd rather eat my hat than start or entertain a fight, so I'm good to go"—I regret to tell you (okay, I don't really regret it) that you're most definitely *not* good to go. That fight you're avoiding will still happen, but it'll be bigger, messier, and more stressful.

Make a decision to communicate with your partner today. If an issue is still on your mind a full 48 hours after it occurs, then you need to talk it out. Thankfully, with the tips I've given you in the previous section, you should be able to do that.

You're always on the defensive.

If you always have to be right in every argument, you have a certain idea of how things should be done, you're quick to jump to your own defense, or you're convinced that you're never the problem in the relationship, there's a very big possibility that your defensive attitude is a source of frustration for your partner.

While it might even be true that you're right most of the time, there's more than one way to be right. Rather than pointing out the 50 ways that you're right, slow down to listen to your partner and consider their point of view. If you're constantly on the defensive, your significant other will feel unheard, isolated, and resentful. You need to quit criticizing and blaming your partner whenever you feel attacked.

You're fond of overgeneralizing.

As an overthinker, it's easy to judge your partner based on their actions and connect said actions to other previous actions. Then you'll find yourself associating them with certain behavior and overgeneralizing. Statements that start with "You always..." or "You never..." should be avoided, especially in the heat of an argument.

If you've noticed a pattern of behavior in your partner, rather than bringing it up while you're arguing and emotions are running high, save it for a later date when you're both calm. Don't bring up past incidents to aggravate current issues.

You're quite the mind-reader.

I'm sure there have been incidents where you analyzed your partner's actions and just "knew" what their intentions were while carrying out those actions. Throw in a healthy dose of speculation and negative thoughts, and *voila!*—you have a relationship headed for the rocks. To be honest, a good amount of conflict could be avoided by simply asking questions and clarifying matters with your partner. I encourage you to, as the popular saying goes, "Assume nothing and question everything."

You don't listen.

Sure, you're present with your partner and you spend as much time as possible with them, but do you listen? I mean, *really* listen. Do you roll your eyes, look at your phone screen, or watch the game while your spouse is trying to tell you something important? Or perhaps you spend that time rehearsing your next debate point in your head instead of listening? These are classic signs of a poor listener.

Why not try active listening? Eliminate distractions whenever you're spending time with your partner. Put the phone or book down, turn off the TV for a moment. You get the idea. Practice mindfulness when you're spending time with your significant other. Ask questions and clarify their statements. This might seem like a trivial tip, but it goes a long way.

You're the Ice King/Queen.

If you're quick to ice out your partner after an argument, or even before an impending argument, you're gravely reducing your chances of settling your disputes amicably. Refusing to discuss a particular issue or even listen to your spouse when they're willing to talk about it shows disrespect and a lack of consideration on your part.

You keep withholding your love.

Treating your partner unkindly after a disagreement is an alarming sign of deterioration in your relationship. Withdrawing your love and affection might seem like a good way to communicate your displeasure, but all it does is drive the wedge between yourself and your spouse deeper.

Maintaining a relationship takes a lot of work, but the best part is that the rewards are plentiful too. If you're guilty of any of these practices, taking intentional steps to change them will improve the quality of your relationship, and you'll see the positive impact almost immediately.

Why Conflicts Should be Resolved in a Timely Manner

What's the silliest thing you've ever argued about? The answers I've heard range from leaving the toilet seat up to chewing noisily in public. I'm sure there are even sillier things you've probably argued about. It's weird, but these petty arguments are often the most annoying ones ever!

Now I want you to think about the *worst* argument you've had with your partner. I mean the biggest knock-down drag-out fight you've experienced. What was it about? How did you resolve it? Was it even truly resolved? How did it affect your relationship?

Study the patterns of both types of arguments—the silly ones and the serious ones. What is the difference between them? How did they start and how were they resolved? It's likely that the silly arguments were never fully resolved; you probably still argue about leaving the toilet seat up or leaving clothes on the floor instead of tossing them into the laundry basket. And that's okay. Some conflicts will never be fully resolved, especially between two people who spend a lot of time together. The key to conflict resolution here is picking your battles wisely.

One big mistake a lot of people make with major conflicts is avoiding the topic and walking on eggshells around each other, hoping that it'll die down. Often, couples like that are likely to go on to have several big arguments revolving around that one elephant in the room. This is because they've missed what is perhaps the most important factor in positive conflict resolution: timing. Resolving the conflict at the best time possible may very well be the key to the health of your relationship.

This might sound unconventional, but there are three possible best times for conflict resolution: before it starts, during the conflict, and after the conflict. Preventing confrontation is the best option, in my opinion. Having a strong bond of friendship and positivity is the key to preventing conflicts before they arise. Showing consistent affection for each other builds up a store of positivity, which helps buffet the relationship during times of conflict.

The next best time to resolve a conflict is during the conflict itself. This requires a strong bond of friendship, communication, and intuition. It will help both of you realize when the argument has become unproductive, which is the minute that the quarrel devolves into other issues that are not connected to the original problem.

You may also notice when the quarrel becomes more about protecting your egos than honest communication. At this point, it's essential to take a small break to figure out where you lost the plot. Then you should reconvene and discuss the matter with the end goal of compromise and preservation in mind.

However, as lovely as resolving conflict before it starts or right in the middle of it sounds, the truth is most of us miss that ship and watch it sail far, far away. This means that the most practical time for conflict resolution, for most people, is after said conflict. This requires striking a delicate balance because attempting to resolve it too soon may lead to further quarrels while waiting too long leads to a buildup of negative emotions and complications.

Conflict is usually accompanied by raw emotions like anger, resentment, and even pain. Attempting to talk to your partner in this state is, at best, unproductive. Letting disputes go unresolved for long periods of time warps the initial negative emotions, and they grow into something ugly and messy. The simple rule of thumb is: the longer conflict is left unchecked, the more difficult it is to actually resolve.

An acceptable time to settle a conflict could be as little as 30 minutes after the conflict to as much as two days after. This is because some distance to process the event is needed. Proper processing of the argument helps both partners cool off, evaluate their emotions, and put things in perspective. As always, different strokes work for different folks, but the bottom line is that conflicts should be resolved as soon as possible after both partners have processed the quarrel.

How to Handle Conflict and Prevent Communication Breaches

If you've not been living under some rock, you've probably heard of Noah and Allie's love story in *The Notebook*. Their love was so passionate and strong that even after 14 years, just as Allie was about to marry someone else, she found Noah, fell in love with him again, and eventually married him.

If you don't know what I'm talking about, *The Notebook* is a book written by Nicholas Sparks which was later adapted into a movie. In the movie, I noticed that Noah and Allie constantly quarreled. They couldn't agree on practically anything, yet their love was so strong that after they got married, they lived happily together for 60 years until Allie got Alzheimer's disease and forgot her husband and family. So Noah did the most romantic thing possible: he wrote a notebook filled with their stories and memories and read it to her each day. Heartwarming, right? I digress.

Back to their constant conflict. One reason they fought a lot was because they were from different backgrounds; another reason is that Noah could have communicated with Allie more respectfully. So why did they still get back together if they couldn't go very long without arguing? My opinion is that they were willing to communicate, and they always kept their love at the forefront of the union.

Of course, you're free to disagree, but the biggest lesson for me from the book was that constant communication and a mutual determination to see your love through to the end can bring the refreshing rays of the sun back to any dark, dead relationship. (A fun fact about this story is that it is based on the true story of a couple the author once met.)

As with anything, communication can be ineffective or effective. It's important to note that communication will look different for different couples because it's largely based on personality types as well as personal differences. The bottom line is that effective and positive communication is the key to sustaining happy relationships for the long term (Tomuletiu et al., 2014).

Before we look at the keys to effective communication, how do you know whether or not you're communicating effectively with your partner? Here are four important signs of poor communication.

Your squabbles become big fights.

Your arguments may often start small, but then the focus switches quickly from one issue to another. For example, an inconsequential fight over leaving the laundry on the floor can quickly become a messy, emotional argument about how one partner is too controlling or always nags, and then it can go quickly into how annoying and lazy the other partner is, and... KA-BOOM!

You never acknowledge or validate each other's feelings.

Picture a scene where you're telling your partner that you didn't like the way they talked down to you at a gathering with mutual friends. How would you feel if they responded by saying that they never talk down to you and that you're being too sensitive and self-conscious, and they refuse to see your point of view ? I'm not a betting man, but I'm sure you'd leave that conversation feeling unheard, annoyed, and maybe even resentful. You don't need to be psychic to know that these unresolved negative feelings will be turning up at the next argument like a bad coin.

You're quick to attribute negative intentions to your partner's words and behaviors.

If you find yourselves ascribing negative meaning to each other's actions, your communication might be going down the drain. For example, if you notice that your partner forgets to buy an appropriate gift for your anniversary, you may conclude that they're cheating on you or that they don't care about your union anymore. Humans are naturally inclined to confirmation bias, so you'll start to look for more evidence to support this claim and most likely start to make wrong connections, which leads to things being blown out of proportion.

You're withdrawing from or avoiding each other.

This is a critical sign in any relationship and should be fixed as soon as possible. Avoiding each other's company and refusing to discuss intimate matters or topics of dissension leads to feelings of emotional and physical loneliness. This can cause one partner to seek an emotional or physical connection outside the partnership. I'm sure we can agree that this is the beginning of a very slippery slope.

If you can identify with any of these signs or you find that your communication patterns with your spouse are getting dangerously close to any of these situations, then you need to fix it—and quickly.

Here are a few ways to fix the communication in your relationship. These steps are also useful if you'd like to improve the quality of your communication:

Take stock of your feelings first.

Are you satisfied with where your relationship is today? Do you think you could improve your communication? How do you feel about the relationship? This step can also be used right before an argument. Are you too angry or emotional to make a rational decision right now? Take a step back to process those emotions before discussing any issue. Ask for a timeout and go for a walk or listen to some music to help you calm down.

Understand your partner.

Talk to your partner about their opinions on communicating effectively. What does it look like for them? How do they feel about it? Are they satisfied with the current contact level? What's their communication style (are they timid, assertive, passive-aggressive, avoidant)? What's yours? Talk about how this affects your relationship.

Settle previously unresolved issues.

This might sound like you're borrowing trouble, but bringing these issues to light, especially if they're still bothering you or your partner, helps to wipe the slate clean. Conflict is typically weighed down by previous unresolved issues, which tends to muddy the waters and make resolution of current issues next to impossible.

Timing is everything.

Carefully consider the best time to bring up an issue. Don't ambush your spouse by springing the conflict on them. Informing your partner ahead of time helps them prepare for the discussion and feel less defensive.

Begin your sentences with "I."

This helps to shift the focus from accusation ("You always/never...") to talking about your feelings. Your spouse is much more likely to respond positively if you tell them how their actions have affected you.

Focus on listening and being heard.

Communicate your points to your significant other in clear, concise statements that are not accusatory. When they're speaking, give them your full attention and process what they've said rather than using that time to think of a reply. Pay attention to your body language as well as your partner's body language. Nodding when they speak, having an encouraging expression, putting down your phone, and even lightly stroking their arm are all great ways to communicate nonverbally with your partner.

Switch your focus to compromise and resolution rather than winning.

Once you're determined to have your argument end in a peaceful resolution, it becomes much easier to compromise.

Establish healthy boundaries.

Boundaries make a relationship healthier, and they are essential for proper communication. Examples could be agreeing not to use sarcastic or hurtful words when communicating or deciding to take a timeout when things get heated. Find what works for your relationship and keep exploring new methods as you progress.

Keep in touch.

Update your partner at different times during your day via text or calls. These regular check-ins might seem mundane, but they help to build a habit of sustained communication and deepen intimacy.

Wrapping Up

It's such a relief to find out that having a fight or two isn't the end of the world, isn't it? Even if you're skeptical about what you just read, take my word for it—it works. Let me know how it goes!

Now, we've talked a lot about you, but we both know that it takes two to tango in every relationship. Let's look at your partner; how does your overthinking affect them, and how can you make sure they come along in your process of improvement? I'll tell you all about this in the next chapter.

Your Quick Workbook

How does being in a conflict with your partner make you feel?

_____

_____

_____

Do you think your past conflicts with your partner have strengthened or harmed your relationship with each other?

_____

_____

_____

_____

Do you agree that your communication with your partner needs to be worked on?

_____

_____

_____

_____

If you haven't been managing your conflicts effectively up till now, do you think what you learned in this chapter can help you manage your conflicts better?

_____

_____

_____

_____

CHAPTER 5

HOW TO PRIORITIZE HEALTHY COMMUNICATION OVER OVERTHINKING

"Be devoted to one another in love. Honor one another above yourselves."

—Romans 12:10

I once had a friend who gave her husband the silent treatment for a week. She was annoyed that he didn't get her a nice gift for their anniversary, just a gift card. Sure, she made dinner, but she rarely talked at the table. She'd go to bed before him and wake up earlier than usual so she didn't have to talk to him.

When they visited me, she made an offhand comment about how marriage could be difficult sometimes. I probed further as to why she said that, and she told me to direct my question to her husband. When I asked him, he said, "I don't know what she's talking about; it's been a great week for me. So much peace and calmness for the first time in a long while."

His wife was stunned. She said, "But I was giving you the silent treatment!"

He said, "Oh, that's what that was? I'd like to order more silent treatment in that case."

We all had a good laugh about it. I encouraged her to get better at expressing her desires.

—Sophia

Respecting Your Partner's Struggles and Personal Issues

I'm sure you'll agree that there's no perfect relationship out there. This sounds like a cliché, but acknowledging and accepting this fact is important, especially if you tend to overthink. You might find yourself feeling anxious about the health of your connection and maybe comparing your partnership to another, seemingly more successful one. But I want you to know that comparison will only steal your joy, and no one really has it figured out. Instead of worrying and comparing, why not focus on what you can control? Why not work to make your relationship better? I think that's the best way to go, don't you?

When it comes to maintaining relationships and working to transform them into healthy ones, one of the most overlooked components for success is respect. It can be quite easy to get so caught up in your own emotions, struggles, and desires that you fail to realize that your partner has those too. This is especially true when there's constant conflict in the partnership. Being intentional about respecting your partner builds the relationship and helps you observe the tiny, intricate details that you might have missed. It helps you recognize that your partner is a person with their own concerns and struggles.

Before you go further, evaluate the current state of the relationship and ask yourself a few questions. You should involve your partner in this exercise as much as possible. These questions are a great place to start:

- What does respect mean to you? What does it mean to your partner?
- Do your expectations look different from your partner's? If so, how do you plan to manage the differences?
- Do you have boundaries in your relationship? Does your partner have boundaries, and do they recognize your boundaries?

- Do you trust your spouse? Can you open up about your feelings and emotions to them?

- Can they trust you to do the same?

- What are clear signs of respect and disrespect for the two of you?

- What is the next step to take if someone feels disrespected?

These questions will help you and your partner start a conversation that should never stop and help you to be cognizant of your other half as a person who needs a safe space to be vulnerable and express themselves.

A big part of respect is being accountable for your actions and their consequences. Realize that sometimes you might unknowingly offend your partner or cross their boundaries. Your actions may hurt your partner. Instead of shifting blame or justifying your actions, why not try apologizing and working with them to see how to avoid future occurrences? Start the habit of daily, weekly, and monthly check-ins. Discuss the heavy stuff, be unflinchingly honest, and reaffirm your commitment to each other.

Once you realize that respect and trust are two sides of the same coin, you'll be less likely to clash with your partner over minor issues. If you trust that they're committed to you, then you should respect them by not looking through their phone, for example, or following them whenever they're out.

A few people I've talked to who have considered this idea came to the realization that they didn't trust their partner. If you're not sure whether or not you trust your partner, then you have to start the journey to rebuilding trust. Trust me, your relationship will be much better for it.

Self-Talk to Remind Yourself That It Takes Two to Tango

"Love is a two-way street constantly under construction."

—*Carroll Bryant*

A lot of people enter relationships with an idea of what their ideal relationship looks like. They come in with set expectations and often find something entirely different than what they expected. One question to ask yourself here is: What forms the basis of your expectations for your relationships?

Oftentimes we form our expectations for romantic partnerships from different sources. They could come from seeing our parents' bond while growing up, or they could come from movies, books, or even culture. Remember that you and your partner are two different people from two different backgrounds with distinct ideas of what your connection should look like, and this needs to be acknowledged and discussed if you want to make any progress in improving the relationship.

The unfortunate part is that when a new romantic relationship starts, because of all the gooey emotions and the feel-good hormones running amok, we often do not take enough time to compare our expectations for the relationship with our partner's, and instead cruise along on the sea of newfound love. I don't know about you, but I think that is a recipe for disaster. Thankfully, most couples are able to balance out their expectations and adjust to the real work of building a life together eventually. But success here depends on a host of factors. The bottom line remains that at some point in your relationship, a reorientation must take place involving both parties for the stability of the partnership.

Now that we've established that we have two different people working together to form one harmonious union, what can you do to reorient your expectations and achieve a deeper, more intimate relationship with your partner? The truth is, you can't go this route alone; your partner needs to be equally committed to the growth and success of the relationship.

As always, the first thing to do is to evaluate yourself. What do you think of yourself? What's that inner voice telling you about yourself and about your relationship? Why is it saying that? I've said this before, but it bears repeating: a positive inner attitude makes it easier to give and receive love. If you have the right amount of self-love and you practice self-compassion frequently, you'll find it easier to extend the same level of love and compassion to your partner as well as to receive love and deep intimacy from them in return.

The work of evaluating yourself isn't something you can accomplish in five minutes; rather, it is an ongoing process that requires your intentional consistency. More often than not, you'll find that your inner voice is sorely lacking in compassion and self-love. The best way to tackle that is to recalibrate and challenge your inner self to advocate for the good of your relationship. The best way to do this is through positive self-talk.

Positive self-talk conditions your mind to accept new facts. The idea of talking your way from a negative mindset to a positive one might sound farfetched or even crazy, but I'm here to tell you that it's entirely possible.

Self-talk is an often-underutilized tool to improve or save your relationship. In fact, using the right self-talk can revitalize your outlook on all your relationships, not just your relationship with your spouse. This simple framework is a great way to identify and recalibrate your negative thoughts and ruminations.

- What am I telling myself?
- What's the root cause of these thoughts?

- Are they helpful thoughts?
- What can I tell myself to overcome this?
- What can I do to overcome this?

For example, let's say you notice that your partner has been distracted recently, keeps coming home late from work, and isn't volunteering to spend time with you unless you ask. Your overthinking brain naturally suspects that they're getting tired of the relationship at best, or maybe even seeing someone else at worst. Using the framework above can help you change your self-talk, and I'll show you how:

- What am I telling myself? "My partner is probably cheating on me because they're tired of the relationship and probably don't love me anymore."
- What's the root cause of these thoughts? "I heard that Shirley and Tom got a divorce. Tom is very good friends with my partner and might have influenced them to look for someone better. I don't think I'm good enough for this relationship."
- Is this thought helpful? "No."
- What can I tell myself to overcome this? "I remember my partner mentioning that a promotion process at work is coming up, so they might be stressed about that."
- What can I do to overcome this? "I can ask my partner about work and offer comfort by running them a bath or offering them a massage. I can then gently express my fears to them."

Self-talk goes a long way to correct negative assumptions about ourselves or our spouses that may not be correct. Without proper evaluation and recalibration, it becomes easy to move from having these unhelpful thoughts to feeling emotions like resentment, anger, jealousy, or self-pity. Positive self-talk helps you become receptive and empathetic towards yourself, your spouse, and others.

Avoiding Self-Centeredness and Asking What Your Partner Needs

This might be difficult for you to admit, but your partner may have accused you of being selfish and now you can't help seeing all the different scenarios that point to it as the truth. Are you really self-centered?

It's possible that you haven't ever considered the fact that you could be self-centered in your relationship. If your partner doesn't complain about it, then everything is good on that front, right? Maybe, maybe not.

Being self-centered means you're more likely to make decisions that favor yourself over those that are more beneficial for the good of your relationship. If you don't consider your significant other while making big decisions or you do things that hurt them, even though you're aware that they don't like it, you might be more selfish than you thought.

In a relationship, if one partner is shy and introverted or the other partner is more aggressive and dominant, it's likely that someone's needs are being overlooked in favor of the other person. In a relationship with two self-centered people, there's a noticeable lack of intimacy and communication. Being self-centered will cause feelings of dissatisfaction, isolation, and resentment in your partner.

The first step in solving this issue is to evaluate yourself and your actions in the relationship. These questions might help:

- Are my actions selfish?
- Do I have a habit of putting myself first?

- Do I naturally expect my partner to do things that please me?

- Do I take time out to pay attention to my partner?

- Has my partner ever accused me of being self-centered?

- Do I give my partner the freedom to grow and express themselves in the relationship?

- Do I feel threatened when my partner spends time with friends and loved ones?

- Would I say that I'm possessive?

Reflecting on these questions and writing down the answers will help you gauge how self-centered you actually are.

The next step is to talk to your partner. Ask them what they think and listen to their honest opinion. If they say that they do think you're selfish, don't panic. Admitting that there's a problem is the first step to solving it. Look back on the behaviors your partner points out and try to find out why you might have acted that way. Intentionally decide to take steps to become less self-centered.

Here are a few tips that will help you become less self-oriented and more committed to the growth of your relationship. As always, being consistent and intentional is necessary.

Pay close attention to your partner.

How often do you really listen to them? Are you meeting their needs? Try to talk to them about their feelings, wants, and needs. Ask for their opinions. A great way to put your partner first is to put yourself in their shoes. Think about what you would want them to do for you and then do the same thing for them.

Realize that your partner has a life outside of you.

If you're being self-centered in your relationship, it's easy to assume your partner's whole world revolves around you. If you find yourself constantly expecting your partner to drop everything to cater to your needs, or you don't mind that they do things for you all the time and you don't reciprocate these gestures, take a step back and think about your partner. Understanding that your partner has a life outside of your relationship is important, as it will help to prevent conflict and help you become more considerate.

Be willing to compromise.

You might be used to getting your own way in your relationship, especially if you feel like you have a more important job or you're somehow the more important person in the relationship. Learning to humble yourself and consciously compromise with your partner is a great way to avoid self-centeredness.

Take your ego out of the equation.

Entertaining your pride will only make you defend your selfish behavior. Instead, pay attention to the fact that your partner deserves to feel safe being vulnerable with you.

Cultivate the habit of generosity.

Learning how to give is a great way to combat self-centeredness. Deliberately decide to be generous with your time, your attention, your words, and your presence in your relationship to make your partner feel special and loved.

Support and celebrate your partner.

If you've become a self-centered person in your relationship, it might be normal for you to forget important anniversaries and events. Making a deliberate attempt to keep track of these days and commemorate them is a great way to make your spouse feel loved and special. Participating in your partner's interests, encouraging them when they're feeling discouraged, and taking time to be present as much as possible are also helpful.

This is not an exhaustive list of ways to curb self-centeredness in your relationship, but these tips will certainly help. As you start implementing these actions, you'll discover even more ways to make your partner feel loved and strengthen your relationship.

How to Cultivate Trust and Avoid Paranoia

Trust is the bedrock of a healthy relationship. Overthinkers tend to have trust issues with their partners, which are worsened if they have experienced traumatic past relationships. These issues might come up in different ways. Recognizing that you do not trust your partner is just the first step to rebuilding confidence. It's not possible to have a long-lasting relationship without trust.

Being able to rely on your partner helps you feel safe and builds intimacy in your relationship. You'll find that you feel free to be as vulnerable and natural as you want because you're sure that your partner is looking out for you no matter what. Trust also helps to minimize conflict; it provides the element of security that is needed in every loving relationship.

Saying that you trust someone means you believe they are reliable and honest. It means you know you're able to depend on them because they have integrity and are faithful to you. On the other hand, here are some of the signs that you don't trust your partner.

You assume the worst.

You find it easy to ascribe the worst possible meaning to your partner's behaviors and intentions, even when they have shown themselves to be reliable in the past.

You're constantly suspicious.

You're always suspicious that your partner is doing something to hurt you in some way.

You don't forgive easily.

When you have trust issues, moving on from past hurts might be very difficult for you. This can affect all aspects of your life and color your interactions with your significant other as well as your family and friends.

You keep a distance between yourself and others.

People with trust issues typically separate themselves from other people and do not let themselves experience true intimacy in a relationship, often because they're afraid of being betrayed or disappointed.

You focus on the negative.

Even though you might have evidence to the contrary, you're more focused on all the things that could go wrong in your relationship and are quick to point out your partner's flaws and weaknesses rather than focusing on their good qualities.

Having trust issues can leave both you and your spouse feeling misunderstood, isolated, and unloved. A lack of trust might be an indicator that your relationship is in distress. In that case, you need to work to rebuild the trust or to solve your trust issues with your partner. To do this, here are some action steps:

Prioritize building trust.

This can look like slowly letting your spouse deeper into your life and having faith in their words, actions, and intentions. It's important to know that as you build confidence with your partner, you must be ready to forgive because mistakes are bound to happen.

Trust yourself.

The best way to trust others is to trust yourself first. Developing a strong sense of self-awareness can help you evaluate other people and interact with them in a more positive way. The fact is, learning how to trust yourself is like a muscle that can be developed with practice, just like all the other muscles in the body.

The ability to forgive yourself must go hand-in-hand with the ability to trust or else you'll end up doing more damage than good.

If you find yourself excessively concerned with monitoring your partner's movements, doubting their intentions, or misjudging their actions, it's possible you're experiencing some paranoia about your relationship. Here's a list of quick tips for tackling paranoia.

1. Identify the reason you're feeling paranoid

Has your partner given you any reason to distrust them in the past? Are you acting this way based on an experience in a previous relationship? Identifying the cause of your paranoia will help you to think more rationally about it.

2. Eliminate stress

Stress is a very common cause of paranoia. Practicing relaxation techniques can help you overcome stress.

3. Practice self-care

A good way to eliminate paranoia is to take time out of your day to practice self-care, even if it's something as simple as a minute or two of deep breathing or a quick walk around the block.

4. Share your fears with your partner

Oftentimes, no matter how much you try to rationalize and counteract the feelings of paranoia, the best and most efficient way to eliminate these feelings is to discuss your paranoid thoughts with your partner. Explain your struggles and their root cause. Don't be shy to ask for the support you need. Both of you can work out strategies to help put your mind at rest.

The Importance of Taking Your Partner at Their Word

In this chapter so far, we've discussed some of the various aspects of communication in a healthy relationship. You've had to do a lot of self-reflection at different points (if you haven't done the exercises yet, this is your cue to go back and do them!), and I'm sure you're committed to doing the work to improve your relationship. However, this last section is perhaps the most critical yet, as it's about something that could destroy all your progress if you're not cautious.

This might sound cliché, but if you're an overthinker, the best way to develop confidence in your partner and silence those nagging thoughts is to trust them. What better way to develop trust than to actually...trust what they say? Doubting your partner's words can be a sneaky way to maintain contact with your overthinking even after you've promised to cut all ties. It's particularly tempting to entertain anxious thoughts about your partner's statements because it's all in your head—who's going to know if you decide to reexamine and second-guess their words?

However, not believing your partner's word is a surefire way to undermine the trust and intimacy in your relationship. You'll almost certainly find yourself feeling resentful of or apathetic towards your partner at the end of the day. Before you know it, these feelings manifest in your attitude and actions towards your significant other.

The bottom line is this: Trusting your partner enough to accept their words at face value helps you to build trust in your relationship. However, before you trust the words, you might benefit from asking your spouse questions to clarify exactly what they mean. This will help to eliminate any doubt or confusion in your mind and also help to manage your expectations.

Don't be afraid to ask your spouse for what you need, and be as honest and direct as possible. And remember to open up to your partner about your feelings, especially if you're struggling with believing them. This might seem difficult and unnecessary, but it actually helps to deepen the intimacy in your relationship.*

Click HERE to get these worksheets that will help you develop healthy relationships.

Wrapping Up

I know this chapter was particularly hard for you because it probably seemed like I asked you to do everything you'd rather not do. I mean, taking your partner at their word?! I know. It could definitely be difficult. But as uncomfortable as it seems now, you'll be happy with yourself for putting in the work when your relationship starts to flourish.

While communication and trust are very important, I would be remiss if we didn't talk about the other elephant in the room. This guy comes along with overthinking and makes himself comfortable. I'm talking about the negativity in your relationship. It might seem like an abstract concept now, but you'll hear all about it in the next chapter and realize why you need to take it seriously.

Your Quick Workbook

Do you solely take all the blame for the issues in your relationship, put all the blame on your partner, or do you both share the blame?

_____

_____

_____

_____

_____

How receptive are you and your partner to each other's needs?

_____

_____

_____

_____

_____

How would you feel if you found out your partner didn't trust you?

_____

_____

_____

_____

Why do you think you find it hard to trust your partner?

_____

_____

_____

_____

CHAPTER 6

DEALING WITH NEGATIVE ENERGY, THOUGHTS, AND HABITS IN YOUR MARRIAGE

"Cast all your anxiety on him because he cares for you."

—1 Peter 5:7

I'll be the first to admit that relationships can be awfully tricky to navigate. Knowing when to commit fully, having the strength to realize that a relationship isn't serving you anymore, or choosing to take a few steps back from your partner even though you'd rather stay isn't for the faint of heart. Finding a delicate balance between trust and self-awareness is necessary for surviving a relationship that may turn out badly for you.

A friend once told me about this woman who was in a seemingly happy relationship with her partner. They had a whirlwind dating period and soon moved in together. But her friends noticed that she was always drained and that she seemed eager to spend time with her friends rather than go home to her significant other. At first, they were concerned that she was being abused, and they gently asked her if everything was all right. She strongly denied any abuse and said everything was fine.

After gentle, persistent probing, she finally admitted that she just didn't enjoy spending time with her partner anymore. Sure, they were still physically intimate, but that was about the only time they saw eye to eye on anything. She said that they argued all the time, they were not as emotionally intimate as they used to be, and she always felt exhausted whenever she had to be around him. Interestingly, she likened her significant other to an "energy vampire" who drained her every time she was around him.

This description stuck with me even though it's been about seven years since I heard that story. I think it was so compelling because of the vivid way she described the negative energy in her relationship. This might sound odd, but it's possible to be in an intimate relationship with negative energy. You or your partner may be injecting negativity into your union as a result of some previous experience that caused emotional damage.

Recognizing Negative Vibes in Your Relationship

Toxic vibes, or negative energy, is pretty easy to spot from the outside, but strangely it becomes difficult to do so when you're neck-deep in the relationship. When the characteristics of your partnership embody the total opposite of everything a healthy union is meant to be, it's most likely toxic. If you realize that there is no intimacy, that you don't support each other, that there is unhealthy competition and disrespect, then your relationship has officially been overtaken by negative vibes.

These signs point towards negativity in your relationship:

Constant fighting

We've covered the idea that conflict can actually be healthy in a relationship, but being unable to successfully compromise for conflict resolution is a sign of toxicity. Constant arguing illuminates a deeper problem with communication, especially if words of disrespect, insults, and harsh language are involved.

Manipulation

This can look like the silent treatment, withdrawal of affection, or trying to make your partner jealous.

Feeling uncomfortable with your partner

The point of being in a relationship is to experience the peaceful, intimate feeling of being emotionally close to someone you trust. You'll most likely stay in a relationship if being with that person makes you happier than being alone. However, if you notice that you're always feeling nervous and uncomfortable or you experience tension around your partner, that could indicate that your relationship is full of negativity.

Constantly complaining about your partner to others

If you find that you never have anything good to say about your relationship or your spouse to anyone, it's likely that your relationship is a toxic one.

No intimacy or affection

Being physically intimate is a nice perk of a long-term relationship, and it also serves to strengthen the emotional connection between you. Avoiding physical intimacy with your partner might be a sign that there's something negative in the works.

Making your friends uncomfortable

If your relationship has deteriorated to the point where you both take potshots at each other while in public with your friends, it's a surefire sign that toxic vibes have taken over your partnership entirely. This might even cause your friends to start taking sides, which means the bad energy has begun to leak outwards.

If you've noticed that your relationship is full of negative vibes, it might be time to take a step back and evaluate it. Are you sure you want to be in that kind of relationship? What part have you played in creating negativity? You must work to overcome this challenge and transform the bad energy into positive vibes.

Improving Your Self-Esteem to Stay Positive and Kind in Your Marriage

"For you created my inmost being;

you knit me together in my mother's womb.

I praise you because I am fearfully and wonderfully made;

your works are wonderful,

I know that fully well."

—Psalm 139:13–14

One of the most popular phrases relating to self-care and self-love is "you can't pour from an empty cup." We've concluded that loving your partner in the way they deserve to be loved begins with loving yourself. You just can't love someone else fully if you don't love *you*. This is where self-esteem comes into play. Self-esteem is simply the way you perceive yourself, and it's very important for a balanced and satisfying life.

If you had to describe yourself honestly to someone else, what would you say?

Do you feel good about yourself, or do you only have negative things to say? What do you think of yourself? People with low self-esteem may find it difficult to have long-lasting, trusting relationships. They might not want to stand up for themselves and might reject any good thing that comes their way.

Low self-esteem can ruin a union in this way. Conversely, developing healthy self-respect sets the bar for how you'll be treated in your relationship and also guides you on how to treat your partner. It means that you're less likely to become unhealthily attached to each other (codependency) and you're able to sort out your own emotional needs alone. A relationship is all about two people coming together to form one unit, true, but it's often necessary to maintain some degree of independence in your relationship to allow for your own experiences and happiness.

Having low self-regard makes you constantly doubt yourself and believe that you're not good enough, which, in turn, leads you to depend on your spouse for approval, love, and validation. This can be dangerous if you are with an inconsiderate or unstable partner.

So, how can you boost your self-esteem?

Focus on yourself.

It goes without saying that building your self-esteem requires you to spend more time alone. Getting to know and accept yourself is essential. A lot of people find it difficult to spend hours and hours by themselves, but start small and build your way up. Do things that you enjoy,* whether that's reading, journaling, listening to music, or pursuing a solo hobby.

*Click HERE and receive these 7 worksheets on self-care and self-compassion.

Claim your space.

Some degree of independence is needed on your journey to reclaiming your self-esteem. Being in a partnership that completely absorbs your identity and doesn't let you differentiate yourself isn't a sign of undying love; it's an unhealthy move for both you and your partner.

Embrace true happiness.

No one can make you truly happy except yourself. Your partner can only improve whatever level of happiness you've already achieved on your own. Relying on your spouse for a level of emotional responsibility beyond what they can handle can cause an imbalance in your relationship that ends with you trying to take way more than your partner might be ready to give. Being in charge of your own happiness means knowing that happiness is a choice you must make every day.

Forgive yourself.

It's natural to have flaws. No one is perfect. These flaws do not make you a terrible or unlovable person, and you need to recognize that and forgive yourself for past mistakes.

See yourself through your partner's eyes.

Try this out. Ask your spouse to describe how they see you and why they love you. This may sound like you're fishing for cheap compliments, but sometimes, taking note of the small ways in which someone notices how amazing you are is a great way to boost your self-esteem.

Find the root cause.

Low self-esteem can be caused by a variety of factors. Taking the time to find out why you're struggling with low self-esteem is a huge step in the right direction.

Keep a journal.

I'm sure you thought you'd heard the last of me advocating for journals, but here we are again. Keeping a journal gives you a safe space to process your thoughts. It's best to write in your journal every day for at least 10 minutes per day.

Some prompts to get you started are:

- What am I feeling right now?

- Why am I feeling this way?

- How does my partner make me feel?

- How would I like to make my partner feel?

- Are there any problems in my relationship right now?

- How would I like my relationship with my partner to improve?

After writing in your journal, it might be best to discuss some of the things you've discovered with your partner.

Building Compassion and Avoiding Blame

Most people are surprised when I tell them that, for the most part, it's possible to develop any character attributes you want as long as you're ready to put your mind to it. I compare these attributes to muscles in the body, which we all know can get bigger when used more often.

In the same way, practicing particular attributes or characteristics will create a habit that you will soon unconsciously start to follow.

However, just as it's possible to develop positive attributes, it's also fairly easy to develop negative attributes through consistent repetition.

A good example of this is the tendency to blame each other. Let's be honest here, nobody wins at the blame game. All it does is shift blame endlessly from one person to the other. It also intensifies feelings of annoyance, isolation, unhappiness, and disappointment. Compromise is very necessary here.

You want to avoid the blame game at all costs. Here are some tips for doing that.

Find your reason.

Think about why you're engaging in blaming your partner. Do you want to correct their behavior, or do you just want to vent and lash out at them? Discovering the intention behind your behavior can help you decide if you are in the wrong or not.

Accept that blaming each other is poor communication.

Blaming your partner isn't an effective way of communicating with them because you are essentially accusing them of wrongdoing, putting them on the defensive. Why not try getting your message across with empathy, love, and compassion? These are ways that have been proven to affect the people around you positively and that can actually trigger a change.

Helping Each Other Through Bad Habits

Okay, let's face it, relationships can be rosy and lovey-dovey, but bad habits can quickly change all that. They might even be the source of conflicts in your relationship. Unfortunately, breaking a bad habit isn't easy, and quarreling with your spouse over a particularly bad habit can stress them out and drive them to continue that habit.

So what's the best way to help your partner break a bad habit? How can your partner support you to break yours? Bear in mind that you have to find a way to break this habit without resorting to further conflict in the relationship. It sounds like a tall order, but it's entirely possible.

The first step is to approach your partner in an empathetic manner and focus on the solution. Most times when we approach our significant other about their bad habit, we attack or confront them, not realizing that this is far from the best way to get a positive response. I mean, would you enjoy being attacked because of something you've been doing habitually? Of course not. It's better to discuss things with your partner in a soft, gentle manner.

Tell your partner exactly how you feel about their habit and show them you understand where they're coming from. Encourage them to drop the habit. Communicate your worry as clearly as possible. A good way to do this is to use statements that explain your reaction to the habit. For example, you can say something like, "When you smoke cigarettes, I get scared for our fertility as a couple." Tell them how relieved and happy you'd feel if they broke that habit.

Make sure to pick the right time to engage with your spouse. Approaching them about a bad habit when they're already in a bad mood might not be the best idea. Pick a time when your partner is relaxed and gently bring up the issue in a non-confrontational manner.

Offer positive reinforcement. Encourage your partner to break the habit by offering an incentive if they do. You must also be ready to hear about your own bad habits as well. This might be because they're feeling defensive about what you've told them. But don't get upset or accuse your partner of changing the subject. Both of you can agree to change your bad behavior and receive a joint reward when you're successful. This is a great way to improve communication and foster intimacy in a relationship.

I love talking about this topic in particular because it shows how teamwork can be used as an instrument to deepen the communication between your spouse and yourself.

Wrapping Up

I'm glad to see that you've made it this far. We've made a lot of progress, and by now, if you've been implementing what we've talked about, you should be seeing a huge difference in your relationship with your significant other, and perhaps even in your other relationships.

But, just like learning to ride a bike, sometimes you may fall off and it seems like the end of the world. Let me just say that it's very possible to slip back into old habits if you're not careful. Relapses are real. In the next chapter, we'll talk about what to do when this happens and how to get over it.

Your Quick Workbook

Has your relationship been emotionally draining, and how is this affecting your life as a whole?

_____

_____

_____

_____

_____

Do you think positivity is a possibility in your relationship?

_____

_____

_____

Have you ever considered your self-limiting thoughts as a reason for the constant negativity in your relationship?

_____

_____

_____

Does your partner have bad habits that annoy you? Has your partner complained about any bad habits of yours? What move have you made towards breaking these bad habits?

_____

_____

_____

PART 3

Preventing Relapses and Keeping Things Going

Identifying a problem and its solution is wonderful. It's commendable, in fact, and I'd like to let you know you're doing great. It's important, however, to keep your growth intact. Now that you have seen just how overthinking might be making your relationship difficult, it's time to look at how to harness the principle of taking it one day at a time and moving forward steadily with your partner. Let's dive in for the final swim.

CHAPTER 7

THE ART OF LISTENING, TRUSTING, AND LOVING FIERCELY

Listening: More Than Just Hearing

When our marriage got to year 13, I felt like my wife stopped listening altogether. Every time I attempted to make conversation with her, she'd be too preoccupied with our financial problems and would not give coherent responses to what I said. This went on for two years, and I felt constantly unheard until I couldn't take it anymore. In a fit of anger, she threatened me with divorce, and I dared her. We both still regret everything we did after that. Our daughter hates us for ruining her life.

—Jason

Isn't it funny how some people seem to have excellent communication skills, yet they really don't? They *hmm* and *aah* at all the right places and always give off the vibe that they know just the right thing to say or the right gesture to make to keep you going. I mean, they stare at you directly, like they're gazing right into your soul, leaning forward and nodding, and you can't possibly doubt that they're listening to you.

If only that were completely true!

Communication skills are very important, as they help you connect better, but if you're not listening effectively, your communication is fundamentally flawed. The truth is, sometimes you're practicing these communication tips, unless you're a natural-born conversationalist, you might be so focused on *showing* someone that you're listening that you end up actually missing a large part of the conversation.

Listening is a skill nobody wants to admit they don't have. I mean, isn't it just hearing whatever someone is saying to you? All you need to do is concentrate and give them your full attention; how hard can that be, right?

Wrong.

Sorry to break it to you, friend, but listening and hearing are two different things, and you can be hearing what a person is saying without actually listening to them. It takes effort and focus to listen. And let's be honest here, although the Bible speaks about being quick to listen, slow to speak, and slow to anger, it's much easier to switch things up and be quick to speak and quick to anger, especially when you've been hurt by the person you're speaking with.

You're probably thinking, "Okay, so hearing is not listening and listening is not hearing. Fine, I get it. What's the difference between hearing and listening, then?"

Simply put, hearing is **passive** while listening is **active**. Hearing is the ability to perceive sound. You can't close your ears or ask them to stop functioning. The most you can do if you don't want to hear someone speaking is leave the room, or ask the person to stop talking if what they're saying is getting on your nerves, or you're in a bad mood and their voice is grating on your ears, or you're preoccupied and what they're saying just goes in one ear and out the other.

Listening, on the other hand, is voluntary. It's a choice you've made to concentrate and give your thoughtful attention to what the other person is saying. When listening for real, you're taking in the information a person is giving you and trying to understand what they're saying from their perspective.

Many times, before listening to their partner's perspective, an overthinker will have already made up their mind about the situation. Before your spouse gets the chance to speak about something, you've imagined different scenarios and drawn up your conclusion. You've made up your mind, and you're just giving your partner a chance to speak so that you can say, "Let it be known that I heard you out," or because it's the Christian thing to do. Well, making up your mind before listening to what your partner wants to say doesn't exactly make for a peaceful relationship, and if you've already decided something about a discussion that hasn't even been had, listening is going to prove difficult for you.

If you nag your partner sometimes for not listening to your needs and feelings, think about whether you're a good listener as well—because, let's face it, you can't expect your partner to listen to you if you won't listen to them.

If you're thinking, "Listening is too hard. I'm reading this book because I overthink a lot, and now you're asking me to set aside my assumptions and thoughts and listen without judgment?"—relax. I understand your concern, but it's possible to become an expert in listening, even if you're struggling with overthinking right now. After all, there are many instances in the Bible where Jesus showed superb listening skills, and hasn't He assured us that what He did, we can do even more?

How to Pay Attention to Your Partner's Nonverbal Communication

The success of any relationship can be said to rest almost solely on how well both parties fare at communication. One study found that 67.5% of marriages that end in divorce are due to communication problems (Boyd, 2022). I guess it's safe to say that communication is the foundation for any healthy relationship that plans to stand the test of time.

Verbal communication is always lauded as the most important aspect of communication, but nonverbal communication, while often overlooked, is just as crucial. If you want a successful marriage with the person you love, you need to master nonverbal communication in all its diverse forms. I'm always excited to talk about nonverbal communication because I love watching people's eyes light up when they realize how profound the effects of nonverbal communication can be. Let's jump right in!

Nonverbal communication, also known as manual communication, is basically speaking with every body part except your mouth. It involves gestures, body movement, and expressions like pulling back when hurt, walking off when annoyed, twirling hair when nervous, biting nails when anxious, and being short with someone when irritated or pissed. Nonverbal communication is the message that gets passed along without any trace of a sound. It could be a look, a nod, a disapproving curl of the lips, a smirk—it all counts.

Oftentimes, we can tell that our partner loves us through nonverbal communication. It's in the little things like preparing a warm bath for you after a long day, surprise gifts and dates, the way their face lights up when you walk into the room, or how they hug you from behind. Likewise, it's easy to know when your partner is upset based on their nonverbal cues—for instance, when they're not talking as much as usual, they give you the cold shoulder, or they go from chatty and bubbly to silent and withdrawn mid-conversation. Perhaps they have the habit of greeting you with a hug and a kiss when they get home at the end of the day, but they've recently stopped doing that, or they offer a halfhearted hug without the kiss. You don't need a therapist to tell you that something's changed.

There's a meme that jokes about what women really need when they say they want space and attention at the same time; it's a bit inane, but one thing we can't deny is the fact that we're complicated creatures, no matter our gender. Needless to say, learning to communicate properly with your partner will go a long way towards helping you unfold the mysteries of human nature.

It's likely that there have been times when you didn't realize your partner was broadcasting their emotions loud and clear without saying a word. You probably couldn't correctly decipher their body language, and of course, arguments won't be far off in situations like that.

Trust me, I know.

I know it can be quite frustrating because you most likely didn't even know they were angry in the first place, and suddenly they're fuming. And then perhaps they get even more upset after they realize that you never even noticed they were angry. Or—this is my favorite—they get annoyed because you didn't apologize for something that upset them that you didn't even *know* you did. I'll be real with you, it's enough to drive any well-meaning person up the wall.

So, what's the way forward?

Maybe it's learning how to listen effectively. Of course, being an effective listener is important for a healthy relationship, but it's not *just* about listening to whatever they say and examining their words over and over for hints of trouble before it starts. Nope. That's heading into overthinking territory, and the whole point here is to avoid that. Effective listening is about listening to what is said, and also what *isn't* said. Now, make no mistake, I'm not asking you to be some sort of mind reader or something weird like that. No need for that because, frankly speaking, it's just not possible.

But if you've been with your partner for a while now, being able to recognize some of their nonverbal tells should be your forte. You should be able to tell when their mouth is saying one thing and their body language is saying something else entirely. If you can, that's great! If you can't, sit tight because I'm about to show you stuff.

Let's take a look at various types of nonverbal communication, shall we?

1. Facial expressions

Some of us have very expressive faces, like me. My wife can immediately tell how I feel about something just by looking at my face when she brings it up. I believe facial expressions are the easiest form of nonverbal communication to understand. Your facial expressions can communicate happiness, sadness, anger, disgust, surprise, and fear. Those emotions are pretty much the same everywhere. If your partner is claiming to be happy and is frowning, it's easy to identify that their words and facial expression don't match. As far as I know, frowning signifies anger or displeasure and a smirk could mean mockery. I'll go out on a limb here and assume it's the same for you too.

Anyway, for people with faces that are hard to read, two solutions come to mind. The first is microexpressions. Microexpressions are facial expressions that are very brief in duration, lasting less than one second (Svetevia, 2016). Research suggests that everyone has microexpressions, no matter who they are, and most microexpressions look the same on different faces. It's fascinating and very useful in behavioral analysis.

The second solution is to look for other nonverbal indicators. Is their face not giving you any clues? Check the rest of their body language. Keep reading to learn more about the other types of body language.

2. Movement and posture

This includes how you sit, stand, and walk, as well as your stance, bearing, and how you basically carry yourself. Did you know you can identify whether someone has feelings for you based on their posture? For example, when they're leaning towards you, or their feet are facing in your direction, it could mean that person has a little crush on you. You can guess that your partner is tense if they're pacing nervously, or if their body is stiff, or their shoulders are squared.

3. Gestures

We use gestures a lot, especially when we're speaking animatedly about something that interests us. Gestures are mostly involuntary. They include things like pointing, beckoning, waving, and running your fingers through your hair.

4. Eye contact

It's important to maintain eye contact to keep the flow of a conversation. You can gauge a listener's interest or lack thereof by how well they make eye contact as you talk. If they have shifty eyes or find it difficult to maintain eye contact, it could mean they're hiding something or lying.

5. Touch

Now, this is an important part of relationships. How your partner feels can be easily communicated through touch. A pat on the back, holding hands, or putting an arm around the other person can be used to convey love and affection. A firm handshake can sometimes be used to assert control. A fist bump is a clear sign of friendship.

6. Space

Depending on your relationship or how you feel about someone in a given moment, it may seem like someone is invading your personal space if they stand too close. Other times, you may feel like they're not close enough. You may be able to guess that your partner is in a sour mood or has something on their mind when they don't want you in their space.

7. Voice

Sometimes, our feelings and emotions can be so overwhelming that they seep out and are evident in our voices. The tone of your voice can sometimes indicate hurt, sarcasm, anger, or even confidence. Paying attention to things like how loud your partner is speaking, their tone, and their inflection will give you valuable information about how your partner feels.

Now that we've covered the different types of nonverbal communication, let's discuss how to observe and identify these signals so you can better understand your partner's feelings, moods, and actions. This will definitely help you to improve your connection with your partner.

Here are some tips to help you decode body language easily:

Watch out for inconsistencies.

These discrepancies may seem insignificant, but they're actually quite important. If your partner is saying something but their body language is saying something else, you might want to look closely into that situation because something doesn't add up. A nonverbal cue should support what the person is saying, not negate it.

Take note of all the nonverbal signals.

While each nonverbal cue could signal one thing or another, a combination of these nonverbal cues can mean something else as a whole. Consider eye contact, tone of voice, posture, and body movement—when taken together, are these signals consistent with what they're saying?

With these tips, evaluating nonverbal cues should become very easy.

So, what should you look for when you're assessing each type of body language?

1. Facial expressions

Check whether the person's facial expression appears mask-like and uninterested, or if their face is expressive and indicates that they're interested in what you have to say. They could also slightly lift their eyebrows to show surprise, discomfort, or skepticism based on the context. The eyebrow lift can also come with a smile, which may indicate that they find what you're saying interesting or are just playing with you.

2. Posture and gesture

Is their body stiff or relaxed and comfortable? Do they keep checking the time or constantly change their posture, showing impatience? They might fidget, which can indicate boredom, anxiety, or irritation. Do their shoulders appear raised, tense, or relaxed? Are their fists clenched and their arms crossed while you're asking them about something? That might mean they're getting defensive.

3. Eye contact

Are they making eye contact or not? And if they are, does it feel natural, or does it seem overly intense?

4. Touch

You should note the presence or absence of physical touch. Sometimes it might not be absent, just reduced. The way they touch you also matters—does it scream possessiveness or just tenderness and care? Is their grip on you a little too tight?

5. Tone and voice

Does their tone sound flat and uninterested? Animated? Or is it sounding a little over the top or like they're forcing it?

6. Timing and place

Timing and place really matter, and nonverbal cues can give you clues as to whether it's the right time and place for a conversation or not. Your partner could slightly shake their head to indicate "not now" or tilt their head to the side as if saying, "Let's go there." Even if they don't give these signs, you can confirm whether or not there's a back-and-forth rapport, or the rate at which your partner gives their nonverbal responses.

That's basically it. However, keep in mind that it's not uncommon to misunderstand nonverbal cues, in which case you can simply ask your partner what they're feeling. Nevertheless, understanding nonverbal cues will help your relationship a lot. Since you can tell a lot about how they're feeling at that moment, you can more easily avoid arguments or uncomfortable situations, settle issues amicably, and figure out the root of the problem when something isn't right.

Using Nonviolent Communication to Improve Your Relationship/Marriage

Listening to and understanding body language helps to enhance effective communication between you and your partner. Clearly, communication is a two-way street. The Bible says wives should be submissive and husbands should love their wives as themselves (Ephesians 5:22, 23). But that can be difficult to do, and gets pretty frustrating when it seems like you're the only one seeing the problem and trying to work on the relationship. We're only human, after all, and sometimes we need a little effort from our partner to show they care. That's why both spouses must work on this together.

Did you know that when you change your mode of communication, you're automatically influencing your relationship with your partner? The important thing here is deciding to change your mode of communication for the better. One great tool I frequently recommend is nonviolent communication (NVC), a set of principles developed in the 1960s by psychologist Marshall Rosenberg. This tool has helped a lot of couples take their communication game to the next level.

Your approach to communication in romantic relationships should be a reflection of the old proverb, "Dig your well before you're thirsty." Thirst here is a metaphor for your need to connect, and for the mutual understanding and trust that is essential for your partnership. Digging the well involves practicing nonviolent communication and becoming skillful at it so that you'll have those tools ready when you need them.

Most people are skeptical about the NVC approach at first; some have accused it of feeling unnatural and scripted. But after they practice it for a while, they frequently have no choice but to admit that it makes a notable difference. They can't seem to stop raving about how much their communication with their partner has improved as well as how their connection to each other has been reinforced.

The mistake most couples make is that they wait till there's a full-blown conflict before they decide to work on their communication skills. Don't wait till you get to that point. Even if you're already in a full-blown conflict, don't worry, the NVC tool can turn things around.

Usually, the way NVC works is that when we find ourselves in distressing situations or situations of conflict, we must take time to think before making our grievances known to our partner.

So, instead of saying, "Derek, you're always leaving your stuff lying around and expecting me to pick up after you like a maid. That's really disgusting. I'm not picking up after you today; clean up your mess yourself!"—NVC instructs you to stop, think, and rephrase that statement. I mean, you don't actually expect Derek to respond well to that, do you? NVC acknowledges that our automatic responses to situations will usually hurt the people we love. It focuses on being more compassionate and empathetic when communicating your feelings.

NVC sounds so simple that you're probably thinking, "Okay, so I just have to think before I speak, right?"

I don't mean to burst your bubble, but it's not that easy. Especially if the reason you want to improve your communication skills is to get your partner to always agree with you. NVC is not a manipulation tool; rather, the key components of this tool are purpose, attention, and intention. The goal of using this strategy is to connect on a deeper level so that contributing to each other's well-being will come easily to you and your partner. It aims to create win-win situations, not an I-must-always-win situation.

I know, I know, I've gone on and on about NVC and how important it is for effective communication and a deeper connection with your partner—but it's just so awesome, I can't help it. All right, let's dive right into the four steps of nonviolent communication.

1. Observe the facts

Most times when we experience distressing situations, like Derek leaving his stuff lying around despite the number of times his partner has spoken to him about it, it's hard to look at the situation objectively. This step entails focusing on the facts without being judgmental, and avoiding the use of words like "always," "often," and "never."

When you stick to the facts, it's easier to connect with the other person without them having to be on the defensive, whereas when you talk about your interpretation or judge the situation, the other person is more likely to hear blame and criticism, and they put their guard up almost immediately. Let's look at these examples:

Observation: "You promised to take the trash out two days ago, and I had to take it out myself just this morning."

Interpretation/judgment: "You're unreliable and never helpful around the house, and even the one thing I asked you to help me with, I ended up doing myself."

2. Note feelings

This second step involves describing the emotions these situations make you feel. Our interpretations and judgments of situations are often a result of our feelings being expressed as thoughts or observations. So, when describing your feelings, don't do it as a mash-up of your interpretation of someone else's actions and your thoughts; instead, share only the emotions you experience.

For instance:

Feelings: "I am excited," "I feel irritated," "I feel frustrated."

Interpretation and thoughts: "You don't care about me. You think I'm worthless."

3. Uncover desires

NVC focuses on needs—after all, most of the emotions we feel center on whether our needs are being met or not. We tend to blame the person or situation that made us feel a certain way. Instead of blaming others for the way you feel, you can find other strategies to satisfy that unmet need. Fortunately, one strategy can satisfy many needs, and a particular need can at times be satisfied by a million different strategies.

Let's look at an example of what I mean by that.

Need: Authenticity

Strategies for meeting this need: Telling your partner what you don't like instead of bottling up your emotions, doing things you feel passionate about, and excusing yourself from uncomfortable situations.

4. Make requests

This final step is about expressing your request clearly and concisely. My wife was telling me how women especially may tend to keep quiet or give vague requests, expecting that their partner will find out what they want them to do on their own. She used to do this to me a lot back when we were younger. However, doing this is setting yourself up for disappointment, as most times, it results in your needs not being fulfilled.

You should also know that making a request is different from demanding something. Asking your spouse to please put the dishes in the dishwasher and saying, "You'd better put your plate in the dishwasher" are two very different things. Also, your request should be doable and clearly state what you want or don't want.

Now, let's combine the four steps to restructure the statement made to Derek earlier:

"Derek, I found your stuff thrown all around the room when I got back from work today, and it made me feel irritated and annoyed. I know that's not your intention; it probably just got to me because I like things to be organized and I had a stressful day at work. Do you think you could pick everything up and put it away instead, please?"

How does that sound? Better, right? You can probably see how using these steps will make communication a lot easier and smoother, and also help you avoid conflict in your relationship.

How to Love Fiercely Despite the Tendency to Overthink

Yes, it's normal to overthink things, and it shouldn't be surprising to find that romantic partnerships, too, are often the subject of a lot of overthinking. However, by this point in the book, you have likely realized that if you're not careful, overthinking could sabotage your relationship. As an overthinker, you might start inventing nonexistent issues about the relationship, which can make you miserable and affect your mental health.

We've already established the common reasons why you might be overthinking your relationship; now the big question is: Is it possible to still love your partner fiercely despite being an overthinker?

Learning to truly listen to what is said and what goes unsaid and practicing nonviolent communication are excellent ways to keep the flame of love burning despite your overthinking tendencies. Letting your partner know what you're feeling and thinking instead of constantly second-guessing yourself or repressing your feelings is important as well. Also, be sure to ask your spouse what they mean when they say or do something that you're not sure how to interpret—or you can simply tell them if they've said or done something that makes you feel uncomfortable.

Since you've acknowledged the fact that you overthink everything, a simple solution to handle these thoughts that pop into your mind is cognitive restructuring. This process turns negative automatic thoughts into positive ones. Cognitive restructuring works by finding evidence to support your assumptions. If you don't find any, it's easier to let go of these thoughts.

A key secret to loving your partner despite your tendency to overthink is trusting them. I know that trust doesn't come easy, especially for overthinkers, that's for sure. But unless your partner has proven untrustworthy, I believe you should give trusting them a go. This is so important because trust lays the foundation for a healthy, happy relationship.

I remember a young woman named Jolene who had a tendency to overthink things. If you merely looked at her the wrong way, *bam*! She'd go off assuming the worst. That was before she got married to Dave. He is one of the sweetest, most caring men I know, and fortunately, he's very compassionate and quite empathetic toward Jolene's overthinking tendencies. But Jolene's previous relationship was with a chronic cheater, sadly. Thus, she didn't trust Dave one bit when they began dating. She was always going through his phone, picking fights if he so much as glanced at another woman, overthinking all his nice gestures—it practically ruined the relationship.

I had to sit her down one day and tell her to open up her heart to trusting Dave, and she admitted that he had never given her a reason to doubt his faithfulness. She really tried—God bless her heart, she did. It took a while, and they're a work in progress, but their relationship is a loving, happy one now, and I couldn't be happier for them.

How to Build Trust in Your Relationship

1. Be honest, accept your emotions, and practice vulnerability

Ask your partner for assurance if you need it. Tell them if you're feeling uneasy. Invite them to get to know you, how you feel about their words or actions, and how you want them to feel. Be honest about your dreams, worries, and aspirations.

2. Assume your partner's intentions are good

If your spouse lets you down, remember that it might not have been on purpose; mistakes can happen. While it's acceptable to speculate about their motivations, remain open to the possibility that they may have made a simple error. Forgive them. Don't forget what the Bible says about forgiveness—forbearing one another and forgiving one another: "If any man has a quarrel against any, even as Christ forgave you, so also do ye" (Colossians 3:13).

3. Talk openly and honestly about important issues

Spend some time each day checking in, facing one another, and considering how things are going. If there are problems in your relationship, address them right away rather than letting them fester. Start off simple, use sentences that start with "I" ("I feel," "I notice," "I wonder"), and be honest. The Bible says not to let the sun set on your anger, but I think you should apply that verse to any issues troubling your relationship, too. Say it and get it off your chest; you'll definitely sleep better that way.

4. Recognize how previous wrongs can lead to mistrust

Consider whether your lack of trust is a result of your partner's behavior, your own fears, or both. Be mindful of any unsolved problems or trauma from previous relationships that might be causing mistrust right now.

5. Practice mending fences after a dispute

If you're feeling overwhelmed during a discussion or argument with your partner, take a quick pause to consider what just transpired. This will give you both some time to cool off and gather your thoughts so you can talk to each other in a more meaningful and productive way.

6. Be aware that stating your needs is not being needy

When our partners fail to satisfy our needs, we tend to become incredibly irate and dissatisfied. But have you stopped to consider whether you've clearly articulated this need to your spouse? Have you given them instructions on how to meet it? Most of the time, our partners can't read our minds; therefore, we have to teach them how to meet our needs and help us feel loved.

So that's it! As long as there's mutual trust in your relationship*, it is completely possible to love your partner fiercely despite being an overthinker. Choose to trust your partner today. You'll be glad you did.

*Click HERE to receive this Bonus on healthy relationship

Wrapping Up

When I discovered just how critical body language is for communication, and what an important tool it can be, it opened up a whole new world of communication for me. The ability of you and your significant other to understand each other's needs and respond to them appropriately brings a new dimension of contentment and happiness to the relationship.

This could be you too. We've learned a lot so far, and I'd like to say that your relationship is worth it. Your happiness is worth it. Your joy is worth it. Keep applying what you've learned, and keep pressing for more. The rewards are unquantifiable.

At this point, maybe you've been wondering: "Okay, so let's say I follow all these steps, improve my relationship with my partner, and reduce my tendency to overthink—but what if I slip back into overthinking when I start feeling anxious again? Is it possible to actually prevent overthinking relapses? Can I stop them from occurring?" I'd turn to the next (and final) chapter to find out. See you there!

Your Quick Workbook

Do your overthinking tendencies tend to get in the way of your ability to listen effectively without being judgmental or doubtful?

_____

_____

_____

_____

_____

Do you and your partner use nonverbal communication a lot? How well do you recognize each other's cues?

_____

_____

_____

_____

_____

What do you think about nonviolent communication (NVC) techniques? Is NVC something you're open to trying out?

_____

_____

_____

_____

_____

CHAPTER 8

PREVENTING OVERTHINKING RELAPSES TO PREVENT CONFLICT AND TRUST ISSUES

"In the multitude of my thoughts within me, Thy comfort delights my soul."

—Psalm 94:19

Anticipating Overthinking Triggers

If overthinking is a long-term habit, you obviously can't just put a lid on it and say adios just like that. Habits can be very hard to break, and it's natural to expect that your overthinking tendencies won't go away instantly.

Overthinking can be triggered by a lot of factors. Let's consider six triggers/possible causes of your overthinking habit:

1. Anxiety disorders

If you've already been diagnosed with an anxiety disorder, you probably know that overthinking is a classic symptom. Anxiety causes you to automatically overthink everything and assume the worst of most things. Keep in mind that although it is tough for a person with an anxiety disorder to get over their overthinking tendencies, it's not impossible.

2. Regrets

Sometimes it's hard to let go of past mistakes, which can be problematic. It's good to reminisce on the past from time to time, especially to relive good memories, but sometimes we tend to stress over mistakes made in the past and wonder how we could have prevented them.

This line of thinking is impractical and a waste of energy. No matter what we do now, we can't undo the past; we can only learn from our mistakes and become better people. Make peace with your past, and if you're still struggling to let go, you can do something that serves as a quick fix. For instance, if you were really unkind to someone in the past, you can try asking for their forgiveness.

3. Childhood trauma

We all know that our childhood experiences can leave a lasting impact on us. Well, overthinking is one of the aftermaths of having a terrible childhood. Kids tend to withdraw into themselves and overthink as coping mechanisms to get them through tough and scary situations. The unfortunate part is that this tendency becomes a habit and persists right through to adulthood. Reframing and resetting these habits might be difficult for an adult, especially one whose mind has been set to naturally overthink things, but it is doable (thank God for that).

4. A need to always be in control

Some people want to be in control of everything. Maybe you want things to go exactly the way you'd prefer, and you believe the only way to pull that off is to try to control everything. That makes a lot of sense; I can't deny that.

Taking control of situations and people has its clear advantages, but it has its cons too. Apart from being an indicator that you lack confidence in other people's skills, which could affect your personal and professional relationships, it also frequently leads to overthinking. Since you want everything to be perfect, you end up stressing about every detail, and whether you got something wrong or not. If you're this kind of person, start letting go gradually. Doing it all at once would be difficult, but start gradually delegating tasks to others. This improves your interpersonal relationships and reduces your overthinking and stress.

5. Personal worries

We all worry about things—our job, health, money, relationships. But believe me, there's a reason why the Lord asks us to cast all our burdens on Him. Worrying too much affects your mental, physical, and spiritual health. And does worrying solve anything? Absolutely not. Instead, you can make a list of the things you're worrying about, set a time to do something about them, and enumerate the steps you can take to solve each problem. Worrying will not solve anything, says the Bible: *"...and which of you with taking thoughts can add to his stature one cubit?"* (Matthew 6:27)

6. Uncertainty

Not knowing what to expect of the future can be scary sometimes. Some people worry about the future more than average—about whether they'll fulfill their dream of working a job they're passionate about, whether they'll have a disabled kid, when their parents might die, and the list goes on and on. But overthinking the future is not helping anyone, especially not you; you'll only end up inventing scenarios in your head for questions you don't have the answer to.

Rather than stress about the uncertain future, why not talk to God about it? After all, He knows the end from the beginning. If your automatic response to new, uncertain situations is panic, it's important to reframe your mindset. The future is unknown to us, so just live every day as if it's your last and stop stressing about the future.

Remember, your overthinking triggers are unique to you. We've all had different life experiences and handle distressing situations differently. Even if you can't relate to any of the reasons listed above, take time to reflect on your unique experiences that may be affecting your tendency to overthink.

If you pay attention to your overthinking patterns, I'm sure you'll notice that you tend to overthink due to specific situations. It may be when you're feeling sad, stressed out, sleep-deprived, or alone. Paying attention to your triggers is one way of preventing your overthinking relapses. So, observe the situations when you catch yourself overthinking and pick out the common triggers during these instances.

Prioritizing Sharing About Each Other's Day

I know I've reiterated this point again and again, but the importance of communication in a healthy relationship cannot be overemphasized. Between going to work, taking care of the kids, cooking, and all the other things that take up our time, communicating with your spouse can be overwhelming. Time flies, and before you know it, you can barely find a spare minute to have meaningful, deep conversations. Suddenly, neither person is making an effort anymore because you're both engrossed in your day-to-day activities. It becomes easy to start thinking that your partner prefers work or playing with the kids to spending time with you. Throw in a few incidents of coming home late and your overthinking brain goes into overdrive and pushes your relationship downhill.

I can hear you asking, "So how do I avoid this? My partner and I are so busy, and it's hard to find time."

The truth is, you have to *make* the time, and you have to prioritize your marriage. If you can't find time to talk because you or your partner spend the whole evening taking care of the kids and you get so tired that you just go to bed immediately, you're not doing something right. Have you ever thought about what goes on in the minds of kids whose parents split up? If your relationship is not solid, there's no teamwork, and it's possible that your kids won't have a family unit anymore if things deteriorate.

So, how do you prioritize your relationship? Spend quality time together.

Talk about your day. Have a bit of alone time together. A great trick for people with busy days is to schedule it right into your day and stick to that schedule. You and your partner should commit to this. It could be something as small as going to bed together a few minutes earlier than usual or planning date nights. Ladies, let your little black dress see the light of day once more. I'm sure when your love was still young and budding, you enjoyed talking about your day with your partner after being apart. It's high time you reignited that spark.

Instead of overthinking how rude your colleague was to you, go on and rant about everything to your partner; after all, they're supposed to be your confidante.

Making Positivity a Daily Habit in Your Home

Several relationship experts continuously emphasize the importance of positivity in our relationships. If you've ever listened to or read something by Pat Love, John Gottman, and many others, then you'll have noticed how they're constantly stressing this fact. And it's true: the adverse effect of negative energy on relationships doesn't need much explanation.

But let's be honest here, being positive all the time is hard. It's like there's always negative energy around. Disappointments, stress from your job, life issues, and the like can make maintaining positivity difficult. We're more inclined to negative thoughts because our brains have been wired for survival. Considering the worst possible scenarios may just be our way of protecting ourselves.

But positivity means a happy, long-lasting relationship, so how do we go about achieving it?

Becoming more positive isn't just about deciding to think positive thoughts. Most of us are inclined to see the negative side of things, so there's a need to reframe your mind and address issues that may be the cause of your negativity.

Here's how to make positivity a daily habit in your home:

1. Take a break from all forms of negativity

I learned this from Harville Hendrix (author of *Getting the Love You Want*, among other books), put it into practice, and trust me, it worked. So how does this work? You and your partner should avoid criticizing, shifting blame, or expressing any shame. No matter how tempting it might be, you have to persevere on this. In fact, during this period you might notice their annoying personality quirks and feel like saying something just a teensy bit critical— but you have to hold back. It can be quite maddening, I know, but don't give up and you'll see the benefits. Another great tip is to focus on things you love about your partner instead of dwelling on the negatives.

2. Compliment and appreciate your partner

Tell your spouse what you appreciate about them. This encourages you to focus on the positive rather than the negative. Saying things like, "I love how you look in that dress," "I appreciate your driving me to and from work because my car acted up," or "I appreciate your sense of humor" are simple ways to start.

3. Reminisce about happy memories

Everyone is always talking about the honeymoon phase in relationships. I doubt there's any relationship that hasn't gone through this phase. You might be wondering how you went from that phase to the current, not-so-lovey-dovey phase you're in, but that's what happens if you're not intentional about the relationship. Looking back at those happy times is great, but don't stop there. Try to recreate those awesome memories; you'll be glad you did.

4. Be realistic

No relationship is perfect, that much is clear. You might not have noticed some flaws in the honeymoon phase, but when that wears off, you'll have to deal with the realities of a long-term committed relationship. Also, you know who you married, and you can't expect your partner to make unrealistic changes.

5. Make clear requests

Your partner is not a mind reader; if you want something or have an issue with how they dealt with something, let them know. Good communication automatically makes a relationship better. And don't forget to practice NVC when doing this—remember, the way you deliver your message matters a lot.

6. Take ownership of your part in a conflict

You shouldn't always assume, or allow your partner to assume, all the responsibility for a conflict. Own your role in it and share what you learned about yourself in the course of the argument. For instance: "I realized during our argument that I was too harsh in trying to correct you; next time I would like to take a softer approach."

7. Create positive responses to negative thoughts

As I mentioned earlier, external stressors are bound to bring about negativity. Try replacing every negative thought with a positive one. After all, you need positive energy if you're going to be practicing positivity.

My partner and I use some of these practices in our relationship. We're not a perfect couple (we're a work in progress), but these practices are doing wonders for our marriage. As you know, a happy relationship means we're also happy in our daily lives. We've made it a habit to appreciate each other constantly and to communicate our issues clearly and gently avoid conflicts. We're also always on the lookout for negativity, and when it arises, we deal with it as a couple.

Practicing all these steps at once may not be practical for you, though, since you're just starting out. Take it one step at a time. Start from those that seem the easiest to you and gradually integrate more of them into your home. Make them a part of your partnership and you'll fall in love with the process, and with your spouse, more and more.

How to Efficiently Prevent Relapses with Your Overthinking

Picture this: You've been waking up at 6:00 a.m. every morning for the past five years, and the first thing you do is drink coffee. You know you're not fully awake without caffeine in your system. Then, you put on your running gear, go for a run, get back home, take a shower, eat breakfast, and hurry to work. One day, after five years of this routine, you decide to take a break from coffee because you read an article that spoke about the dangers of excessive caffeine intake. I can bet your first day would be hellish. You'd probably have a headache, feel irritable and tired, and be tempted to take just one sip of coffee. But you make it through nine caffeine-free days (and you swear that those days are the hardest), and now you're confident that you can function perfectly without caffeine. Then one morning, weeks later, after you're sure you've conquered the need for caffeine, you wake up with an unexpected, serious craving for coffee—what do you do?

Humans are creatures of habit, and habits die hard, that's for sure. You've been overthinking for so long, and now you're making an effort to stop; does that mean you'll never feel the urge to overthink a situation again? That's doubtful.

Since you've identified your overthinking triggers, when you experience them, you can easily prevent a relapse based on these tips:

1. Find a distraction

Engage in something you enjoy to stop yourself from overthinking. I'm sure you have a lot of hobbies or activities that interest you and will keep your mind off these negative thoughts for a while. It could be creative, like attempting a new recipe or picking up some new cooking techniques, or you might have to work it out by going to your preferred exercise class. You could also try to acquire a new interest, like painting or pottery, or do volunteer work with a neighborhood organization to make a change. By the time you're done, you'll probably have forgotten what you were thinking about.

You should put some of these activities in your schedule; they'll help you reduce your anxiety level and stop focusing on negativity.

2. Get help from friends, loved ones, or your partner

If you keep overthinking a situation or occurrence, you can ask your friends or partner to weigh in on the matter. They may give you a fresh perspective or help you find a solution to the issue so that you won't have to continue stressing about it.

3. Challenge your thoughts

You don't have to believe your thoughts 100%. After viewing them objectively, you might realize that the thought is baseless. Find out if there's any evidence in support of or against the thought. That way, you can easily determine if it's logical or helpful. It's easy to squash your overthinking when you realize that what you're thinking is not supported by any facts. Then consider an alternative possibility for a broader, more balanced perspective on the situation.

4. Practice self-compassion

Being compassionate towards your friends or your partner probably comes easy to you. What about towards yourself, though? How does your internal monologue sound when you're dealing with an issue or challenge?

What does practicing self-compassion mean? It's about being able to show oneself love, kindness, and forgiveness. You will truly calm your body's internal threat system by doing that, which will give you a clearer head to address any issues.

5. Find comfort in God's Word

The Bible says, "In the multitude of my thoughts within me, thy comfort delights my soul" (Psalm 94:19). Often, it's only in God's Word that we can find true comfort. God's Word will bring you peace and put an end to your ruminating thoughts.

Communication Exercises to Strengthen Your Relationship with Your Partner

Talking, listening, being open, and understanding each other make for effective communication. Trust, love, and communication are the foundation of a successful relationship, which is why communication exercises are necessary tools for couples who want to improve their partnership.

One thing about these exercises, though: you must be willing to actually do them, and also get your partner on board. It's understandable that you and your partner barely have time for any extra activities with your busy schedule, so I won't waste your time with exercises that might not work. These exercises have been proven effective over and over again and have helped many people to greatly improve their relationships. In fact, a lot of couples have printed copies of these exercises to share the good news with those who might be in need of it.

Try each of these exercises out one by one, and choose the one that works best for you to continue implementing in your relationship.

1. Taking turns

Have you ever witnessed conversations where one person doesn't allow the other to complete what they're saying before speaking? This frequently happens in group conversations among friends, but it can happen between spouses as well. This exercise addresses that, giving both partners the opportunity to speak and be listened to.

Decide who will speak first and set a timer for three to five minutes. When the timer starts, one person begins speaking without interruption from the other. The other partner is not allowed to speak during this time, but they may express acknowledgment, understanding, and empathy through nonverbal cues.

Once the first person has completed speaking, the second asks questions to clarify what they have just heard (for example, "How did you feel when you told me that?" or "What can I do next time to make things better?" or even "Why is this so important to you?"). After these queries have been addressed and clarified, it is the other spouse's turn to speak without interruption.

This exercise teaches the pair of you to wait patiently for your turn and to respect each other's time and viewpoints.

2. Mirroring

When you mirror your spouse, you pay attention to his or her ideas and emotions before repeating what was said back to them and asking, "Did I get that right?" You can keep asking questions until your partner feels like they've been sufficiently heard, at which point they can either affirm or deny that you got it right. The listener might then support their partner by stating something like, "That makes sense" or "I'm glad you clarified that for me." Even if you don't quite agree with what was stated, at least now that you've heard them out, you can approach the argument with more understanding.

3. The "I" statement

One of the most well-known communication exercises for couples is the "I" statement technique. Here, you want to avoid accusing, blaming, criticizing, and shaming one another—all of which are frequent tactics couples use when they're at odds with one another. The issue with blaming and shaming is that rather than enhancing the relationship, it might cause distance or detachment.

Using "I" statements when you're angry or upset about something might help you take ownership of your emotions while lessening the amount of blame you place on your partner. In fact, studies have demonstrated that using the pronoun "I" rather than "you" lessens the possibility that conversations about conflict may result in a violent encounter. Finally, using "I" statements can enable us to forge stronger bonds with all the people in our lives, not only our romantic partners (Shane et al., 2022).

4. The 40-20-40 method

A specific communication exercise for compassionate listening and helpful conflict resolution is the 40-20-40 method. With this technique, the conversation's focus is divided into two parts: each person's feelings receive 40% of the attention, with 20% left over to talk about the relationship.

The aim is for each person to listen with the intention of understanding the other rather than defending themselves. Each person uses their allotted time to speak about their own feelings. In order to avoid seeming accusatory, it's best to only discuss how each person is feeling. The objective here is to show kindness and empathy to one another.

5. Fireside conversation

The term "fireside" connotes warmth, openness, and a say-anything attitude. President Franklin D. Roosevelt hosted what he called "fireside chats" over the radio to engage with the American people during World War II, bringing to mind the image of a friendly discussion with the president in front of a crackling fire. With this in mind, pick a place where you and your spouse feel at ease, order or prepare something yummy for both of you, and sit down together for a cozy conversation.

In order to give each other your entire attention during these conversations and to feel free to express whatever is on your mind, it is crucial that you remove all outside distractions.

You'll notice that these exercises cover verbal, nonverbal, and listening skills. They will help you and your partner learn more about each other and also help you clear the emotions, issues, and misunderstandings you've been piling up over time. Try to schedule one of these exercises as frequently as possible (at least once a week), and in no time, your relationship will improve due to effective communication.

Wrapping Up

Some of the strategies in this chapter might be common knowledge, but you've almost certainly learned one or two new things. While I'm sure that following the guidelines set out here will help a lot, it's entirely understandable if you get overwhelmed. Especially if you're reading this for the first time and trying to get your head around everything in the book all at once.

Here's my advice: take it slow and use the workbook sections. You can come back to these tips as many times as you want. Remember that it's not a sprint, but a marathon.

Your Quick Workbook

How do you feel when, despite all your hard work, you relapse (or almost relapse) into your overthinking habits?

_____

_____

_____

Do you think spending quality time with your partner regularly is a habit you can make stick? Why or why not?

_____

_____

_____

Practicing positivity despite all the negativity around you might prove difficult; how are you feeling about it?

_____

_____

_____

What methods or strategies have you practiced in the past to help you handle your overthinking tendencies? Were they helpful?

_____

_____

_____

Conclusion

Getting lost in your own negative, anxious thoughts can be damaging; it's like you're being sucked into a vortex, and you can't see or hear clearly, which makes you unable to view things objectively. You already have your own definitive thoughts about a situation, so whatever anyone else says doesn't make much sense to you.

Being trapped in a black hole of your own thoughts can be overwhelming. It gets even more terrifying when you realize that the vortex can show up at any time and swallow you up, stealing your time, happiness, and peace—and worst of all, holding you back from having a deeper connection with your partner.

How would you feel if all of that negativity and anxiety completely disappeared from your life? Or if you were able to prevent yourself from being sucked in in the first place? Freeing, right? Yep, freedom, love, laughter, and deeper connection are the keys to a happy life. And do you know the best part? You really can leave all your negativity behind you for good. It might be a lot of work, but the positivity you'll enjoy afterwards makes it totally worth it. You'll be able to enjoy the happiness and deep connection that comes with being in a healthy, long-lasting, committed relationship, maybe even enjoy that long-forgotten honeymoon phase again, and a lot of other couples around you will probably wonder how you and your partner are thriving.

That's the value you're getting from this book—the ability to let go of overthinking and all negativity and connect more deeply with your partner.

And you know what the best part is? You can read this book over and over again to gain more insights; after all, it's yours.

Now that you know that your overthinking tendencies and anxiety are what have been putting a damper on your relationship and preventing you from communicating effectively with your partner, all that's left to do is utilize the tools packed in this book for a better, stronger, long-lasting relationship. Being fiercely in love is not only for those who have just fallen in love. You can also experience this, even if you've been with your spouse for decades.

Putting an end to your overthinking habits, managing your anxiety, and learning how to be a better communicator is important because once you tame the negativity and start practicing effective communication, it will propel your partner to make an effort too.

You should know that the journey won't be simple, though. Changing a long-term habit is no walk in the park. But as long as you can recognize your triggers and stop the thoughts before you enter another negative thought spiral, you're good to go.

The first step is becoming aware of your overthinking, which you have successfully done.

The next step involves dealing with all the negativity—your overthinking spirals, negative thoughts, negative energy, and conflict with your partner—which you can do using the tools we've discussed in this book. Then you can begin learning and practicing the art of effective communication and how to avoid relapsing. Acknowledging your issues, removing every trace of negativity from your thoughts, and preventing relapse might seem like a tall order, but don't give up. Having a happy relationship and life is definitely worth all the stress.

Remaining positive despite all the external stressors around you is going to prove challenging. Everything going on in the world right now is enough to put anyone in a sour mood for days. But the fact that you've made it to the end of the book shows how determined you are to improve your relationship. I know that managing to stay positive in this negative world is something you can do as well.

This book is the perfect guide to help you communicate and connect with your partner. Now that you have all the tools you need, go out there and use them. You're just a few steps away from enjoying the best years of your relationship.

If you got value from this book and enjoyed reading it, please leave a review on Amazon so other amazing people can have access to the tools in this book and improve their relationships as well. Gracias, amigo.

13 Scriptures to Find Comfort in When Overthinking

1. 2 Corinthians 10:5: "We destroy every proud obstacle that keeps people from knowing God. We capture their rebellious thoughts and teach them to obey Christ."

2. Proverbs 12:25: "Anxiety weighs down the heart, but a kind word cheers it up."

3. Romans 12:2: "Don't copy the behavior and customs of this world, but let God transform you into a new person by changing the way you think. Then you will learn to know God's will for you, which is good and pleasing and perfect."

4. Isaiah 35:4: "Say to those with fearful hearts, 'Be strong, do not fear; your God will come, he will come with a vengeance; with divine retribution, he will come to save you.'"

5. 1 Peter 1:13: "So prepare your minds for action and exercise self-control. Put all your hope in the gracious salvation that will come to you when Jesus Christ is revealed to the world."

6. Philippians 4:8: "Fix your thoughts on what is true, and honorable, and right, and pure, and lovely, and admirable. Think about things that are excellent and worthy of praise."

7. Psalm 94:19: "When anxiety was great within me, your consolation brought me joy."

8. Psalm 139:23-24: "Search me, O God, and know my heart; test me and know my anxious thoughts. Point out anything in me that offends you, and lead me along the path of everlasting life."

9. Colossians 3:2: "Think about the things of heaven, not the things of earth."

10. Jeremiah 29:11: "'For I know the plans I have for you,' declares the Lord, 'plans to prosper you and not to harm you, plans to give you hope and a future.'"

11. Hebrews 12:1-2: "...let us run with endurance the race God has set before us. We do this by keeping our eyes on Jesus, the champion who initiates and perfects our faith..."

12. Luke 12:25: "Who of you by worrying can add a single hour to your life?"

13. Psalm 119:76: "May your unfailing love be my comfort, according to your promise to your servant."

11 Overthinking Quotes to Remember

1. "I get anxious about everything. I just can't stop thinking about things all the time. And here's the really destructive part—it's always retrospective. I waste time thinking of what I should have said or done."—Hugh Laurie

2. "Take time to deliberate, but when the time for action has arrived, stop thinking and go in."—Napoleon Bonaparte

3. "Thinking too much leads to paralysis by analysis. It's important to think things through, but many use thinking as a means of avoiding action."—Robert Herjavek

4. "Worrying is like paying a debt you don't owe."—Mark Twain

5. "Don't brood. Get on with living and loving. You don't have forever."—Leo Buscaglia

6. "Spend 80% of your time focusing on the opportunities of tomorrow rather than the problems of yesterday."—Brian Tracy

7. "Don't get too deep, it leads to overthinking, and overthinking leads to problems that doesn't even exist in the first place."—Jayson Engay

8. "I think and think and think, I've thought myself out of happiness one million times, but never once into it."—Jonathan Safran Foer

9. "You don't have to see the whole staircase, just take the first step."—Martin Luther King, Jr.

10. "The sharpest minds often ruin their lives by overthinking the next step, while the dull win the race with eyes closed."—Bethany Brookbank

11. "If you treat every situation as a life and death matter, you'll die a lot of times."—Dean Smith

BOOK #3

Overthinking Is Not the Solution

25 Ways to Reduce Stress, Eliminate Negative Thinking, Develop Mental Clarity and Master Your Emotions to Live on Purpose

Robert J. Charles, PhD, DMin

INTRODUCTION

Have you been feeling stressed lately? Do you struggle to quiet your racing thoughts? Do you feel lost in your own world, exhausted by constant worry? If so, you might be a chronic overthinker.

Overthinking can be described as excessive mental activity and worrying. It is essentially when your thoughts are running in circles and never letting you catch a break. You can overthink anything, from an upsetting memory to a pause in the conversation, and it often leads to anxiety—which can quickly have a negative impact on your wellbeing.

Today, overthinking is endemic to our global society. It is estimated that 60 million people in the United States alone suffer from anxiety. Although they come from different backgrounds and have varying personalities, almost all share one thing: overthinking. We live in demanding times that require a great deal of mental ability to function and succeed. Family responsibilities, financial constraints, mental trauma, relationship problems, and other issues may keep our minds working nearly 24 hours a day. Unfortunately, this state of constant stress frequently leads to anxiety, fear, and negative outcomes. At this point, too much thinking becomes a huge problem.

I can empathize with what you've been through. I understand the stressful predicament you've created for yourself, and how you've been sucked into the worry trap. But I also know that you're an empathic, driven individual who is struggling to navigate your life and to believe in yourself along the way. That's why I wrote this book, which is full of strategies to guide you through the difficulties and assist you in rewiring your brain, regaining control of your thoughts, and altering your mental patterns. Throughout this guide, I will present you with science-backed tips to get control of your emotions, achieve personal and professional fulfillment, and transform your life by putting an end to destructive thought patterns.

With the assistance of this book, you can not only overcome your repetitious, unhelpful negative thoughts, but also replace them with positive ones that bring peace, joy, and love into your life. This applies to how you approach everything, from small questions like "Should I buy these flowers?" to large ones such as "How am I going to spend the rest of my life?"

This book will show you how to shake off the burden of negative thoughts. You can reset your brain with unique mind training routines, allowing you to stop worrying and stressing all the time. Follow the simple exercises found in this book if you want to rewire your brain to stop overthinking and reduce stress and anxiety. This guide is the solution you've been seeking. Why not begin a new chapter in your life—one without space for tension, anxiety, or negativity? In this book you'll find new and healthier habits to declutter your mind and achieve inner balance.

While it's true that several books on the topic of overthinking have been written already, I want to point out why I believe writing another one was worthwhile and what this book provides that is unique. Overthinking is destroying lives around the world; in this book, I offer a fresh perspective on this problem: a spiritual perspective. I wanted to create a dependable, practical guide for disciples of Christ on how to conquer self-destructive thinking, avoid perfectionism, and rewire your brain. In researching useful techniques for overcoming stress and fostering positive habits, I left no stone unturned. When you reach the end of this game-changing book, you will recognize your own tendency to overthink and be able to take simple actions to rewire your brain, develop new, positive thought patterns, and stop undermining every decision you make by second-guessing yourself.

Our mind is simply incredible. No other word can better define it. It is capable of amazing things, both psychologically and physiologically. However, if we allow the constant upheaval of negative thoughts and anxiety to set up camp in our head, we'll end up with completely out-of-control, negative, disturbing thoughts that create feelings of helplessness, sorrow, confusion, and depression. Until you can learn how to control these thoughts and think effectively, you will never be at peace with yourself.

Effective thinking assists you in steering your life in the desired direction. A mind that overthinks is unproductive; it chases away opportunities for joy and peace that present themselves to you. Stop allowing your mind to entrap you. Reclaim control of your thoughts. The lessons contained in this book will take you from where you are now to where you want to be by not only teaching you how to make wise choices but also discussing why your current way of thinking is detrimental to your wellbeing and how positivity can significantly improve your outlook.

If you can relate to the feelings of anxiety and helplessness described above, and if you wish to change them, keep reading this book.

CHAPTER ONE

OVERTHINKING

"Don't worry about anything; instead, pray about everything. Tell God what you need, and thank him for all he has done."

Philippians 4:6 (NLT)

Lesson from Shakespeare: A beautiful flower may bloom from a very difficult situation

In April 1564, in Stratford-upon-Avon, north of London, England, Shakespeare was born. The single biggest worry of Shakespeare's time was public health and hygiene. Specifically, everyone was afraid of the bubonic plague—and they had good reason to be worried. The plague was a horrific and fatal infectious disease. The terrible outbreaks of the plague took the lives of vast numbers of individuals. In fact, millions upon millions of people in Europe ended up dying from the plague over the centuries.

At the time, no one fully understood the plague; medical authorities did not know exactly where the disease had originated, how it spread, or how to cure it. However, they did realize that a large sum of people crowded together increased the infection rate.

This situation took place throughout Shakespeare's lifetime. With strict quarantines and the help of the weather, the epidemic would slow, and social activities would resume their ordinary course; however, after a break of a few years, the disease would inevitably return and ravage the country once again. When the death rate reached a specific number in London, city authorities shut the theaters down, including the Globe, which was famous for producing Shakespeare's plays. They could not resume their activities until the death rates decreased.

Why have I recounted this story here? Well, Shakespeare lived his entire life under the dark cloud of the bubonic plague, but despite the gloomy outlook, he continued to follow his passion and worked hard to write and produce many plays. Not only did thousands gather to watch his plays in 16th century London, but his work went on to have a massive impact on the English language, on playwriting, and on culture as a whole. As a young boy, Abraham Lincoln read Shakespeare to master English. Hundreds of words and phrases we use every day first appeared in his writings, and many people believe Shakespeare was the best English writer of all time.

Shakespeare took action and overcame his situation. No matter how depressing a situation can be, do not lose your focus and passion to the trap of overthinking. Even in difficult times, something remarkable may still arise. A beautiful flower may bloom from a very unexpected place. A masterpiece can come from chaotic circumstances. Do not despair in your difficult moments. Keep your faith in God. He will bring you through whatever obstacle you currently face.

Before we can fully understand this, we first need to learn what overthinking is and how it takes a toll on our life. Once you understand what's holding you back, you can start the journey of becoming victorious, joyful, and at peace.

What Is Overthinking?

What is overthinking? It can be anxiety about the past, fear of the present, or worries for the future. It is a cognitive process that involves excessive or obsessive thinking about something, whether it's an event, a decision, a conversation, or an idea. This usually results in even more stress for the overthinker, who feels there are too many possible outcomes if a situation does not work out correctly, leaving them feeling helpless. Overthinking generally causes us to spend too much time ruminating with no action taken to solve the problem, thus having either a neutral or a negative effect on our wellbeing.

When you overthink, one of two main outcomes can take place:

1. You become so immersed in ruminating on the problem at hand that you lose track of time. You struggle with insomnia for nights on end because you cannot shut off your mind when you lie down in bed. This negatively affects your mental and physical health.

2. You eventually realize that the solution to the problem was right in front of you all along; however, you lose interest in solving it because you've already made up your mind about the outcome and are convinced things will turn out badly, even though many other possibilities could occur.

These outcomes indicate how harmful overthinking can be and why you need to stop.

Overthinking leads to mental and physical stress. It also leads to frustration. Here's an example: let's say you're a brand-new business owner and you're getting ready to showcase your new brand to the public for the first time. You may feel anxious about what people are going to think of it compared to other products on the market. You may worry about whether they will like it at all, which leads you to worrying about failing in your business and having nothing to show for your hard work. You continue to overthink until you completely lose passion for debuting your brand because you've already decided how things are going to go down (badly) instead of taking a chance on the outcome. Unlike Shakespeare, you've allowed your circumstances to infiltrate your thoughts and take away your passion.

Does this sound like you?

Do you find yourself constantly asking, "Should I do this?", "Did I do the right thing?", or "How am I supposed to do that?" ... and then questioning your answer? Do you stay in this indecisive stage for extended periods of time? If so, it may indicate that you're overthinking. Here are a few other criteria you can use to determine whether or not you're an overthinker:

- a need for perfectionism
- constantly seeking the opinions of others
- insomnia
- burnout
- irritability
- hypochondria
- prolonged sadness
- a belief that you do not have control over your life

Since you're reading this book, let's assume you are, in fact, an overthinker. What can you do about it?

The answer to this is simple: thoughts are either conscious or unconscious, and you must take control of the conscious ones (to the best of your ability) in order to improve the unconscious ones. Unconscious thoughts just sort of bubble up without any interference on our part and usually center on negative events and feelings like worry, anxiety, or regret. In your conscious thoughts, however, you can work on making the best of your situation.

Causes and Symptoms

The next step is to evaluate and solve the problem of overthinking in your life. First, it is essential to know what makes you overthink. That can be challenging. Perhaps it's mental issues, such as depression and anxiety. Maybe your fear of embarrassment pushes you to overthink what you wear or how you act in front of other people. Other factors that can cause chronic overthinking include childhood abuse or neglect, trauma, perfectionism, or a genetic predisposition to overthinking. These factors can affect the quality of our decisions in different ways. We will discuss these causes in the following paragraphs.

Holding on to excessive worry

Research shows that severe anxiety is widespread among American teenagers (Garcia & O'Neil, 2021). Most of them are afraid of failing in their lives. They worry too much about the world around them, about their image in the eyes of others. It's no surprise that they worry about what others think about them, and this tendency often continues into adulthood.

The habit of constantly worrying that things could go wrong will push you to overthink. The negative images you develop in your mind will often feature the fear of failure. This drains your energy and your ability to make good decisions.

Instead of worrying about the future, understand that thinking positively and constructively about accomplishing your goals is more productive. Remember, the future is uncertain for everybody. No one knows what will happen tomorrow, and Christ told us not to worry about tomorrow (Matthew 6:34). Therefore, the best thing you can do about the future is pray, plan for it, and then let whatever happens happen.

Changing your mentality to focus more on your goals and achieving them will motivate you to live a life with a sense of direction. The best part is that the sense of optimism you develop will help you see all aspects of your life from a positive perspective, increasing your overall sense of happiness.

Negativity

Studies have shown that negativity is a common trait among those diagnosed with anxiety and depression (Kalin, 2020). Past research has found that people who have a higher occurrence of these types of negative thoughts experience more stress and anxiety, which leads to subconscious patterns of overthinking and concentration problems.

The problem isn't the level of stress or anxiety, but how often this kind of thought occurs and what you do about it. People who are prone to overthinking might want to prepare themselves for these negative thoughts and find coping mechanisms to keep their minds in check.

Headaches and dizziness

A headache is a sign that your mind and body need rest. If you pay attention to your thinking, you might notice that you're thinking about similar matters repeatedly. Dizziness, likewise, is a common symptom of the tension brought about by worry and might happen when you're stressed. Sometimes the dizziness can be so intense that it causes concentration, vision, and task performance problems. If you're experiencing headaches and dizziness on a regular basis, it's possible that you're over-analyzing things.

Of course, it's possible that these are symptoms of an underlying health problem, so it's wise to get these symptoms checked by a professional;

however, if you are otherwise healthy, these symptoms might be a sign that you're worrying too much and having issues with anxiety.

Negative emotions

You can know whether you are overthinking by checking for the symptoms of depression. Subconscious negative thoughts can be a symptom of clinical depression. (Note that not everyone who has negative thoughts is clinically depressed, but it's something to watch out for.)

Other symptoms of depression include sadness, irritability, and an overall lack of interest in things that make you happy. You might also feel completely overwhelmed by the responsibilities your day-to-day life. It might feel easier to just stay in bed all day.

You could also have trouble concentrating and focusing on things around you. You might feel a lack of motivation to do anything but feel guilty for not doing anything, and even avoid social interactions with other people. If you are experiencing any of these symptoms, please seek help from a professional to get yourself feeling better.

Abstract thinking

This refers to thinking which goes beyond concrete realities. When you formulate theories to explain your observations, you engage in abstract thinking. This can be a useful skill, but it can also be detrimental if you're an overthinker. For example, when your business is not performing well, you might jump to the conclusion that it's because you're doing something wrong and begin ruminating over your shortcomings instead of considering other possibilities.

Avoidance

Avoidance means that you try to avoid doing something by using the decision-making process as an excuse; that is, you spend so much time going back and forth between options because you want to avoid having to choose anything at all.

Neglecting intuition

This occurs when you don't take into consideration the things you already know at the core of your being, and instead opt to overthink. Instead of following your gut instinct, you end up second-guessing your intuition and could make the wrong decisions.

Creating problems

You may also think in a way that creates problems that are not there. Certain situations are not as complex as you may perceive them to be. The problem at hand may only require a couple of minutes to solve, but when you overthink it, you make it much more complicated than it needs to be.

It is vital to focus on the bigger picture and not nitpick at the details. Try to see things as they are; don't complicate your life by thinking of potential problems.

Magnifying the issue

Usually, small problems require simple solutions. Unfortunately, sometimes we amplify these problems and develop overly complex ways to solve them. This is another form of overthinking. You're wasting your mental resources to come up with huge, elaborate solutions that don't match the scale of the problems you're experiencing.

Fear of failure

Fear of failure is not a new concept to most people. This motivates many of us to work hard. But for an overthinker, instead of letting that fear drive you to work towards a bright future, you let that fear grow inside you and consume your thoughts.

Fear of failing can be crippling. It can cause you to rethink your actions and motivations. It can prevent you from taking the initial step. It can cruelly eat away at your self-confidence if you allow it to, leaving you feeling utterly incapable of taking the necessary action to realize your goals.

A certain amount of dread can inspire you if you remain focused on the end objective. (For example, think of a public speaker who turns their nerves into excitement and motivation to give a fantastic speech.) Despite these nagging anxious thoughts, you can use the nervous energy to force yourself toward your goal.

Failure can be a helpful learning experience if we allow it to be. We all must fail occasionally to develop as individuals and improve.

Making irrelevant decisions

An overthinker may believe it is vital to make certain decisions that they are not actually required to make. For instance, you might be convinced that you need to plan out all of your major life decisions for the next several years right at this very moment, when in fact it is just fine to let life unfold before you and make decisions one at a time as they are presented to you.

Now that we've explored some of the symptoms and causes of overthinking, let's examine the three main forms of overthinking.

Three Forms of Overthinking

There are three dangerous forms of overthinking: ruminating, fear, and excessive worrying. Let's dive into each of these.

Ruminating—Rehashing the Past

Ruminating is obsessively going over a thought or problem repeatedly without ever coming to a conclusion. Whether it be repeating an old argument in your mind over and over or mentally replaying a mistake you made like a broken record, you just cannot seem to let the thought go no matter what. Ruminating is heavily connected with depression because this mental health condition causes you to remember the worst aspects of yourself continually.

You can see the self-defeating aspect of ruminating. It's one of the most dangerous things about overthinking because it paralyzes you and prevents you from taking action. What's the point if (according to your mind) you're just going to fail, no matter how hard you try, or it's already too late to turn things around from a previous bad decision? As you can see, rumination reflects how you view yourself and is thus deeply rooted in self-esteem and self-image.

If you've experienced any form of abuse, neglect, or trauma, it could result in lower self-esteem or self-image. This is further exacerbated if you have a history of academic, athletic, or social underperformance during your formative years and have been constantly compared to your higher-performing peers. Without any obvious talents to make you think otherwise, it's easy to feel like you're a nobody.

Fear for the Present

Fear for the present actually stems from the past. It is a reminder that things can be taken away in an instant and there is nothing you can do about it. If you find yourself constantly in a state of fear about what could happen to you or a loved one at any moment, you are experiencing this form of overthinking.

This feeling activates when you have something important on your mind and don't want anything else to stand in its way, whether it's a relationship or a work project. The fear hinders your productivity because you're constantly worrying about danger or failure. The anxiousness associated with this fear makes it difficult to concentrate on key tasks.

Another reason we may find it difficult to live in the present is that it is constantly filled with reminders of our mortality. Whether we realize it or not, we become acutely aware of life's relentless course. Change is the only constant.

However, if you relive the same scenario over and over again, whether it's about to happen or has already happened, you are being consumed by your thoughts. If you tend to get caught up in negative visions of the future, you are locked in "worry mode." We all do this to some degree, but the critical question is whether or not you have moved into addictive thinking territory. Just like an addiction to substances consumes a person with anxiety, worry, and doubt, being addicted to overthinking and overanalyzing creates a sense of being bound to suffering. It takes you over, and it isn't very easy to be present and in your body.

Why does this happen? Because underneath the fear, subtle or not, emotions are begging to be processed. For example, if you are nervous about an upcoming conversation, rather than being with and facing the fear, your brain will run every possible scenario to try to make you feel that you can control the outcome—to try to make you feel secure. This is not realistic. Don't be trapped by this false promise. The reality is, we can't control what happens in life and it's better to learn to live without the fear.

Excessive Worrying—Predicting the Future Negatively

Worry is your brain anticipating potential problems in order to avoid them, but this tends to lead to negative, usually disastrous future predictions:

- I'm going to fail the test tomorrow. I'll blank out, forget everything, and end up failing out of school.

- I'll never get my dream job. There's always going to be someone better than me. I should play it safe and work a stable and well-paying career I hate.

As you can see, ruminating and worrying are closely related; both cause one to think negatively, whether it be about oneself or a situation.

You may feel stressed about your presentation tomorrow, so you start to tell yourself that you won't do a good job. The more you think about it, the more you worry about what could go wrong, and the worse you feel. Or perhaps you have low self-esteem and feel that you aren't good enough, so you constantly worry that your spouse or partner will find someone else and leave you. Because you don't believe in yourself, you don't have confidence in how things will turn out; you are therefore always worrying about the future—fear of the unknown.

Rescuing Yourself from Overthinking

Overthinking is such a common cause of stress and anxiety that nearly everyone does it from time to time. At this point, you're probably wondering how you can put an end to all of this overthinking and the misery it can cause. Good news: the time for help is here. It's rescue time!

If you have identified yourself as an overthinker, here are some ideas for resolving the problem.

Be aware of the problem

Becoming aware of this problem is the first step to solving it. If you're not aware that your mind is wandering down negative paths towards anxiety and stress, how can you expect to stop it? Keeping track of your thoughts can help you see when you're getting stuck in a negative mental cycle, whether it's wondering what might happen if a specific event occurs or ruminating about what someone said to you yesterday.

Research shows that positive self-talk can positively impact your general wellbeing (Grzybowski, 2021). However, the impact of self-talk is only clear when you use it positively and consistently. The power of self-talk can lead to an overall boost in your self-esteem and confidence. If you convince your inner-self that you are calm, confident, and capable of rising above any situation, you will find it easier to overcome the emotions that seem to weigh you down.

Prevent negative thoughts

Next, you can take preventative measures against your thoughts by preparing yourself for the worst. The best way to do this is to think through what would happen if the worst-case scenario were to occur. Run this scenario in your mind all the way through to the end.

For example, if you have a job performance review coming up and you're feeling extreme anxiety about it, follow your anxiety to its conclusion. What is the worst-case scenario? You might get a bad review. What's the worst thing that could happen if you got a bad review? You might be fired. Then what would you do? You could start polishing up your resume and applying for other jobs. If you play out the scenario like this, you might discover that even in the very worst case, you have the strength to overcome the situation. It might also be helpful to make a list of exactly what you'll do if you're left with limited options. Having a strategy for the worst-case scenario will put your mind at ease and help you see that there's always something that can be done, even in the scariest situations.

Talk to someone

Talking to someone about what's going on in your head can help calm your worries and ease your anxiety. If you have a trusted friend or family member you can confide in, this is one of the best ways to get your thoughts out in the open and find out exactly what's going through your head. Telling a friend about your feelings can help you see you aren't alone in your struggles and put things into perspective. It also allows your friend to offer advice and comfort. Finally, it will make you aware of how overthinking can affect your mental state so you'll be better prepared to prevent that negative spiral.

Take some time for yourself

It's essential to get some time for yourself each day or every week, even if it's just for 15 minutes. Do something that will make you feel more in control of your mind. Finding these coping mechanisms helps keep your thoughts and emotions in check when you're going through a rough time. If you're feeling spaced out, read a book, listen to music, or go for a walk. These things can help prop up your mood and relax your body.

Change your habits

Set a goal for what you want to accomplish each day or week, and try not to dedicate too much time to one thing. Keep your goals short and simple. For example, if your goal is to read each day, block out just 15 minutes a day for reading. If you make your goal too big and complex, you're less likely to follow through and this can lead to more stress and anxiety. Achieving small goals on a daily basis will help your concentration and improve your focus.

Take care of your health

Another important way to take control of your mind is to take care of your overall health. Get plenty of rest each night and exercise regularly. Try to get around eight hours of sleep every night. Of course, if you're already experiencing insomnia as a result of your overthinking, this might be easier said than done, but do what you can to make your bedroom a peaceful and relaxing place so that you can rest even if you're not asleep. These things are important for improving your mood and overall wellbeing. Eating healthy food can also help keep you feeling balanced and in control of your emotions. If you're not taking care of yourself, you're not giving yourself the best chance to combat overthinking.

Talk to God

You can always talk to God about how you feel. He will always listen to your prayers and answer them because He knows what is best for you. Sometimes all it takes is a simple prayer to make things better again if you're feeling stressed out or worried.

God transforms believers. He will assist you with your mental confinement. As Luke chapter 4 tells us, Jesus is coming to liberate the captives. Jesus wants to deliver you from your mental jail. He has this power. He wants to help you in your battles. Remember that nothing is impossible with God. You can have your life back—you just need to trust Him.

The Apostle Paul wrote:

"Be anxious for nothing, but in everything by prayer and supplication, with thanksgiving, let your requests be made known to God; and the peace of God, which surpasses all understanding, will guard your hearts and minds through Christ Jesus."

Philippians 4:6-7 (NKJV)

Paul wrote these words as he was in jail, facing various horrible challenges that could have pushed him to overthink his situation and be filled with fear and anxiety. However, knowing that God is with him, he believes, and he dares to say to the Philippians, "Be anxious for nothing."

These two verses invite us to:

- Seek help from the Lord
- Praise God for His goodness
- Put your situations in God's hands
- Meditate and reflect on the good things around you.

Doing these things will give you peace. All of this is possible in Christ, and this attitude will help you overcome your tendency to overthink.

I want to remind you today, as Paul did the Philippians: "Be anxious for nothing."

Key Takeaways

- Overthinking can be anxiety about the past, fear of the present, or worries for the future. It is a cognitive process that involves excessive or obsessive thoughts about something, such as an event, decision, or idea.

- Rumination is a pattern of cyclical thinking over something that happened in the past. It is characterized by repeating the same thought without reaching a conclusion, usually accompanied by negative feelings and anxiety.

- Fear is a reaction to a present, perceived threat, and it impacts us both physically and emotionally. We find it difficult to live in the present if we are constantly filled with fear.

- Worrying about the future or about current events creates a stress response in the brain.

- Worrying itself is the process of expecting a negative outcome that may never occur. Once you've accepted the idea of something bad happening, it will constantly be in your mind.

- It's best to stop ruminating over negative thoughts, no matter how hard it is to let them go, because ruminating has detrimental effects on your life.

- The best thing you can do to rescue yourself from the negative thoughts is to pray and trust in God. He will help you through every situation.

Time to Take Action

I want you to realize you can do something right now to help you cope with overthinking. It's time to stop thinking about what occurred in the past or worrying about what will happen in the future and start living in the present.

This is the perfect time to take action. Don't let negative thoughts destroy your life. If you're ready to change your life for the better, then you can choose right now to live the best possible life you can.

If you're serious about taking your life back from those negative thoughts, you have to change. A new way of reasoning is required. It's best to start by taking some notes about what keeps your mind busy.

In the next chapter, we'll dive into the undesirable consequences of overthinking to demonstrate to gain a clear understanding of its effects on our mental and physical health as well as our relationships.

CHAPTER TWO

UNDESIRABLE CONSEQUENCES OF OVERTHINKING

"A merry heart does good, like medicine, But a broken spirit dries the bones."

Proverbs 17:22 (NKJV)

In case you're not already convinced of the serious impact that overthinking can have on your life, let's look at an example of how it can affect you over the course of your life.

Lia's overthinking journey

It all started when Lia was about 10 years old. It started with the small things, like picking a subject to start on for her homework or deciding which color pencil to use. Every time Lia had to make a choice, she spent lots of time considering which one would be best and what the outcomes might be.

In school, she was scared to disappoint her teachers, as her parents always told her school was her responsibility, and she was expected to have good grades. She was afraid of not being good enough, and she often prayed to be good. Because of all this stress and overthinking, Lia spent her childhood days feeling tired and lacking energy despite sleeping an adequate number of hours every night.

The tiredness turned into anxiety once Lia grew up and became a young lady. During her last years of high school, she had to choose a university, and during university she had to choose a career path, and every choice presented to her only added to her anxiety and doubts. She wanted everything to be perfect and wanted everyone around her to be happy. But, because of this, Lia spent way too much time thinking about her choices and about every little thing that could go wrong, over and over and over again.

By the time Lia started working her first job, her stomach had started to rebel. She frequently got really bad stomachaches, and eventually found out she had ulcers after a pretty severe case of stress and anxiety due to a problem she had at work. All Lia wanted was to be perfect, to please everyone, but in doing so, she spent too much time inside her head, worrying, and in turn, she had made her body sick too.

It took Lia a very long time to realize all her symptoms could be traced back to her overthinking. But once she did, she turned back to what she knew best: religion. She went to the Lord and asked Him for guidance, asked Him to help her to trust the process more and worry less about the outcome.

Lia had forgotten she was meant to trust, to believe. So, slowly, she worked on herself and tried to overthink less. The results didn't show up immediately, but Lia gradually found tips and tricks to help her live a better life, one free from overthinking.

Do you, like Lia, feel sick all the time? Have you lost sleep? Is your stomach constantly in knots? Have you had trouble finishing projects? If you've ruled out any physical causes of your symptoms, it's likely that you are overthinking and experiencing excessive stress and anxiety.

It was once thought that overthinking was merely an indication that one was worrying too much about what they were doing. Unfortunately, it has been found to have a lot more severe consequences than people originally thought. Overthinking hurts. Below is a list of the consequences that come with overthinking.

How Does Overthinking Affect Life?

Overthinking can be such a burden. Whether you're contemplating your next career move or thinking about your current relationship, it can be hard not to create an endless stream of worry and doubt. If you are indeed an overthinker, you overanalyze everything around you. You may try to find a deeper meaning in each of your experiences. When meeting new people, you may focus on how other people are perceiving you instead of engaging in productive communication. If someone gives you an unusual look, you may make assumptions about what they're thinking about you based on that glance.

Essentially, overthinking consumes you. You end up wasting a lot of energy trying to make sense of the world around you. What you don't recognize is that not everything has a deeper meaning. Sometimes a look from a colleague is just a casual look with no thought behind it, and sometimes people say things flippantly without having any deeper meaning.

As an overthinker, you've probably experienced something called "analysis paralysis." This is a scenario where you think so much about the outcomes of a decision and spend so much time weighing the options that you end up doing absolutely nothing—you're paralyzed by fear and anxiety. You may then find yourself in a vicious circle of thinking a lot, but doing very little. Perhaps the best strategy to prevent yourself from falling into this type of thinking trap is to try out each of the alternatives. The simple decision to act—no matter what that action is—will make a huge difference.

To understand why overthinking is one of the leading factors in anxiety and depression, you first need to know what's happening in your brain when you're worrying. When something bad arises or someone says something negative, our brains respond by releasing stress hormones like cortisol into the bloodstream. Cortisol speeds up the heart rate, raises blood pressure and tells the brain to release many other stress hormones. Overthinking can thus have many undesirable consequences on your life.

Can cause depression, ulcers, and colitis

Depression is a psychological condition that may manifest itself in various ways. It is a common, chronic illness. Estimates suggest that 1% of the global population is suffering from depression (Shah, Mohammad, Qureshi, Abbas, & Aleem, 2021).

To try to alleviate some of the worldwide burden of depression, the World Health Organization released a statement that defines depression as "a common mental disorder portrayed by persistent sadness or low mood that affects [one's] ability to function." A single factor or a combination of factors may bring depression about. Since every individual is unique, what motivates and depresses them differs.

The term "depression" is frequently portrayed as tragic, disheartening, sad, fractious, unmotivated. In general, it means the absence of intrigue or delight in life, which is often impacted by overthinking. When these feelings only exist for a brief timeframe, it might be a passing instance of "the blues." But if they continue over many days and begin to interfere with your ordinary daily life, chances are you might be clinically depressed.

Depression is more than a persistent state of bitterness. It is a psychological issue that requires professional care. Significant depression can manifest itself in a variety of ways; it can not only impact your emotions, but impact you physiologically as well. People with clinical depression are in danger of experiencing serious negative outcomes, especially individuals between 15 and 24 years old, as indicated by the American Psychological Association (APA) (Kalin, 2021).

People who are diagnosed with depression may struggle to eat, sleep, or do many other daily tasks. Having a significant amount of stress as a result increases the risk of heart disease, ulcers, and colitis, a chronic digestive disorder characterized by inflammation of the colon's inner lining.

Affects the heart

Symptoms of high stress levels often include an increased heart rate or a fast heartbeat. One study that examined the association between stress and rapid heartbeats discovered that a person's heart rate is much higher when going through a stressful situation (Low & McCraty, 2018).

When you can't stop your mind from ruminating and you're constantly thinking about stressful scenarios, the stress accumulates in your heart. While you're sitting there trying to think of all the things that could go wrong, your heart beats harder out of fear. As a result, the blood flow to your heart increases, causing an increase in pressure. This can eventually lead to a condition called hypertensive heart disease, when the arteries in one or both of your heart chambers become narrowed or blocked. As blood continues to travel through those blocked arteries, it can cause a heart attack.

You must realize that what we're talking about here is significant stress over prolonged periods of time. Naturally, a bit of stress and a racing heart here and there isn't going to cause any permanent harm. It's when you let the overthinking get out of control for weeks, months, and years that your health becomes jeopardized.

Increases cancer risk

When you keep thinking about negative issues and reinforcing a feeling of fear, your body can release chemicals that disrupt the normal balance of hormones. The disruption of this balance increases your risk of developing cancer.

One of the most obvious victims of overthinking and stress is the brain—that's a no-brainer (forgive the pun). Stress has a significant impact on this organ. Cortisol (the stress hormone) can harm and even kill brain cells in the hippocampus. Chronic overthinking can change the structure and connectivity of the brain, altering its functions. Chronic stress also causes mental difficulties like anxiety and mood disorders (Andersson, Carlbring, Titov, & Lindefors, 2019).

Gets you stuck in analysis paralysis

We often cling to denial to prevent ourselves from having to endure the reality of stressful situations and uncomfortable or painful emotions. This manifests for many people in the form of addiction; they use distractions like drugs, alcohol, exercise, or work so that they don't have to face the truth. Unfortunately, this only exacerbates the problem because these shortcuts are not the solution. In a similar manner, some people become "addicted" to thinking, which leads to overthinking because they cannot or do not want to accept the truth.

Because of the aspiration for perfection, overthinkers continuously examine and re-examine any situation. They are afraid of making the wrong choice, and they're out of touch with their instincts. Therefore, they take a lot of time to make decisions, don't have confidence in their choices, and often end up not choosing anything at all—resulting in the previously discussed "analysis paralysis."

Social media and the internet only exacerbate the analysis paralysis an overthinker may experience by providing an unrealistic and idealized version of life. The result is a "perfect" standard that we feel obligated to meet to fit in, but of which we always fall short no matter what, resulting once again in endless anxiety, worry, and self-doubt. (If you want to see examples of this unrealistic standard, look no further than your Instagram feed.)

If you do not take control of the thoughts that are causing you to worry excessively, you'll end up with more stress, which (as discussed previously) is a leading cause of mental health problems. Providentially, this book will give you insights on how to stop worrying and therefore decrease the chance of any health problems arising so that you can live a healthier, happier life. If you make a "bad" decision, remind yourself that it's okay; it happens to everyone. The important thing is that you gained a lesson from your mistake.

Leads to anxiety

Anxiety is a physiological stress response that may be beneficial or harmful based on the level of the reaction. Everyone encounters anxiety from time to time; in fact, it is an imperative piece of our physiological makeup. It can encourage us to recognize and deal with difficult situations. Basically, anxiety allows us to distinguish and react to peril by entering "fight or flight" mode. The "ideal" amount of anxiety can actually assist us in performing better and overcoming challenges.

However, there is another side of anxiety. Certain people have intense and overwhelming anxiety responses that essentially hijack their brains and block them from rationally or reasonably processing their experiences.

Persistent anxiety causes genuine problems and can even lead to physical illness or anxiety disorders such as panic attacks, phobias, and obsessive-compulsive behaviors. Anxiety at this level can have a troubling and weakening effect on our lives and our physical and mental wellbeing, prompting a wide range of physical manifestations like headaches, digestive issues, and heart palpitations. The consequences of unchecked anxiety can be even more serious in the long haul, possibly causing permanent damage to our bodies.

Alarmingly, around 1 in 5 individuals report feeling anxious "almost constantly" or "much of the time." As a whole, it seems that we as a society perceive ourselves as being more anxious than in the past (Swift et al., 2014). A study by the Mental Health Foundation shows that money and responsibilities are two of the most common sources of anxiety. Anxiety is one of the most universally recognized mental medical issues globally, and it is essentially an epidemic in modern society; however, it is still under-studied, under-reported, and under-treated.

A decent capacity to adapt to anxiety is vital to withstanding whatever life tosses at us. Allowing extreme anxiety to build within us again and again increases our chances of being overcome by fear, unable to discover balance in our lives, or to relax and recoup.*

*Click HERE to receive these 7 worksheets on self-care and self-compassion.

Can kill relationships

You should grab the opportunity, whenever it's presented to you, to develop emotionally and personally with your spouse or partner. Only through this type of intimate partnership can you understand how to become more empathetic and present. Unfortunately, overthinking is one of the primary causes of conflict between partners, friends, and family members. While some people can talk out their issues, others avoid confronting their problems head-on, instead ruminating about them and growing cold or distant in the relationship.

This is a mistake. It's time for you to take responsibility for your actions and confront the source of your frustration. Most people overthink because they feel overwhelmed by the number of things in their lives that are out of their control.

Remember, there will never be a perfect relationship; your partner has flaws just as you do. Therefore, instead of turning to someone else to improve your relationships, a great place to begin is within yourself. Minimizing your own tension and anxiety will significantly boost your own quality of life and, by extension, the quality of your relationships.

Deciding to take back control of your thoughts is the start of a mindful partnership that will restore bonding instead of fostering conflict and disunity.

Signs of overthinking in a relationship

It's easy to drift through the day thinking about your significant other when you're in a relationship, especially if it's new and exciting. Thoughts about your coupledom are valid even as the relationship evolves and becomes more stable.

When those thoughts become increasingly negative or intrusive, however, and consume more and more of your time when you should be concentrating on other things, it's time to reign them in a little. When you obsess over minor details, over things expressed and things unsaid, what your partner did or did not do, your mind might fool you into thinking things that aren't true. These are symptoms of excessive thinking about a relationship:

- You continually imagine the worst-case scenario (for example, worrying about harm befalling your partner)

- You conjure up implausible scenarios in your head (such as unfaithfulness even though your partner has given you no reason to doubt him or her)

- You become illogical (for example, asking your partner to do things to "prove" his or her loyalty)

- You are unreasonably suspicious

- You have a rich imagination, but you use it to imagine negative situations

"What if" makes life miserable

It is astonishing to see the number of people who feel lonely these days. Even those with active social lives, who spend a lot of time with people, often develop a sense of loneliness. During the pandemic, these feelings of isolation have only increased throughout society. If a person does not have a supportive family, good friends, or even good neighbors, they can easily begin to feel lonely. Persistent feelings of isolation can lead to depression, and sometimes it also leads to excessive "What if?" thinking.

For example, you may begin to worry about things happening that have never happened before or imagine yourself in situations that have never occurred. You might catch yourself asking, "What if I say something wrong?", "What if it rains and I have to cancel my plans?", "What if so-and-so thinks such-and-such about me?", and so on. You're overthinking a situation before it even happens. And sadly, most of the time, your inner dialogue is negative. It's time to change that.

Avoiding taking action when you should

You may think the reason you're overthinking is because you want to make the best possible choice, but many times, you're actually avoiding taking action. When you're confronted with an issue that requires action, your first instinct is to overthink about what to do instead of simply doing something.

Think about the last few conversations you had that involved an issue you wanted to take action on or a problem you needed to solve. You probably thought about every aspect of the problem and came up with a list of reasons you couldn't solve it. This is essentially a form of procrastination. You're afraid of facing whatever the outcome might be, so you just avoid doing anything altogether.

Not accepting reality

Sometimes, people allow their emotions and bad memories to come into play when overthinking. When you have thoughts like "I'm terrible at handling challenges" or "I'm inadequate," this shows that your negative emotions are getting in the way. Accept the reality that you're not perfect and that sometimes people make mistakes, including you. Otherwise, your mind will create fear-based scenarios that will ultimately cause your emotions to control you instead of the other way around.

The Solution: Avoid Negativity

Doing anything negative, including overthinking, puts a barrier between you and the reality of the world around you. It also puts a barrier between you and God. When something negative happens, remind yourself that it's okay, and that life is not perfect. Overthinking only prolongs the bad feelings that are part of this reality. It's time to act instead of overthinking.

Think about the last time you overthought a problem. What was it? What did you tell yourself? How did it make you feel? Overthinking doesn't make any situation better, so don't think about any one issue for too long. Instead, set yourself a time limit to think over and confront the problem logically; then, take action on what you've learned or decided and don't look back.

Your thoughts need a curfew. Fill your mind with God's Living Word and you will have no space for the enemy's lies. God has many wonderful promises for you:

"Even to your old age, I am He,
And even to gray hairs I will carry you!
I have made, and I will bear;
Even I will carry, and will deliver you."

Isaiah 46:4 (NKJV)

"No weapon formed against you shall prosper,
And every tongue which rises against you in judgment
You shall condemn.
This is the heritage of the servants of the Lord,
And their righteousness is from Me,
Says the Lord."

Isaiah 54:17 (NKJV)

"Though the mountains be shaken
and the hills be removed,
yet my unfailing love for you will not be shaken
nor my covenant of peace be removed,
says the Lord, who has compassion on you."

Isaiah 54:10 (NIV)

Key Takeaways

- Overthinking is often used as an easy way to avoid taking action.

- Overthinking can be caused by negative thoughts and emotions that distract you from reality.

- Not confronting issues is a form of overthinking, which prevents you from moving on with your life.

- Taking action on the problem at hand will allow you to move on with your life instead of thinking about it for too long.

- God has worked miracles for you in the past. He wants to do this for you again in the future, if you let Him.

Time to Take Action

Only when you take action can your mind turn positive thoughts into reality. The more you take action to solve your problems, the better life gets.

And, of course, the better you get at doing this, the more likely you are to be successful at it again. This is how habits are created. You can utilize the power of habits negatively (by letting yourself overthink and become stuck in anxiety and fear) or positively (by consistently taking action to improve your life).

It's clear that overthinking affects our lives very much. Is there a solution to this disease? In the next chapter, we will examine how to eliminate negative thinking and have that happy life you desire.

CHAPTER THREE

HOW TO ELIMINATE NEGATIVE THINKING AND LIVE HAPPILY

"For God has not given us a spirit of timidity, but of power and love and discipline."

2 Timothy 1:7 (NKJV)

Lisa had reached the end of her rope. She was fed up with people telling her to stop being so negative as if she were being negative by choice.

Tom knew that his negativity was weighing him down, but hearing too many clichés like "life is what you make it" caused him to become even more anxious and cut himself off from the world completely.

The pandemic filled Jason with so much fear and negativity that he became agoraphobic and couldn't bring himself to leave the house.

Sammi had reached a point where she wasn't sure that life was worth fighting for, as every moment of her life seemed so bleak.

There are hundreds of thousands, if not millions, of people in the world today who are personally struggling with negativity. You're not alone. The problem with negativity is that it isn't simply a bad mood that you can shake off when you feel like it. Once rumination starts, the mind begins to dwell on only the negative aspects of a situation, and fear and anxiety take over.

We look for inspiration in the world, anything to shine a bit of light on our gloomy thoughts, but that doesn't happen. Over time, you start to notice more negative thinking going on than positive, like a sponge soaking up all the bad. Sadly, negative thinking can easily become a permanent state of mind that can wreak havoc on all areas of your life.

If you feel like you're walking on the very edge of a cliff and one more issue is likely to cause you to fall into a pit of depression and paralyzing fear, you aren't alone.

According to the National Science Foundation, 80% of our thoughts are negative (Kaida & Kaida, 2019). That is exhausting, to say the least. We are literally swimming in our negative thoughts, and many of us are drowning.

Negativity isn't like a broken leg or a skin rash. You can't see it, but you carry it around with you all the time. Not everyone can afford therapy or is comfortable with the idea of talking to a stranger about their innermost thoughts. Others are worried that they will be slapped with a mental illness label and just given antidepressants. So, how can you combat the negativity in order to bring happiness and joy back into your life?

Negative Thoughts

Negative thoughts are toxic to a healthy life and lead to deep unhappiness.

Thus, the first thing we have to gain control over is berating ourselves for our negative thought patterns. All those people who have told you that you're just a negative person and you aren't putting enough effort into being positive are wrong. Science tells us that our brain is trained to pay more attention to our negative thoughts. To an extent, there is a good reason for this.

When we are stressed or feeling scared, our brain releases cortisol and adrenaline hormones. These two hormones play a crucial role in the fight or flight response, which is a built-in biological response that protects us from danger. If your child starts crossing the street, for example, your first response is to grab their hand and probably shout at them because you fear an accident—even if no car is coming. Your brain and stress hormones are helping your body jump into action in order to protect you (or your loved ones). On the other hand, too much cortisol can have numerous consequences on our health. Some of these include:

- Weight gain

- Acne

- Thinning, easily-bruised skin

- Muscle weakness

- Severe fatigue

- High blood pressure

- Headaches

Increased blood pressure, headaches, weight gain, and severe anxiety are symptoms of too much adrenaline. This also puts you at greater risk of heart attacks and strokes. So, the release of cortisol and adrenaline is natural and is generally a good thing, but as soon as negative thinking becomes a severe issue, we are putting our health at risk.

There is another problem with an overactive fight or flight response. An increase in cortisol increases white matter in the brain. White matter is good for communication between the brain's gray matter, but it's the gray matter that carries out processes. Gray matter is necessary to cope with stress effectively. When white matter dominates and increases stress and fear, it becomes harder to decipher complex problems.

Those who don't suffer from negative thinking might be able to take a step back and view situations from alternative perspectives. In our heightened state of stress, this is much more difficult. Essentially, it is not your fault that your mind automatically jumps to negative conclusions.

We also have to consider that although our brain is an organ, it acts as a muscle: it needs training. Our brain has been trained in the wrong way through no fault of our own. Thanks to technology that scans the brain, we know that people who suffer from depression have an overdeveloped right prefrontal cortex, where negative thoughts are processed, and an underdeveloped left prefrontal cortex. Imagine lifting weights with only your right arm—your left will never be able to keep up. That's what happens to the brain when we continuously think negatively.

But as the brain is not a muscle, how does this actually work? The brain has approximately 100 billion neurons, and each neuron has an average of 7,000 synapses (connections to other neurons). All our negative thoughts and experiences get stored as memories. Every time we recall a memory, the synapses are strengthened. The more often these memories are accessed, the quicker and easier it is for negative thoughts to reappear.

Rewire Your Thought Process

Without wanting to bombard your mind with statistics, I feel it is crucial to help you understand how much stress affects us. Because we all seem to be under stress, it has almost become the norm rather than something that only occurs once in a while. In reality, our bodies aren't designed to cope with constant stress, and we are starting to see how damaging this is.

Some of the statistics below are shocking, but perhaps exactly what we need to help us realize that we have to start moving toward a less-stressed lifestyle.

- Americans between ages 30 and 49 are the most stressed.

- 52% of Generation Z has been diagnosed with mental health issues.

- 83% of U.S. workers suffer from work-related stress.

- 1 million individuals miss work every day because of stress.

- Depression costs companies $51 billion in absenteeism.

- Healthcare costs from stress cost $190 billion annually.

- Work-related stress causes 120,000 deaths in the U.S. each year.

(The American Institute of Stress, 2019)

We do not want to be a part of any of the above statistics! So, we must take control of stress and see it for what it is: fuel for unhappiness, negativity, and health problems and not something that we can afford to accept.

What the neuroscientists tell us

So, you're stressed out and feel like you're on the verge of exploding? Something has to give, and you don't want to cause a scene or breakdown. The good news is that there are four instant stress busters that you may or may not have heard of. The problem is because they are so simple, you might not feel they are powerful enough to work. For this reason, I have included neuroscience research to help convince you (Reeve & Lee, 2019).

1. Tense and relax your facial muscles

There is a communication loop between your brain and your body. When the gray matter in your brain creates stress, various muscles tense up. Once your muscles are tense, a message is sent back to the brain to let it know that the message has been received.

If you've tried asking your brain to stop stressing and it hasn't worked, you need to break the loop by making your body tell your brain that you are not stressed anymore. Consciously releasing the tension in your facial muscles sends that message. As you might imagine, the facial muscles are the best to use because they are more closely linked to our emotions. That being said, your hands, stomach, and, more surprisingly, your bum muscles will also send the right messages to the brain.

2. Do deep breathing

This may surprise you because we generally focus on the benefits of slow breathing, which can also be used to help reduce stress and feel calmer. But what about when we need to feel more excited, and get that adrenaline rush to work in our favor? Deep breathing (which is even used by Navy Seal recruits) activates the parasympathetic nervous system, necessary to conserve energy, and helps turn that stress into positive feelings.

3. Jolt your vagus nerve

The vagus nerve is the longest nerve in the body. It extends from the brain to the large intestine and is responsible for many critical body functions. In particular, it lowers heart rate and manages stress and anxiety. If this nerve is damaged, you may suffer from reduced attention and even depression.

Your vagus nerve is attached to your vocal cords. Therefore, singing or chanting can jolt your vagus nerve and offer some relief from stress. Alternatively, you can splash your face with cold water—a classic example of a traditional technique that you may have previously dismissed.

4. Listen to classical music

If you put on your all-time favorite tunes, you'll be tempted to sing, waking up the vagus nerve. But music can also help stress levels in other ways. Music engages a large part of the limbic system in the brain, which is responsible for our emotional responses. Music also increases heart rate (and, science aside, you know certain songs just make you feel better no matter what mood you're in!). Making music of your own, whether singing or playing an instrument, has an even more substantial effect on the limbic system.

Spiritual music can also ease your stress. In Samuel 16:14-23, we see music's therapeutic effect. When David plays the harp for King Saul, the king instantly feels better.

Next time you start to feel stress building up, remember these four highly effective brain tricks. Naturally, if you're in the middle of a meeting, you probably don't want to start making strange faces to release tension or burst out into song, but squeezing your bum muscles is a subtle alternative. You can also excuse yourself to the bathroom and splash your face with cold water to quickly alter your mindset. None of these solutions takes more than a couple of minutes.

Process of Negative Thoughts

Many people suffer from negative thoughts that sometimes turn into cognitive distortions. These are patterns of thinking that distort your view of reality and can have a detrimental effect on your psychological wellbeing.

No matter how great your life is, there will always be things you aren't happy with. This is normal. But if you let these thoughts get the better of you and they start causing real problems in your life, they need to be addressed. That's why it can be helpful to learn about them, so you're aware of when these patterns of thinking start popping up in your daily life. Here are some common negative thoughts and their distorted counterparts:

i. Jumping to conclusions

This is when you think a particular event means something it actually doesn't mean. You might create a very detailed scenario in your head of how something happened, often without checking for facts that could prove or disprove your assumptions. When you rush to conclusions and negatively interpret an event or circumstance based on a lack of evidence, you end up reacting to your false belief instead of the reality.

This distortion arises from the erroneous notion that we can read other people's mind and know their intentions. Of course, we can get a sense of what other people are thinking, but the distortion here pertains to the negative interpretations we make. When you jump to conclusions or attempt to "mind-read," it's usually in response to a persistent idea or concern. For instance, you may be anxious about your relationship or believe your partner is losing interest in you, and thus you always jump to the conclusion that he or she is being unfaithful.

ii. Catastrophizing

This is when you think something terrible is bound to happen when, realistically, the chances of such an event are really low. You might imagine a particular situation will end up very badly, (e.g., in death, divorce, or imprisonment).

When confronted with the unknown, this flawed thinking causes people to fear the worst. Common fears can suddenly increase when people catastrophize.

For example, let's say an expected check does not appear in the mail. Catastrophizing would lead you to conclude that it will never arrive and that, as a result, your family will be evicted from your home because you'll be unable to pay the rent. A more logical approach would be to assume that the check will show up in the next few days.

It's tempting for those who have not experienced it to dismiss catastrophizing as a hysterical overreaction; however, people who have developed this cognitive distortion may have been exposed to so many negative occurrences—such as chronic pain or childhood trauma—that they automatically fear the worst in various circumstances.

iii. Overgeneralization

Overgeneralization is a cognitive distortion involving believing that one event, or a single negative experience, reflects an entire category of people or events. Any negative experience can trigger this type of thinking, and it's very dangerous because it can make you feel so bad about the world around you that you become depressed or angry.

When people overgeneralize, they judge one occurrence and then apply that conclusion inappropriately to all situations. If you get a terrible score on one math test, for example, you might assume that you're just bad at math in general. Or if you have one traumatic relationship experience involving your partner cheating on you, you may come to believe that this is what will happen with all of your future relationships.

Post-traumatic stress disorder and other anxiety disorders have been linked to overgeneralization.

iv. Labeling

Labeling is a widespread cognitive distortion that all of us engage in to some extent. It is the process of defining oneself and others based on a particular trait, behavior, or event. Labeling someone in your mind can be both positive and negative. The harm of labeling occurs when people limit themselves or others to a single (generally negative) attribute or descriptor, such as "drunk" or "failure."

People can become self-critical as a result of being labeled. It can also lead to misinterpretation or underestimation of others by the thinker. This misunderstanding can lead to serious interpersonal issues. No one wants to be assigned a label.

v. "Should" statements

In general, "should" statements are used to manipulate others into doing what you want. They take the form of sentences like "You should have done this," or "you must" statements like "You must be a loser if you don't..."

A cognitive distortion is likely at work when people think only in terms of what "should" or "ought" to be said or done. It's rarely beneficial to berate yourself for not performing well at something you "should" be able to achieve. "Should" and "need" phrases are commonly used to adopt a negative picture of your life or the lives of others.

Internalized cultural or family expectations are often at the basis of these types of thoughts, which may or may not be suitable for your actual situation. Such beliefs can lower your self-esteem and increase your worry.

vi. Emotional reasoning

"I feel depressed, so it must be true that I'm a failure."

What's distorted about this thought is the assumption that what you feel is an accurate reflection of reality. Many people are unhappy when they're feeling unfulfilled in their lives. That dissatisfaction often reflects the gap between who you are and who you want to be, and thus is not a reflection of your real situation. Emotional reasoning is a thought pattern commonly fallen into by people with anxiety or depression (Howard, 2019).

Emotional reasoning is the delusion that your feelings are true—that how you feel about a situation is a trustworthy sign of reality. While listening to, affirming, and expressing your emotions is necessary, it's also critical to appraise reality based on facts.

vii. Personalization and blame

"It's my fault that I failed."

"It's my fault that they're upset."

"It's my fault that I've been single for so long."

The above statements are all examples of personalization. Personalization occurs when you assume full responsibility for an event even though other factors contributed to the outcome. If you suffer from personalization, you'll more than likely believe things such as "I'm a bad person" or "I'll never be successful." Alternatively, you may mistakenly believe you've been targeted or excluded by others on purpose.

Taking everything personally when it isn't associated with or influenced by you is one of the most common cognitive errors. If you frequently blame yourself for things that aren't your fault or are out of your control, you may be engaging in the personalization cognitive distortion. Personalization has been linked to increased anxiety and feelings of despair.

Replace Negative Thoughts with New Attitudes

The best way to alter a negative thought is to replace it with a positive one. The following techniques, based on a cognitive behavioral therapy (CBT) approach, can help you completely transform your outlook on life:

i. Ask yourself if the thought is realistic.

You must be able to recognize the error you're making in order to change an unproductive mental pattern. Detecting the untrue ideas that cause your negative feelings and mindsets is crucial to resetting your cognitive processes.

It's also helpful to track when and where your thoughts appear. Certain settings may make you more susceptible to cognitive distortions. Knowing what those scenarios are will help you plan to avoid them ahead of time, or identify and correct the negative thought before it overwhelms you.

Some folks find that journaling as part of the process is beneficial. Writing down your thoughts can help you spot a cognitive distortion even if you're not sure what's causing your anxiety at first.

You'll likely notice skewed thought tendencies more quickly when you practice self-monitoring.

ii. Think of similar situations in the past and evaluate if your thoughts align with what took place.

Learning to examine your views and assumptions, particularly those which get in the way of leading a productive life, is an essential aspect of cognitive restructuring. This can help you discover how your unconscious thoughts are prejudiced or unreasonable.

Ask yourself the following questions:

- Is this a feeling or a fact-based thought?

- What proof do I have that this belief is correct?

- What evidence do I have that it's *incorrect?*

- How could I put this theory to the test?

- What are the worst-case scenarios? What would I do if anything terrible happened?

- How else can the data I'm receiving be interpreted?

- Is this a black-and-white situation, or are there shades of gray?

If you're suffering from the cognitive distortion known as catastrophizing (discussed above), you might be imagining the worst possible conclusion in a stressful circumstance. You could challenge this cognitive pattern by making a list of all conceivable outcomes and considering the likelihood of each scenario.

Questioning helps you evaluate alternate outcomes that aren't as disastrous as the ones you're afraid of.

iii. Actively challenge the thought and look for alternative explanations.

Gathering evidence is an important part of cognitive reorganization. You might want to keep track of the circumstances that cause a reaction in you, such as who you were with and what you were doing. Make note of how powerful each response was and what memories or fears were triggered as a result.

You should also try to acquire evidence to support or refute your ideas. Cognitive distortions are not only erroneous and biased, they're often profoundly ingrained in our mind. Challenging them and substituting them with other explanations will show you how irrational they are. You may also need to make a list of the facts (if any) that support your distorted belief and compare it against the facts that support an alternate belief.

If you suffer from the cognitive distortion of personalization, for example, you may tend to blame yourself for matters which aren't your fault. If you challenge this belief and consider the alternative—that you are not the cause of other people's behaviors—you may benefit greatly.

iv. Think of what you gain versus what you lose by continuing to believe the thought.

This method involves weighing the benefits and drawbacks of maintaining a cognitive distortion. Consider the following questions:

- What good does it do to believe I am unintelligent or incapable?
- What does this thought pattern cost me in terms of emotional distress and wasted time?
- What will be the long-term consequences of holding this belief?
- What impact does this mental pattern have on those around me?
- In what ways does it help or hinder my job performance?

Seeing the benefits and drawbacks side by side can help you decide whether changing the pattern is worthwhile (and it probably is!).

v. Recognize whether your thoughts are the result of a cognitive distortion.

The reason we benefit from cognitive restructuring is it allows us to see things in new ways. Part of the technique entails recognizing the cognitive distortion you're falling prey to and then coming up with rational, constructive alternative explanations to replace the distortions that have become entrenched over time.

Let's say you didn't do well on a math test and you start thinking that you're just terrible at math (overgeneralizing) and you're going to fail out of school (catastrophizing). You then catch yourself, identify these two patterns of cognitive distortion, and decide to look into ways to improve your study habits instead of continuing the negative thought process.

Another example: A group of coworkers stops chatting when you enter the room. Immediately, you think to yourself, "They must have been talking about me. I must've done something wrong." Once you realize that you've fallen into the trap of several distortions (including jumping to conclusions and personalization), you start thinking about other possible reasons that your coworkers stopped talking. You may discover that it had nothing to do with you or that you misread what was going on.

Develop Endurance

Endurance can be defined as the body's ability to function for extended periods of time without becoming exhausted. For example, if you're able to run a long distance, such as running a marathon, you have good physical endurance.

We need more than just physical endurance in this life, however. It presents many challenges, and you need mental, emotional, and spiritual endurance to get through them. Think of your life as a sailboat on the ocean. You will face storms. Certain circumstances or news will shake you to your very core. You have to set your mind to stay strong, no matter the situation. You have to develop endurance to succeed.

You don't have much control over what happens to you, but you *can* control how to react to each situation. Your state of mind will determine your reaction. In the first century AD, the Stoic philosopher Seneca wrote: "Fire tests gold, suffering tests brave men." Problems, and yes, suffering, will come to test you. No huge tree can become profoundly rooted in the ground if strong winds do not blast against it. Your adversities and your suffering will strengthen your tree by allowing it to plant its roots deeper into the ground, and will ultimately make you stronger—if you put your faith more deeply in Jesus.

In the situation you are in right now, ask God to help develop your endurance. Do not let anger take over your emotions. Remember what scripture tells us about going through challenging times: "And not only that, but we also glory in tribulations, knowing that tribulation produces perseverance; and perseverance, character; and character, hope." (Romans 5:3-4, NKJV)

No matter what you are going through, focus on your goals and focus on God, and He will help you to weather the storm.

Become Unbreakable

In the Bible, God said, "Send men to spy out the land of Canaan, which I am giving to the children of Israel; from each tribe of their fathers, you shall send a man, every one a leader among them." (Numbers 13:2, NKJV) After receiving this command from the Lord, twelve spies went to the borders of Canaan territory to explore and examine the region.

Ten of the twelve (all except Joshua and Caleb) had negative thinking. They said things like:

- The people of Canaan are more powerful than Israel. (Verse 28)

- We are not able to go up against the people, for they are stronger than we. (Verse 31)

- The land through which we have gone as spies is a land that devours its inhabitants. (Verse 32)

- All the people whom we saw in it are men of great stature. (Verse 32)

- There we saw the giants (the descendants of Anak came from the giants), and we were like grasshoppers in our own sight, and so we were in their sight. (Verse 33)

These ten spies gave multiple reasons why they could not go and take Canaan. Because of the ten spies' negative thinking, they and the people of Israel (except Joshua and Caleb) did not enter Canaan. Even though God said He had given this land to Israel (Numbers 13:2), the spies' negative thinking messed up God's plan. They forgot all that God had done for them in the past. They certainly had to face many obstacles, but the only thing they had to do in order to succeed was move forward with faith, relying on God's promises.

This story shows us that people who dwell in negative thinking forget or deny God's promises. Your negative thinking can destroy God's plan for your life, and your influence can be disastrous for others. You are better than that. Let's face our battles with faith.

Like the ten spies, the stressful situations in your life may feel like huge giants before you. The challenges may seem like way more than you can handle. But with the help of God Almighty, no battle is too difficult for you. Face your challenges with faith; He brought you this far, and He will not fail you here.

Perspective is everything.

When faced with the same situation as the ten spies who did not trust in God, Caleb said, "Let us go up at once and take possession, for we are well able to overcome it" (Numbers 13:30). It's about time to be like Joshua and Caleb. You can face any challenge with God's help.

Ask the Lord to remove your negative thinking from your mind. Despite your giants, your future is bright in Jesus. God says to you:

"For I know the thoughts that I think toward you says the Lord,

thoughts of peace and not of evil, to give you a future and a hope."

Jeremiah 29:11 (NKJV)

With Jesus, you are unbreakable. Paul writes:

"Yet in all these things we are more than conquerors

through Him who loved us."

Romans 8:37 (NKJV)

Key Takeaways

- The first step toward change is becoming aware of the situation, recognizing your cognitive distortions, and developing endurance through difficulties.

- Making positive changes to your life can be challenging, but it is also very rewarding. Keep going forward, and do not get discouraged by the small setbacks you may experience along the way. If you stay dedicated and determined, there is no reason you cannot achieve the results you want and deserve in life.

- Remind yourself that with God, you are unbreakable. You should be proud of how far you've progressed in your journey with this book.

Time to Take Action

Negative thinking is a cycle that can be broken with hard work, commitment, and lots of practice. You don't need to suffer with the negative thoughts, stress, and anxiety forever; you can change and reframe these patterns. In this chapter, you have learned to identify and understand your negative thinking patterns, transform them into more positive ways of thinking, and utilize some coping techniques to manage the worries and anxieties that can result from your thoughts and feelings.

What's more, you have hopefully learned how to see the joy in your life once again and how to find the little things that make you happy. However, the work is not over. It is essential to keep going with these techniques, as change takes time and does not happen overnight.

Permanent changes require gradual and consistent steps to ensure they are cemented in your new mindset. Do not be tempted to rush, as you're only at the beginning of a long but extremely rewarding journey.

With time and patience, you can achieve all the goals you've set out to achieve and ensure that you reap the rewards of your hard work. As you continue along your path, you'll notice many significant areas of your life begin to improve.

Put your faith in God. With His help, you will be victorious.

Mental clarity is all it takes—but how do you develop mental clarity? The next chapter will help you dissect this concept and open up your mind to have a better understanding of your next steps.

CHAPTER FOUR

HOW TO DEVELOP MENTAL CLARITY IN A NOISY WORLD

"For I know the plans I have for you, declares the LORD, plans for welfare and not for evil, to give you a future and a hope."

Jeremiah 29:11(NIV)

Nat's brain fog dilemma

Let's look at another story to see an example of how to develop mental clarity.

It was what felt like just another day at the office as Nat sat at her desk, staring at her computer screen but unable to concentrate on what she was looking at.

"Nat, is everything okay?" Luke, one of her colleagues, asked.

They had been working together in the data analysis office for a few years, so Luke knew it wasn't usual for Nat to be stuck on a project. She was one of the best because she was always so focused and usually got the best and most important projects and clients.

"I just can't seem to concentrate on this project," Nat replied with a worried look. "I'm not sure what I'm trying to do. It almost feels like my mind is clouded, and I'm just so tired..." She yawned before she continued, "I'd better go make a coffee. Do you want one?"

Luke shook his head and stopped Nat with an extended hand.

"Nat, I don't think coffee is the answer. I know how stressed and anxious you've been lately with the new workload, and I think what you need is to clear your mind."

"To clear my mind?" Nat looked skeptical.

"Yes. I've been where you are. I'm a massive overthinker, and it caused so many problems for me that I now work on developing mental clarity every day. Do you want some advice?"

"Sure, anything to get rid of this brain fog," Nat said as she sat down again.

"One of the best things you can do is to make sure you're sleeping enough and getting the rest you need. Track your sleep if you need to, but make sure you're sleeping about eight hours every night. You've got to work on your nutrition too, and make sure your body is well-nourished. Eat balanced meals, and drink plenty of water throughout the day. And finally, work on the things that generate anxiety for you to make sure they don't overwhelm you. If you do all that, your mind will start to clear up again."

Nat thanked Luke for the advice, and that night, she started planning her sleep schedule as well as a new nutrition plan. She knew her mind wasn't the way she'd like it to be, and she understood now that she needed to put in the work to make sure things got better. Luke was right; her mind hadn't been clear, and she had to turn the situation around.

If you're interested in cognitive development, self-improvement, or just want to sharpen your mind a little, this section is for you.

We'll dig into what mental clarity is and provide a variety of ways to increase it. We'll also look at the different types of brain fog and detail their causes and effects.

Mental Clarity

Mental clarity is a feeling of deep focus, knowledge, or wisdom. It doesn't refer to the absence of mental illness, but rather the ability to be mentally stable and to focus on what you're doing. Someone who has clarity can typically think more clearly and make good decisions. They are also better at understanding themselves and others. Clarity is a trait that is often desired by people who are depressed or stressed, as they tend to suffer from brain fog.

Some people describe clarity as an elevated state of being. It's often associated with other terms such as focus, empowerment, mindfulness, and even inspiration. Clarity can be achieved in many ways, and it's often dependent on a person's specific needs. Some methods are more effective than others for achieving it, but regardless, achieving clarity requires a certain mindset. So, you're probably wondering what exactly goes into achieving this mental state.

In order to achieve mental clarity, you must have an open mind, a positive attitude, and confidence. You should be curious about the world around you and learn how things work.

Are You Lacking Mental Clarity?

Your brain is an amazing organ. It's responsible for thinking and making decisions and controlling emotions like fear and happiness. It's also a storage facility for our memories, thoughts, and dreams. However, sometimes stress and other factors can bog down the brain and dampen a person's mental clarity.

If you've ever felt lost and confused or felt like life is passing you by, it may be time to check your mental clarity. Does your mind frequently wander, and do you leave tasks half-done, or not done at all? Do you experience brain fog, a feeling of "fuzziness" inside your head that prevents you from thinking clearly?

Here are some of the signs that you're experiencing a lack of mental clarity:

i. Inability to focus or concentrate

Mental clarity is the ability to stay on task and in the moment. It requires that you hold your attention on something for extended periods of time. An inability to focus over an extended period of time can indicate that you might lack mental clarity.

Concentration occurs naturally and without effort when we are mentally healthy. Pay attention to how much work it takes you to concentrate. This can offer an indication of how powerful your current mental state is.

ii. Physical or mental exhaustion

If you're experiencing physical or mental fatigue, it could signify that you lack mental clarity. Exhaustion is often caused by poor diet, lack of sleep, and stress. When the energetic resources of our minds are drained, the rest of the body generally follows suit.

Physical and mental exhaustion are possible side effects of low mental clarity, and they may indicate that it's time to make a behavioral change. A lack of mental clarity may well be the cause of you feeling tired and lethargic after even the simplest tasks.

iii. Loss of interest and lack of motivation

Lack of motivation can also be a sign of a lack of mental clarity. If you lack initiative, you're likely to have low energy, feel unmotivated, and have low self-esteem.

Another sign of low mental clarity is a loss of interest in things or tasks that used to offer you joy. When our minds are clear and powerful, we have a natural desire to study. Your lack of motivation could indicate that your mind is in need of rejuvenation.

iv. Memory problems

Memory problems can also be a symptom of low mental clarity. You might find yourself misplacing things, having trouble remembering names and numbers, or unable to recall events. Poor memory recall is a clear symptom of low mental performance, just as a great ability to recollect memories is a sign of excellent mental performance.

Memory retention should never be an issue when our thoughts are healthy and clear. Checking the sharpness of your memory recall is a wonderful approach to keeping track of your mental health.

Causes of Decreased Mental Clarity

Before we can understand how to improve mental clarity, we must first examine the possible causes or triggers that affect it. These factors exhaust our mental resources, making mental performance considerably more difficult. If any of these seem familiar, you've probably figured out what's to blame.

i. Lack of sleep

Have you ever woken up feeling unprepared for the day? A lack of sleep can also cause lack of mental clarity, as you're less alert and your brain isn't functioning smoothly. You might find your ability to think and your focus diminished after a sleepless night. This can in turn lead to excessive caffeine or sugar consumption in an attempt to keep the brain alert, which only creates more mental fog.

An excellent circadian rhythm is an essential component of human health. The mind and body struggle to work at their best when you don't get seven or more hours of sleep each night.

Some of us have trouble sleeping because of stress, while others have poor sleep hygiene. People who work irregular hours are at higher risk of developing sleep disorders. You may be jeopardizing your mental health if you do not give your body the rest it needs.

ii. Stress and anxiety

Stress is probably the most common cause of mental fog. Stress can cause your mind to shut down to protect itself from the demands you place on it. It also makes it difficult to process information and make decisions. We are all aware that stress is harmful to our health (although sometimes a little stress can be a good motivator), but it can also be a powerful mental foe.

High cortisol levels are a result of chronic stress, which signifies decreased circulation—and poor circulation causes your heart to send less oxygen to your brain. This might lead to a loss of mental clarity, which can exacerbate your stress and worry. If left untreated, it can become a vicious cycle.

iii. Poor nutrition

Another major cause of mental fog is poor nutrition. The nutrients in the foods you eat affect your brain, behavior, and even how you feel. Your brain needs essential fatty acids, vitamin B, vitamin C, and vitamin E that are found in nuts and vegetables.

There are a variety of foods that can help you focus and think clearly, but many of us have poor nutrition due to a lack of variety in our diet or a high intake of processed foods. Too little or the wrong kinds of nutrients can cause brain fog and low mental clarity. A poor diet can also cause a lack of nutrition. It's hard to think clearly when blood sugar levels aren't regulated and nutrients aren't absorbed properly by the body.

Vitamin B-12, in particular, offers numerous brain and immune system benefits. Fish, meat, poultry, eggs, and dairy products all contain this vitamin. Omega-3 fatty acids and other healthy fats also benefit the brain, particularly when it comes to minor memory loss and depression. (But remember to consume in moderation! You can have too much of a good thing. Consume too much of omega-3 or vitamin B, and you could have negative effects like mental fuzziness, headaches and maybe even nausea.)

Importance of Mental Clarity

Mental clarity is essential because it offers us a sense of empowerment and helps us to function in the world. Mental clarity is greatly affected by our physical health: what we eat, how much we exercise, and how well we sleep all impacts how our mind works on a daily basis.

When you don't have mental clarity, it's tough to enjoy your life and be productive because you can't make good decisions, stick to your plans, or work towards fulfilling the goals you've set for yourself. Both in and out of the office, mental clarity is essential for productivity and fulfillment. To solve problems and stay on top of whatever obstacles come our way, we need a clear mind.

So, how can mental clarity help you achieve your personal and professional objectives? Let's have a look.

i. Helps you make better decisions

Mental clarity helps you think more clearly, which in turn will improve your decision-making skills. When you're mentally clear and focused, you can see things from different perspectives and make choices that are in your own and other people's best interests. You'll also be better at evaluating situations and problem-solving.

A cloudy mind leads to cloudy judgment. If you want to make good decisions in life, you need to have good judgment.

ii. Helps you find focus and direction

If you have poor mental clarity, you're more likely to get distracted by the irrelevant and the trivial. You'll also find it harder to stay focused, which can cause unanticipated consequences. If your mind is cluttered with thoughts, memories, and experiences, it will be harder to focus. Clarity of the mind will help you think more clearly and focus on the task at hand.

iii. Makes it easier to organize tasks and prioritize

When your mind is clear, you'll be more likely to feel in control of your life and be able to live it in the best way possible. This will make it easier for you to organize tasks and prioritize. "A crowded desk is a symptom of a cluttered mind," as the old saying goes.

Organizing becomes second nature when your mind is operating at peak performance. A well-organized mind can approach things more efficiently and complete them in the sequence in which they were assigned.

iv. Helps you enjoy life more

Being able to focus, make good decisions, organize your thoughts efficiently, and stick to your plans helps you to enjoy life more. Lack of mental clarity can make you feel confused and uncertain about what you should do next. When your mind is clear, it will be easier for you to make the right choices and feel in control of your life. With mental clarity, you'll get more out of life in terms of purpose and happiness.

We can perceive life more clearly and prioritize what's most essential to us when we have mental clarity. This includes spending quality time with family and friends as well as pursuing personal development.

Improving Your Mental Clarity for Personal Growth

When your mental state is clear, you'll be able to process information more effectively and make better decisions. You might find it easier to identify problems and come up with solutions that work for you. Your ability to be productive will improve and you'll enjoy life more.

Meditation and prayer can help to improve your mental clarity in the long term by clearing out the clutter and making way for positive thoughts and experiences.

In short, mental clarity is at the heart of health, productivity, and performance, regardless of where you are in life, and your own mental clarity contributes to the clarity of those around you, whether at work or within your family.

Taking care of your mental health is an important aspect of living a happy and whole life. There are numerous straightforward techniques to develop mental clarity for personal growth and success in whatever endeavor you set your mind to, as we've learned.

What happens if your head is unclear?

When you don't have mental clarity, even the simplest things become difficult. Low mental performance can manifest itself in a variety of ways, both in the body and in the mind.

i. Struggling to perform well at work

When your mind is foggy, one of the first things to suffer is your work performance. Because employment necessitates mental acuity, a lack of clarity will make work more difficult than it needs to be. If your work performance standards are slipping, it's possible that you're coping with a muddled mind.

ii. Isolation and detachment from loved ones

Your emotional wellbeing influences your mental clarity. Many people with poor mental clarity experience feelings of loneliness or isolation. This occurs as a natural self-preservation mechanism. You waste less mental energy on maintaining relationships when there are fewer people around you.

iii. Depression and low self-esteem

A combination of low mental energy, poor job performance, and isolation from friends and family can swiftly lead to mental illness.

When you know you aren't performing at your best, it might be difficult to see yourself in a good light. As a result, you're more likely to develop self-doubt, low self-esteem, and even imposter syndrome. If not handled, this can lead to depression.

iv. Sleep disturbances

Sleep deprivation and mental stress are very closely associated. When you're anxious, it's likely you'll have difficulty sleeping, which only contributes to more stress.

Your sleep schedule is influenced by your mental acuity. You may find that you're sleeping too little or too much if your mental health is suffering. This can cause brain fog in a variety of ways.

Your natural circadian rhythm, or your internal body clock, is disrupted by poor sleep hygiene, such as irregular sleep and wake times, having fewer than seven to eight hours of sleep per night, or blue light exposure before bed.

Blue light reduces the melatonin hormone required for deep REM sleep, and to consolidate and integrate memories from the day, both REM and non-REM sleep are needed. Additionally, because your body and brain detox the most between the hours of 10 p.m. and 2 a.m., staying awake during this time disrupts the body's natural detoxification process and can contribute to mental fogginess.

An early morning wake time that does not coincide with the end of a sleep cycle can also impair cognitive performance and make you feel sleepy and foggy during the day. One way to deal with this is to download an app like Sleep Cycle, which tracks your movement throughout the night to determine what stage of sleep you're in. Then, it sets your alarm to go off at the end of your sleep cycle, ensuring you don't wake up in the middle of a cycle. Note also that pushing the snooze button after your alarm goes off will not help you feel more rested; instead, it will increase your chances of falling asleep and being awakened once again.

How to Develop Mental Clarity

Despite the difficulties you may experience if you have poor mental clarity, there are a variety of strategies you can employ to encourage attentive engagement. You have the power to make things better for yourself.

These eight mental clarity methods are all simple to include in your everyday routine. They can aid in the development of a keen, active, and clear mind.

1. Get plenty of restful sleep.

The amount of sleep you get determines how much energy you have during the day. Both mental and physical energy are affected by this. You must prevent generating a backlog of fatigue (or "sleep debt") and ensure that your mental performance is on point all day long by maintaining a consistent and healthy sleep routine. One approach to ensuring you get adequate, quality sleep is to use a sleep tracker.

2. Take control of your tension.

Knowing how to successfully manage stress levels will have a significant impact on your mental clarity. Finding individualized tension release and relaxation strategies is an important part of stress management. You can also use a stress tracker device to keep track of your stress levels throughout the day. Being conscious of your stress levels will help you maintain mental sharpness and achieve your best potential.

3. Develop a mindfulness practice.

Mindfulness is the attitude of living in the present moment. You can better regulate your energy by slowing down and being aware of your body, environment, and activities.

4. Strike an excellent work-life balance.

Work-life balance entails making time for both work and recreation. You may drain your energy levels and experience burnout if you spend too much time at the office. Similarly, if you concentrate solely on relaxing and having fun, you'll get very little done and be unable to achieve your goals. Knowing how to improve mental clarity requires striking a healthy balance between the two.

5. Take care of yourself.

Self-care is an essential part of life. You can control your stress levels and stay productive by finding the activities, settings, and people that make you feel comfortable and supported. Taking time out of your week to do something that brings you joy is beneficial to your mental health. It will also help you maintain a flexible and robust mindset.

6. Get your body moving.

Moving your body regularly is an essential component of overall health, both emotionally and physically. Sweating out impurities and activating the circulatory system can keep your mind busy. Even simple exercises such as walking or swimming might help you achieve mental clarity.

7. Eat a balanced diet.

That's right—you can actually eat your way to a sharper mind. Nutrition and mental health are inextricably intertwined, which is why eating a balanced diet is so critical for general wellness. Many foods can provide you with all of the nutrients you require to cultivate mental vigor.

8. Seek assistance.

Many people find it difficult to seek out help when they're going through a difficult period. However, asking for help is one of the most self-empowering things a person can do. It's not uncommon to get stressed out by mental fogginess. Ask for help from friends, family, or a healthcare professional if you need it. They will make you feel acknowledged and understood.

9. Seek God daily.

A daily encounter with God in prayer will help you. He has the power to give you all the mental clarity you require.

I remember a time when I was in my late twenties; I was in a confusing situation. I did not have the clarity of mind necessary to make a significant decision. One day, I was in a meeting with some pastors. One of them gave me a text that would change my life forever:

"I will instruct you and teach you in the way you should go;

I will guide you with My eye.

Do not be like the horse or like the mule,

Which have no understanding,

Which must be harnessed with bit and bridle,

Else they will not come near you."

Psalm 32:8-9 (NKJV)

God promises to instruct you, teach you, and guide you. With God's help, you will receive the mental clarity you need to navigate any confusing situation.

Key Takeaways

- Mental clarity comes from the development and maintenance of certain mental, emotional, cognitive, and spiritual traits. A lack of mental clarity may be due to stress, poor sleep, or poor nutrition, and can affect work performance, relationships, and mental health.

- Improving your mental clarity will ultimately make you happier, more organized, and more fulfilled.

- Understanding the advantages of mental clarity allows us to improve our own lives by sharpening our brain's performance through good sleep, diet, exercise, and spiritual practices.

- An increased capacity for mental clarity results in significant personal growth, both professionally and in your everyday life.

- Seek God daily and ask Him to give you the mental clarity you need.

Time to Take Action

Overwhelming thoughts are some of the most significant barriers to personal growth. We all have moments where we overthink or worry about something instead of taking action. These habits are often detrimental to our mental clarity, emotional wellbeing, and sense of fulfillment.

Be mindful of your thoughts. Take note of the types of thoughts that are passing through your mind throughout the day. Are they clear? Are they rational? Or are they foggy and vague? You might even consider writing down some of these thoughts. This exercise is beneficial because it allows you to be accountable to yourself and understand clearly which thought patterns are not supportive of your aims. Realize that not every thought you have is important or should be taken seriously, and then use the tips in this chapter to improve your mental clarity.

Once you've opened the door to mental clarity, the next step is stress management. What are the sources of stress, and what can you do to manage it? The next chapter will guide you on the journey of stress management.

CHAPTER FIVE

STEPS FOR PERSONAL STRESS MANAGEMENT

"You shall not fear them, for it is the LORD your God who fights for you."
Deuteronomy 3:22 (NKJV)

Lucy's therapy session

This short story will give you an example of everyday stressors and how to manage them:

"I don't know what to do," Lucy said to her therapist as tears streamed down her cheeks. There were so many things on her plate right now that she didn't know where to start.

"First, take a deep breath with me," Ms. Peters said. "Now, let's list the things that are stressing you out, okay?"

"Well, to start, I have three exams coming up in the next two weeks. Then I need to finish a lab report, and my mom is organizing a party that she keeps insisting she needs help with. Also, Alan is complaining that it's been a while since we hung out and says I don't give him enough time. But I don't *have* time!" Lucy cried.

"Okay, okay, breathe," Ms. Peters said softly. Lucy took a deep breath and waited for her therapist's wisdom.

"There are two things I want you to do. First, organize those tasks in order of urgency. Which one needs to be done first? Then organize them in order of importance. Some might be both important and urgent, while some might be important but not under a tight deadline. Also, Alan needs to understand that sometimes you're going to be busy and have less time for him. It's important that through it all, you make time for yourself. You can't make other people your priority. *You* have to be your priority, okay?"

Lucy nodded.

"Write things down," added Ms. Peters. "Write what you need to do, your top priority, and then just do it. Also, pay attention to which of those things stresses you out the most, as you might want to get those out of the way faster too. And finally, when you're doing one of those tasks, forget about the rest. The moment you pick a task, that task is all that matters, okay?"

"Okay," Lucy replied, feeling a little bit more hopeful with a plan in sight.

This story brings out several aspects of stress. We'll discuss how to tackle them in detail—but first, we need an understanding of the sources of stress.

Sources of Stress

There are four primary sources of stress in our lives:

1. **Environmental:** The environment can present you with a barrage of competing demands. Weather, noise, crowds, pollution, traffic, dangerous and poor housing, and crime are all examples of environmental stressors.

2. **Social:** The pressures of our various social responsibilities, such as being a parent, spouse, caregiver, and employee, can cause us to suffer from stress. Deadlines, financial troubles, job interviews, presentations, conflicts, demands for your time and attention, loss of a loved one, divorce, and co-parenting are all instances of social stressors.

3. **Physiological:** Physiological stresses are circumstances that affect our bodies. Adolescence, menopause, disease, aging, giving birth, accidents, lack of exercise, poor nutrition, and sleep disorders are all examples of physiological stressors.

4. **Mental:** Your brain classifies situations as stressful, challenging, painful, or enjoyable. Some life situations are stressful, but oftentimes our thoughts determine whether or not they are an issue for us.

Tackle the Common Stressors

Stress is a common part of life, and it may help you get things done. Even extreme stress caused by serious disease, job loss, a family tragedy, or a traumatic life event can be normal. You may feel depressed or anxious for a period, which is natural, and then begin to recover. If you're feeling low or nervous for more than a few weeks, however, or if it's interfering with your home or work life, check with your doctor. Therapy, medicine, and other approaches may be beneficial.

Stress can be a healthy reaction to a given situation, but it can also become a problem if it affects your everyday activities. Excessive stress can interfere with your health as well as your relationships. So, how do you properly manage your stress, and what are the best ways to avoid it? Keep reading to find out!

Academics and work

The first thing you should do is try to harmonize your personal life with your academic and/or work responsibilities. Try to plan out a schedule that fits these different aspects of your life. You should have a set time for homework or answering emails, a set time to go to bed at night, etc. This will help you organize your time and feel more balanced. Avoid rushing through school or work tasks; block out enough time in your day so that you can complete them comfortably. Stick to your schedule as much as you can to avoid getting stressed out by tasks piling up.

Time and task management

Time management is key to stress control. If you don't effectively manage your time and priorities, you can easily become overwhelmed. People frequently experience stress when they believe they are running out of time to finish a task. Simple time management practices might help you feel more comfortable and focused. So, how do you manage your time properly?

First, make a list of everything that is important and needs to be completed. These are usually your daily or weekly responsibilities. Once you have created this list, prioritize the items from most to least important. Then, try to complete these items one at a time in order of priority. Be sure to tackle the essential things first, then work your way down the list. This will help you feel more accomplished throughout your day.

In addition, create a timeframe within which to accomplish these tasks. For example, if it is a one-hour task, plan on spending one hour on this particular activity; once the period is over, reward yourself and take a break! This will help you stay motivated and organized throughout your regular activities.

Consider developing a written timetable, segmenting your duties into reasonable time periods, planning accordingly, and scheduling time for relaxation or socializing each day. Divide your job into critical versus unimportant tasks, as well as urgent versus non-urgent.

Look on the bright side

One of the best ways to reduce stress is to accept it and look at the good things in your life. Focusing on the positives can help you relax by diverting your attention away from your unpleasant thoughts or releasing built-up tension. When you are stressed out and frustrated, think about what's working for you now instead of the negative aspects. For example, don't think about the fact that you cracked your phone screen and were late to pick up your child from school; instead, think about how lucky you are to have a smartphone and how much your child makes you laugh.

You can also try to look at things from a positive perspective by optimistically visualizing them. For example, imagine you're going to the beach for vacation. When you get there and look out over the horizon, instead of looking at all the bad parts of this beach, just look at the beautiful waves and the glittering white sand. This will make you feel much more relaxed and excited.

If you feel stressed over school or work, think about positive outcomes for the things stressing you out. For example, if you're stressed about an upcoming exam, think of how confident you'll feel when graduation day finally comes. Or, if a particular part of your job is making you frustrated, remember the positive aspects of your job that make it worth doing at the end of the day.

Exercise

Going for a walk or run can be very effective in reducing stress. Not only will it help you to feel much less stressed, but it will also give you time to think about how to handle your problems logically and rationally. Running will help you to clear your head and get rid of all the distractions that stress brings.

If you have time to work out for an extended period, try doing a high-intensity circuit training workout. This kind of exercise is perfect because it encourages the release of endorphins, which are feel-good neurotransmitters that are released in the brain while exercising. These endorphins can give a natural feeling of euphoria or relaxation. This type of high-intensity exercise also demands your attention, which can distract you from your fears and anxieties.

Relax

Learning relaxation techniques can assist you in dealing with both mental and physical fears. Simply lowering your shoulders and inhaling deeply, then exhaling slowly can help. Consider imagining yourself in a relaxed environment, like a beach, as described above.

Eat healthily

Eat a lot of fruits and vegetables, good proteins, healthy fats and whole grains, and limit your sugar intake. If you eat too much sugar (or drink sugary beverages), the resulting drop in your blood sugar can make you feel anxious. Caffeine can also increase anxiety levels, so if possible, consider reducing your caffeine intake as well.

Avoid alcohol

Some people call alcohol "liquid courage," but the after-effects of alcohol can make you feel even more afraid or anxious. Thus, it's probably best to use other strategies when you're feeling anxious at a social event rather than relying on alcohol to get you through.

Turn to God in prayer

God can help you through any stressful situation. Nothing is too complicated for Him to handle. He is good, and He wants the best for you. God said in His Word, "The Lord will fight for you, and you shall hold your peace" (Exodus 14:14, NKJV). God will fight for you in your anxious situation.

And Jesus tells us:

"Come to Me, all you who labor and are heavily laden, and I will give you rest."

Matthew 11:28 (NKJV)

Key Takeaways

- Try to control your stress by managing your schedule and setting priorities.

- If you're having trouble dealing with stress, take things one at a time, focusing on the most important projects first.

- Learn how to enjoy life and look on the bright side. Seeking the positive moments in your day will help you to relax.

- Pay attention to how you're eating and try to incorporate daily exercise to keep yourself healthy and strong. A healthy body will contribute to a healthy mind.

- Exercise can help you feel less stressed and soothe your nerves. Try to walk or jog as much as possible, even if only for a short time each day. You don't need to go for long distances at a time.

- Remember, God wants to fight for you. Ask Him for help and you will receive it.

Time to Take Action

Stress is a regular and valuable part of life. It helps us cope with dangerous or frightening situations and allows us to react appropriately in these situations. However, if you're feeling stressed for long periods, it can be dangerous for your health and lead to physical and mental problems.

If you've been feeling stressed lately, consider trying one or all of the following strategies:

- Take some time off from work

- Consider clinical therapy

- Improve your diet by incorporating a balanced variety of healthy foods

- Make exercise part of your daily routine, even if only for 10 minutes

- Incorporate prayer into all aspects of your day

In the next chapter, we will discuss how to maintain a balanced life and achieve relief from fear and anxiety.

CHAPTER SIX

A BALANCED LIFE WILL GIVE YOU RELIEF

"Be diligent to present yourself approved to God, a worker who does not need to be ashamed, rightly dividing the word of truth."

2 Timothy 2:15 (NKJV)

Jim's desk

Let's look at an example of how decluttering your environment in your everyday life can give you relief from stress and anxiety:

Jim was sitting at his messy desk, trying to finish up a work project, but his mind was all over the place. His empty coffee mug was calling for him to wash it, the pile of papers he still hadn't graded seemed to be mocking him, and the various objects scattered around and collecting dust were just a reminder that he still hadn't gotten around to deep cleaning the house.

He tried to type something and then got distracted by another tab he had opened. He watched a YouTube video for a few minutes before realizing he wasn't even attempting to work anymore.

Twenty minutes passed like this, with Jim coming back to the file and getting distracted again. In all that time, the file remained unchanged. Jim simply couldn't concentrate. Finally deciding to do something about it, he got up. He took the coffee mug to the kitchen, washed it, and put it away, then put the ungraded papers in a drawer with a note stating the deadline. He also cleaned up all the little trinkets and things scattered around the wooden desk surface. After that, he wiped the desk and made sure there wasn't anything in his line of sight that could distract him. He left only his computer, a notepad, and a pen on the desk.

Finally, content with how things were looking, he sat back down and re-opened the file. Before he started working, though, he closed all the other tabs and windows on the computer, decluttering his screen as well as the physical space in which he was working. He knew all those things could distract him too, and he needed to be rid of them.

And so, with a clear space and a clear mind, Jim began his work.

Jim hadn't realized that the clutter and mess around him was the one thing distracting him from what he was supposed to be doing. But eventually, it clicked, and he tidied up his space before tackling the important tasks. Getting rid of the clutter made him more proactive and productive because fewer things could distract him. All the unnecessary things around him were merely sources of worry that caused Jim to overthink about the other things he had to do, so getting rid of them logically got rid of the problem too.

Like Jim, you probably have a lot of things that are cluttering your life. Many of us have things to do that cause mental clutter. Every day, there are new fires to put out, and it's easy to push the panic button as we worry about what we're going to do. Worrying, however, does not help things but instead makes them worse. The important thing we need to focus on is dealing with our mental clutter because that is the way we can go forward with our lives. But before we do that, we need to discover how mental clutter affects us in the first place.

What Is Mental Clutter?

Mental clutter includes anything that enters our lives that causes us to feel burdened or flustered. It consists of the things on our to-do list, regrets over things we've done in the past, unfinished work, messages to be sent, and bills to be paid, among other things. We tend to worry about many things, even if we don't know whether or not they'll happen. Worrying, being anxious, and even complaining can also be sources of mental clutter. Finally, perfectionism affects our ability to move forward because we fear failure, and thus it can contribute to mental clutter as well.

Once you're able to identify the sources of your mental clutter, what can you do about it?

Define Your Core Values

When you stay focused on your core values, you'll be able to clear up the mental clutter and pursue your most important goals. For some people, faith or religion defines their core values. For others, personal freedom might be their number one value, as they believe that restrictions on these things will cause more harm than good. For others, the importance of family may supersede all other considerations.

For me, the most important thing I believe in is Jesus and His teachings. If you are also a person of faith, it will be fairly easy to define your core values based on the principles found in the Bible.

Why are core values so important?

Much of modern life is busy and hectic, with people doing more than they can take on, resulting in excessive stress. When we add too much to our to-do list, we often stress more because we don't think we'll be able to get everything done. But when we focus on the important things in light of our core values, we can lighten our loads and free ourselves of the unnecessary mental clutter. Try to ease the burdens currently in your life by taking on fewer tasks. This will enable you to do a lot more and be more efficient.

Get rid of physical clutter to reduce mental clutter

Nowadays, our homes are filled with things we never use—books we don't read, DVDs we'll never watch again, gadgets picking up dust, clothes we never wear. Even our email inboxes are filled with unread messages, and our phones continually alert us that we're running low on storage space.

As we fill our homes with more things than we need, we also clutter our minds with more stress. Information is all around us, but we don't know how to handle all the input in our lives. With the click of a mouse, we can order anything we want, from a bicycle to cleaning supplies. We don't even have to leave the house. But then, as we accumulate more and more "stuff," we need to find more places to store all that stuff. It's a never-ending cycle. You can see how emotionally and mentally exhausting all this is for you and your family.

In order to be mentally free of clutter, we must get rid of the physical things that are cluttering our lives. It is crucial to get rid of the junk that's stopping you from pursuing your life's core value and purpose. Release the stress of the past as you release your hold on all the trinkets and gadgets you've been needlessly keeping over the years. Forgive people who have wronged you as you forgive yourself for letting junk pile up in your house, and move on. That's easier said than done, but it will help you improve your overall mental state and contribute to your overall happiness.

Clarify your life priorities

Many of us suffer from procrastination. While this is a fairly common human behavior, it's also frequently a cause of significant stress in our lives. The more we put off doing things that need to be done, the more stressed we become. But the thing is, we're always putting things we don't want to do on the back burner because we imagine they'll be too difficult or time-consuming to complete, and then we end up not getting them done at all or having to do them hastily with poor quality.

Unfortunately, this seems to be a modern problem that is not easily fixed. Think about it: Let's say an employee trying to finish a certain project by the deadline but has been putting it off over the past few days. The deadline approaches, and he realizes he cannot complete the work on time because he's been procrastinating for so long. He asks for an extension and is unable to receive it, leading him to rush to throw together the project, with lackluster results.

This is a fairly typical scenario for the average employee. We are always chasing deadlines, even though we are fully capable of managing our time. You simply need to have a to-do list and stick to it. Prioritizing the items on your to-do list is the most fundamental thing you can do to avoid procrastination.

There are six main areas of your life in which you should establish your priorities and determine how you want to spend your time while having clarity in your life.

1. Spiritual/personal growth

The Bible says in 2 Chronicles 32:8, "With him is only the arm of flesh, but with us is the LORD our God to help us and to fight our battles" (NKJV).

Without God, we can do nothing. But with God, we can do everything. One of the best antidotes to low self-esteem and low self-confidence is faith in

God. Yes, one of the most powerful things you can have in life is faith in God. Faith is what empowers you to feel that you can do anything.

Whatever plans you have, always remember God is still the one who decides what's best for you. So, surrender your plans to God. Proverbs 20:24 tells us, "The LORD directs a man's steps." You plan, but let God direct your steps.

Start your day by reading the Bible, even if only for 5 to 10 minutes each day. Talk to God first before anything else; release your worries to Him. Pray for good health, protection, love, joy, peace, happiness, enthusiasm, and abundance for you and your family.

Do this every single day, and you will discover the secret to gaining confidence and self-esteem: faith in God. In addition to listening to God's Spirit, you must also listen to your heart.

Psalm 37:4-5 (NKJV) states: "Delight yourself also in the LORD, and He shall give you the desires of your heart. Commit your way to the LORD, trust also in Him, and he shall bring it to pass."

God gives us the desires of our heart for a reason. We all have different hopes. My hopes may differ from yours, and your wishes may be different from mine.

If you want to know God's will for your life, listen to what your heart is telling you. God created our hearts to discern things that He wants us to do or not to do. Your heart gives you signals, or warnings, about whether what you're about to do is in God's plan for you or not.

2. Marriage and family

Many studies prove that the number one predictor of happiness is the quality of your social relationships, both at home with your loved ones and at work. Science has shown that bonds with others make us happier and more productive, committed, energetic, and resilient. When we have a network of people we can count on, we recover faster from setbacks.

Thanks to relationships, we achieve more, and we have a greater sense of purpose. Relationships are a necessity. No one can survive or prosper without connections, and they make a real difference in mental health. Being happy and sharing this happiness with others will improve your relationships.

Similarly, when you go through hardships and difficulties, your social support system will help you overcome them. Indeed, the most important relationships are those with your nearest and dearest. Family is not only important—it's everything!

3. Health and fitness

Go for a run or a walk in the morning hours, and it will energize you for the whole day. Take the time to walk through the woods or on the beach to disconnect from the fast and stressful rhythm of the lives we lead. Watch a sunset or a sunrise. Listening to the silence and peace will help you to relax. Taking a walk will re-energize your body, mind, and soul.

A Stanford study concluded that walking improves creative thinking (Wong, 2014), and that walking for just half an hour a day, every day, is just as good as exercising in terms of the health benefits. Walking 30 minutes a day will decrease cholesterol, improve performance, lower stress levels, improve immune system, eliminate fat, and boost mood. It might even shield you against burnout. Even better, you can analyze your emotions while you're walking (just as long as you don't start overthinking them, of course!). Finally, taking a daily walk will allow you to fall asleep more comfortably and have a better and more refreshing sleep at night.

So when are you going to start walking for half an hour every day? Try it for just 30 days and see how this makes you feel! In fact, after only a week, you might see significant improvements in your health and mood.

The benefits of exercising at least every other day are countless:

- Increased self-esteem
- Less stress and anxiety
- Better mood and higher energy
- Enhanced work performance
- Improved sleep quality
- Weight loss
- Less risk of physical diseases

The likelihood of diabetes, osteoporosis, heart failure, high cholesterol, and even particular forms of cancer reduces significantly through exercise. After a run, your brain is more open to creating new neural pathways. Your memory improves, meaning that you retain the material you have learned much better, and you become much more creative.

4. Life management and self-improvement

The best thing you can do to decrease mental clutter and enhance your personal and professional growth is to invest in yourself. Make a firm commitment to becoming the best person you can be. Invest some of your earnings in books, training, or other personal development tools. Keep an open mind and a desire to learn new things and improve yourself.

One possible effect of investing in your personal development is that you may become more beneficial to your organization due to your increased knowledge. There are numerous options available, including in-person and online trainings, that will enable you to enhance a number of different skills. You can learn effective strategies or tools that will transform your life in a two- or four-hour workshop style class. You can also decide to go all-in and hire a life coach to help you work on yourself.

However, feel free to start with easier and less expensive methods, like reading a book, listening to an audiobook, or taking an online course. Some people make it a habit to read at least one book per week, take a new class every two months, and/or enroll in at least one seminar or training course per year.

Be careful, though. Don't fall into the trap of thinking that you always need to take just one more course or read just one more book before starting your dream project. It is imperative that you apply what you learn as soon as possible after receiving training or education. Many people take one class after another and never stop to assess or implemented what they've learned. It's as if they're waiting until they become perfect at a particular skill before they'll attempt to use their knowledge. My friend, this is a colossal mistake and is called sabotaging yourself.

5. Leisure/social

Are you unsure whether you should declutter? There are a few signals you can use to assess whether your social life is in need of decluttering. Consider the following to determine which of the three warning indicators you should be on the lookout for:

1. Mindless scrolling

What percentage of your time do you spend looking through your social media feeds and scrolling mindlessly through post after post? While we may be unaware of it, technology is increasingly encroaching on our lives and our mental health. We require technology to facilitate our life, but we should not allow it to devour too much of our precious time.

2. Online 24/7

Do you log out of your social media accounts after you've used them? Nowadays, no one ever logs out; they're online 24 hours a day, and our phones are constantly updating us about new posts, comments, likes, and chats. The thing is, when our social networking apps are in standby mode like this, we're more inclined to check in on our gadgets mindlessly every minute or so (literally).

3. Immediately clicking on notifications

How frequently do you immediately check out a new post/instant message upon receiving a notification? It may be faster to count the number of times we have disregarded an alert instead. Most of the notifications we click instantly cannot be regarded as remotely necessary, and doing so may even be detrimental to your mental health.

If you find yourself engaging in these behaviors, your online habits may have gotten out of control. It might be time to reassess your use of social media and the internet and declutter by evaluating your online connections, notification settings, and privacy settings to give yourself more of a break.

Mindful Goal Setting

Mindful goal setting entails creating timely, measurable, and specific goals. If you are determined to achieve something in your life, then I'm sure you understand what goal setting is and how it works.

We've all tried to set goals for ourselves one way or another. We end every year with New Year's Resolutions. Some goals last a few months, and some don't even survive January. We're so used to failing to reach the goals that, at some point, we give up on setting them. After all, they don't work, right? At the beginning of every year, we get excited about change; we decide we'll "lose X pounds of fat this year and build Y pounds of muscle" or "make Z amount of money." But we don't, and it's depressing.

I'll let you in on a small secret to setting goals that do work, and that's what we've been building up to in this book. Most of the goals we choose are based on physical or performance-related achievements. We want to look a certain way, save a certain amount of money, or perform so well at our jobs that we'll inevitably get a promotion. While those are the results we want, we're approaching the goal-setting process from completely the wrong direction.

We often look at goals simply as paths to the rewards we'll get from them, but we give very little thought to who we'll become by achieving these goals. It's important to recognize that the results of a goal that goes against our nature or identity won't stick around for too long. So, instead of the goal of losing X pounds a month, why not set a goal of becoming a fit person with a healthy lifestyle? Instead of wanting to make X amount of money, how about deciding to become the type of person who can make X amount of money?

Setting a goal that focuses on the journey instead of the end result makes all the difference in the world. The wrong approach will make each step a struggle until you either give up on the goal (because it's going against your nature) or use up every ounce of willpower on this goal, discarding everything else in your life. The right approach focuses on who you'll become due to this goal. It builds a constructive framework of habits to paint the bigger picture, so you can grow in every aspect of your being, one step at a time. It is possible to be content in the present while still planning for the future. The idea is to savor every moment while mindfully planning your future and appreciating each step along the way.

Essentially, you need to discover what gets you up in the morning. What keeps you going? What drives you? You should deeply consider what you want to do with your life, how you want to live, and your unique goals and aspirations. Don't let anyone get in the way of your journey, and don't hold back when it comes to doing whatever it takes to become the best version of yourself.

To set identity-based goals, choose an identity you want to achieve. The choice of a new identity can be based on several things. You can decide where you want to go and become the kind of person who'd be able to go there, or you can focus on where you're stuck in life and set out to change the current version of yourself. However, what works best is to build your new identity based on your vision of who you want to be and your desire to stop feeling stuck.

Then you need to prove to yourself that you can, indeed, become this person. Identify the habits or behaviors that are preventing you from becoming that person, and form new habits that will help you develop the desired identity. All it takes is one small win in the direction of the goal for you to start believing you can achieve it. Make this identity the central point for building your framework of habits, which will all integrate into your lifestyle. By taking these steps slowly but surely, you'll instill belief and rewire the habits in your brain in the most effective way possible.

Before you know it, you'll have developed all the habits you desired, and overcome the ones that were keeping you stuck. You'll experience your new identity, enjoying the new life you've created for yourself.

In the process of achieving your new identity, there are a few things you can do to make the journey a little smoother. We'll discuss them below.

Create quarterly SMART goals

It's best practice to break down your overarching goals into smaller ones and prioritize the goals you want to accomplish on a daily, weekly, or monthly basis. Apply the SMART formula to each of your goals. SMART provides a good guideline for achieving your dreams. The acronym SMART stands for:

- **Specific:** Does your goal include who, what, where, when, and why?
- **Measurable:** Does your goal use accurate timeframes, numbers, or other units of measurement?
- **Attainable:** Does your goal push the boundaries of what you think you can do without being outside the realm of possibility?
- **Relevant:** Is your goal in line with your true desires?
- **Time-bound:** Does your goal have definite deadlines?

Aligning your goals with the SMART framework and setting quarterly (rather than yearly) timelines to achieve them makes it easier for you to do everything you set out to do.

Here's how to make your SMART ideas a reality:

1. Determine what is most important to you; concentrate on three to four areas of your life maximum to avoid becoming overwhelmed.

2. Focus on three-month goals. Life is in continual flux, and long-term goals can be too vague and discouraging, which is why people often give up on their New Year's resolutions.

3. Create a schedule using a weekly review. Make a weekly action plan that considers your duties, priorities, and available time.

4. Take action on your goals. Convert each goal into a project by working backward from your target deadline. Schedule opportunities to work on your goals, and convert them into deliverables by working on your key objectives first thing in the morning (or whenever you feel most energized). Schedule time for individual actions by grouping them together.

5. Review your goals daily to keep them fresh in your memory.

6. Examine your quarterly objectives. Ask yourself, "Have I gotten the desired result? Which strategies were successful and which were not? Am I devoting 100 percent of my effort to achieving these objectives?"

Identify what's important to you

Below are a few tips to help you focus on the important things in your life to help you achieve your goals.

- Everything you experience is based on your mind; train it on a daily basis!

- Detachment from intrusive thoughts and emotions can be achieved through focused breathing and meditation.

- Take control of your thoughts by interrupting, rephrasing, and challenging them in order to reduce their power over you.

- Make goals centered on your core principles to help you take focused action and maintain your self-esteem.

- Be present and conscious in your relationships to avoid many of the tensions and emotional pain that come with human interaction.

- Keep your home and digital life organized to avoid being distracted from your values, priorities, and ambitions.

Create an environment of clarity

Do you look forward to your weekends because you're always dying to get out of the office? Are you bored with your job? Do you dread gloomy Mondays? Your answers to these questions will help you get on the right track to finding meaningful work for your life, contributing to your happiness and fulfillment.

As you think about your motivation, consider what will make you happy in the long run. What talent or special skills do you possess that will be helpful in a particular job? What interests do you have that can benefit you in your desired position? Think about the things that light you on fire and help you contribute to others and their development, and you will experience mental clarity and a better life.

God wants to bless you. The blessing of Jacob is also for you. Reclaim it today:

"By the God of your father who will help you,

And by the Almighty who will bless you

With blessings of heaven above,

Blessings of the deep that lies beneath,

Blessings of the breasts and of the womb."

Genesis 49:25 (NKJV)

No matter what the situation you are going through, this promise is for you in Christ. God wants to give you His blessings. In God's Word, we read:

"He remembers his covenant forever,

the promise he made, for a thousand generations"

1 Chronicles 16:15 (NIV)

As Paul said in Galatians 4:28, "Now we, brethren, as Isaac was, are children of promise." That means you can claim all the promises of the heirs of Abraham. With God's promises, you will have the power to pass through stormy days. It's time to have a balanced life and stand on the promises of our Heavenly Father.

Key Takeaways

- Mental clutter can be caused by stress and anxiety, but it can also be impacted by a cluttered physical environment.

- To reduce mental clutter, clean up your physical space as well as your digital space. Consider logging out of social media and allowing your mind time to find clarity away from the busyness of daily life.

- Defining your core priorities and values will help you find balance because you'll be able to focus on what's truly important to you.

- Setting SMART (specific, measurable, attainable, relevant, and time-bound) goals each quarter will keep you on track to attaining the balanced, fulfilled life you desire.

- Remember that God wants to bless you, and if you rely on Him, you will find it easier to achieve a harmonious and peaceful life.

Time to Take Action

It is essential to realize that the journey to becoming a more positive and balanced person is a process. It will not look the same for everyone. Some people require more time to process and get over past situations, and others need help in decluttering their physical and mental environment; however, once you're able to move past these challenges, you'll find you can focus on becoming more positive.

Don't be discouraged if nothing changes for a little while even after you start implementing the tips in this chapter. It takes practice. If you're used to always being negative and dwelling on pessimistic, anxiety-driven thoughts in your head, it will take a little while for you to transform that into positivity and mental clarity. Be patient with yourself. Recognize that things can change, but it takes time.

Life is short. We have to take advantage of every opportunity to find joy and meaning in life because that's what is most important. Life isn't about having a fancy job, making a lot of money, or accumulating a lot of stuff. Rather, it's about appreciating the simple everyday treasures life offers and finding a deeper purpose.

This requires having a thankful heart that is willing to take in every moment and savor the goodness of it while finding time to say "thank you" to God for the blessings you have. Once you do that, you'll experience freedom and joy like never before. It will free you from all your anxieties and stress and lead you to a more delightful and prosperous future. You'll experience a fantastic transformation in your life.

A balanced life will help you overcome overthinking and cultivate a new attitude. The next chapter dives into the psychology of stress and managing the anger that often comes with stress. Then we will discuss dialectical behavior therapy, endurance, and steps towards success.

CHAPTER SEVEN

OVERCOME OVERTHINKING BY CULTIVATING NEW ATTITUDES

"Can any one of you by worrying add a single hour to your life?"
Matthew 6:27 (NIV)

Lesson from the vision of Lu Xun: Face your reality

On September 25, 1881, in Shaoxing, China, Lu Xun was born. After some misfortunes, he left his town in 1898 to study at the Jiangnan Naval Academy. Four years later, after graduating with the third-highest scores of his class, he received a Chinese government scholarship to get a Western-style education in Japan. He went there to study medicine.

During Lu Xun's life, China was at its darkest and most helpless time. The Japanese had defeated the country in 1894. Japan's ambition was to be the leader of East Asia. Thus, Lu Xun was humiliated and frustrated by his identity as a Chinese citizen living in Japan. One day during his medical studies, he was shocked by a slideshow in which some Japanese executed a Chinese man. This event pushed him to radically challenge the situation of his country. Instead of becoming a doctor, he became a writer in order to help his country face reality and pursue change.

In 1909, he returned to China to become a writer, essayist, poet, and literary critic. He is among the most talented writers of 20th-century Chinese literature. Lu Xun's top priority was to rejuvenate his fellow Chinese by asking them to face China's harsh reality and explore change through his writings. Today, China has surpassed Japan and is the second-largest economy in the world.

The story of Lu Xun brings out the concept of facing reality and overcoming challenges. In times of crisis, many people are tempted to flee from scenarios that could get them into trouble or put them in an unfortunate situation. However, it is not always possible to prevent a problem from happening. Sometimes you have to face those problems head-on. It is, therefore, best to figure out ways that you can respond to the things that are stressing you out.

The next time you're in this type of situation, remember the story of Lu Xun. Persevere, and do not worry. There is hope. Your challenge may be overwhelming, but do not overthink it, and do not stay in despair. Face the reality and remember that there is always hope. Talk to God when you're at your lowest points. He will always make a way.

The Psychology of Stress

Stress is a powerful force in our everyday lives. It's impossible to pretend that it doesn't exist. It is natural to have periods of stress, but too much can be harmful to your health and affect your happiness, relationships, and overall quality of life. Stress impacts so many aspects of our lives that understanding its psychology may help us keep it at bay in the future. If you can identify the sources of stress in your life and how they impact you, it will help you to reduce your stress. The best way you can deal with stress is to prepare yourself for it.

Facing the stress

The first step to avoiding stress is going through it in the first place. If you cannot anticipate the sources of stress in your life, you will have no way of dealing with them effectively.

When faced with hardship and possible loss, we often hold back on what we're passionate about. For example, you may take a job that isn't exactly fulfilling because you're stressed about not having enough money to support your family. However, sometimes facing the stress and going through that difficult situation is necessary for growth.

To experience profound change within yourself, it's essential that you face up to the things that may negatively impact you. Pay attention to the sources of stress in your life and then find ways to solve those problems.

One thing that makes us so unique as humans is our ability to take a negative experience and turn it into a positive one. In order to do this effectively, you must face your problems head-on.

Coping with stressful times

To master stress, you must first learn to relax in stressful situations. We often find ourselves experiencing stress because of our reactions to the things that happen to us. It is essential to understand why you are stressed and what you can do about it. Once you've taken control of your reactions, you'll find the situation is less likely to cause emotional distress. Facing the source of stress before it begins will prepare you for dealing with the stresses that come your way later on.

Anger and Stress Management

Anger is a normal, active emotion, neither good nor bad. It conveys a message like any other emotion, telling you that a situation is perturbing, unjust, or threatening. However, if your reaction to anger is to explode, that message never has an opportunity to be passed on. So, while feeling angry when you've been wronged or when you're stressed is perfectly normal, anger becomes an issue when you're expressing it in a way that harms yourself or others.

You may feel that expressing your anger is beneficial, that those around you are overly sensitive, and your anger is justifiable, or that you need to exhibit your rage to gain respect. But the real issue is that anger is much more likely to affect how other people see you, impair your judgment, and hamper success.

Controlling your anger

Anger can be a helpful tool, or it can be hideously destructive. It's like a fire. Some situations require an immediate response fueled by righteous anger, such as witnessing some type of abuse or bullying, whether physical or psychological. But in other cases, small things might cause your anger to build to the point where you risk losing control over your emotions unjustifiably.

If you feel that this is happening to you, try the following strategies:

1. **Walk away.** If you're in the middle of an extremely uncomfortable or stressful situation that sparks anger, it's hard not to say the first thing that comes to mind, but you may regret it later. Thus, it may be best to remove yourself from the situation.

2. **Use deep breathing.** Deep breathing has been found to be one of the quickest ways to reduce the intensity of your anger (Thomas & Aiken, 2019).

3. **Practice relaxation.** Immerse yourself in something you enjoy. Look for something to engage in that will divert your attention and help you to calm down once you take a break from the situation. Try reading, listening to music, or any other relaxing activity.

4. **Exercise.** Non-strenuous exercise is a good option. Take a walk, ride your bike, or stretch your muscles. This might help you relax by releasing tension in your muscles.

Dialectical Behavior Therapy

Dialectical behavior therapy (DBT) teaches techniques for managing uncomfortable emotions like stress and anger and reducing relationship conflict. DBT consists of four main areas:

1. *Mindfulness*, which aims to improve a person's ability to admit fault and be aware of the reality of the present situation;

2. *Distress tolerance*, which aims to increase a person's endurance rather than letting them avoid the negativity of the situation;

3. *Self-control*, which refers to methods for coping with and changing strong emotions that are producing challenges in one's life; and

4. *Interpersonal effectiveness*, which refers to the skills that enable a person to engage with others confidently, have self-respect, and build relationships.

Our emotions influence our goals and behavior. The brain internalizes these messages from our emotions—perhaps we think we need to be successful, we need to be perfect, we need to be rich, and so on, and that anything outside this equation is a failure. Anything other than perfection is a threat. When we do not achieve these high standards, it creates more stress and anger. We cannot expect our brains to differentiate between real-life threats and imagined ones. Worrying about an event taking place in the future could trigger the same threat response as a very real tornado coming at you in the moment. Because of the brain's physiology, these negative emotions are thus triggered many times throughout the day if we dwell on stressful thoughts.

DBT's Core Actionable Skills

Let's dive into the four critical skills of DBT as defined in the previous section: mindfulness, distress tolerance, mood management, and interpersonal effectiveness.

Mindfulness

Mindfulness is defined as being aware of and focused on the current moment rather than the past or the future (Brown & Ryan, 2003). The following are some DBT skills for practicing mindfulness:

- Concentrate on the present moment.
- Without passing judgment, observe your thoughts, emotions, and bodily sensations.
- Engage in mindful breathing to bring yourself into the present moment.
- During attentive meditation, be friendly and sympathetic to yourself.

Distress tolerance

When people are overwhelmed by emotions, they often try to deal with them to feel better in the moment. Unfortunately, this can include using substances to numb the pain or engaging in some form of self-destructive behavior. However, these tactics create even more emotional distress in the long run. Learning to better manage those overpowering feelings is what distress tolerance is all about.

The following DBT skills can help you enhance your distress tolerance:

- Divert your attention away from undesirable ideas and feelings.

- Accept what you can't change and focus on what you can change (referred to as "radical acceptance").

- Utilize self-soothing techniques, such as paying attention to your five senses to relax and soothe yourself.

- Visualize a safe, serene location, such as the beach or the mountains.

- Use your spirituality to empower yourself.

Emotional control

When an individual has a history of trauma or feels threatened or abandoned, they may experience emotional extremes that they cannot control. Emotional dysregulation is the term for this. The person may become excessively reactive and self-destructive when triggered or emotionally overwhelmed. Brain researchers have discovered that patients with emotional dysregulation may have abnormalities in the neurocircuitry in the brain that governs emotion. However, these abnormalities can be dealt with using some coping skills to help with emotional regulation.

The following are some DBT emotion management skills:

- Recognize and name the feelings you're experiencing.

- Recognize how your emotions are influenced by your beliefs and behavior.

- Acknowledge and address self-destructive behavior.

- Boost pleasant feelings.

- Manage strong feelings.

Emotions are chemical and physical signals that communicate your feelings and what's going on in your body. Extreme reactive emotions are helpful when confronted with an immediate threat or danger, but they are less useful in relationships and at work. DBT was created to assist people who are experiencing strong emotions in learning how to manage them and better their lives.

Interpersonal effectiveness

Interpersonal effectiveness techniques are all about increasing one's social skills. Setting limits and controlling disagreements while respecting others is necessary for managing emotions and emotional reactivity in partnerships.

Among the interpersonal effectiveness skills taught in DBT are:

- Paying close attention to people so you can comprehend what they're thinking and experiencing

- Making straightforward requests for what you want while maintaining your relationships

- Listening actively rather than passively

Life Skills for Endurance and Resilience

"'So do not fear; I will provide for you and your little ones.' Thus he comforted them and spoke kindly to them."

Genesis 50:21 (NKJV)

Surround yourself with success

The entrepreneur and motivational speaker Jim Rohn once said, "You are the average of the five people you spend the most time with." Reread that sentence.

What kind of crowd do you run with? What kind of audience do you have? You will become more and more like the people you associate with. Do you spend your time with winners or with people who make excuses? Do you spend your time with people who blame others or people who take responsibility for their actions? Do you spend time with cowards who flee from their fears or people who bravely face their challenges?

Suppose you're hanging out with the correct people. You'll embrace their way of thinking and habits. You'll begin to focus on your goals daily, and anything you think about regularly will manifest in your life. Are you aware of this? It's time to take a look at your entourage.

People who are sincerely committed to conquering fear and realizing their goals surround themselves with people who share their thinking or are on the same level as them (or a higher one). These are people who will inspire you and drive you to reach your objectives. To be free of fear, you must raise the bar and your standards while allowing others to hold you accountable, which means running among winners.

Adopt a growth mindset

When scared, we have a tendency to isolate ourselves. What happens if you make a blunder? What if you fail? Maybe you begin to believe that you can't grow and improve at all, that you're not capable of doing so. That is the fear that is preventing you from moving forward.

Adopting a growth mindset is one of the most effective ways to overcome fear and anxiety. It's not about reaching your objectives immediately and being flawless at all times. Stop striving for perfection. Be at ease with what you don't know, and push on regardless. A growth mindset is built on this foundation.

As you attempt to overcome your fear of failure, you'll notice there are many ups and downs along the route. You'll be one step closer to achieving your objectives if you realize that the road to success entails growth and change. Always remember that mistakes are part of life, and adopt the mindset of learning from criticism and feedback.

Find valuable insight in pain

No one enjoys being in agony or feeling stressed and angry all the time. The majority of people go to considerable lengths to avoid it. Pain, however, is a powerful teacher. Painful experiences become excellent opportunities for growth if you understand that your life and sometimes efforts to achieve your goals will be painful. When you stop seeing pain (or stress) as a danger to your life, it loses its potency and becomes a new instrument for dealing with fear and obstacles.

Everyone faces difficulties from time to time, whether the setbacks are personal or professional. What is important is what you learn from your experiences and how you apply those lessons in the future. Rather than allowing sorrow and fear to govern the game and your actions, actively learn from those terrible experiences to take charge of your own life.

Decide right now that you're going to run your life, not the other way around. Consider that pain is a profound teacher. Rather than allowing sorrow and fear to influence your actions, deliberately choose to learn from those difficult experiences so that you may take charge of your life. Reframe your fear and give it a new meaning so that it becomes your ally and guides you to progress to the next level.

Visualize your goals

You've already done the mental work of discovering the genuine reasons you're limiting yourself and defining your life's "must-haves." However, overcoming fear takes daily practice of these habits to result in real change. Recognize your problems, but devote your strength and efforts to finding answers.

One of these solutions is goal visualization. It is used by some of the world's most prominent athletes, entertainers, and businesspeople.

Visualizing your goal establishes your concentration and focus. Visualize yourself succeeding and fully commit to your goal. You can also meditate on achieving your goal. You'll begin to train your brain to believe that anything is possible—a necessary step toward conquering fear.

How to Manage Your Time and Energy to Move Forward

Every day, we face a barrage of deadlines, tasks, and appointments. We're just busy living our lives. We have less time and energy to spend on ourselves. This leads to stress, confusion, and exhaustion. However, if we can learn how to work smarter and not more complicated, we can lead a more fulfilling life with the time we do have.

You've probably heard the cliché that we need to spend our time doing what we love, but maybe you often find yourself with little relief from the tedious tasks that make up most of your day-to-day life. Managing your time and energy in this situation is vital in order to develop efficient ways to get things done with minimum effort.

The three D's

There are different methods you can use to prepare for the future or plan your schedule, but first, take inventory of how you currently manage your time based on the three D's: days, distractions, and decisions. These three D's are essential for managing your time.

Days: First, calculate how many hours per week are available to you. Include any extra time that could potentially be added to your schedule.

Distractions: Consider who or what might distract you from achieving your goals. Then find ways to minimize their interference. For example, if your significant other always complains about you not spending time with them, it might be a good idea to schedule some time in the evenings to focus on your relationship.

Decisions: A big part of time management is making a realistic yet efficient schedule. Make a list of the top priorities you want to accomplish for the week. Put the tasks in order of importance, with the most important first. This is a significant step in time management because it helps you determine if the things on your list are really what you want to accomplish or if they are time-wasters. You may have a lot of things going on at work but decide that prioritizing the pursuit of a hobby or personal interest a few hours per week will make you much happier.

Find happiness

Are you ready to say yes to happy choices? Deciding to have more happiness in your life is a serious matter. After all, your happiness affects your whole life: your self-esteem, relationships, physical and mental health, and maybe even the amount of time you have left to live.

Yes—it's really that important.

Don't let stress get the best of you. Life is tough. You will need strength and courage in difficult times. God knows that. After the death of Moses, Joshua had to lead the people of Israel and fight many kings. This task was monumental. God said to Joshua:

"Be strong and courageous because you will lead these people to inherit the land,

I swore to their ancestors to give them.

Be strong and very courageous.

Be careful to obey all the law my servant Moses gave you;

do not turn from it to the right or the left,

that you may be successful wherever you go.

Keep this Book of the Law always on your lips;

meditate on it day and night so that you may be careful

to do everything written in it.

Then you will be prosperous and successful.

Have I not commanded you? Be strong and courageous.

Do not be afraid; do not be discouraged,

for the Lord your God will be with you wherever you go."

Joshua 1:6-9 (NKJV)

God commands Joshua to "Be strong and very courageous" three times (verses 6, 7, 9). But in verse 9, God said this is not just advice; it's a command ("Have I not commanded you?").

We read in Joshua 12:24 that Joshua defeated 31 kings. That means 31 dangerous fights—31 periods of high stress. But it's also 31 times that God showed His power against the enemy, 31 times that God kept His promises, and 31 times that God saved His people.

Today, you may be fighting many battles: Fighting to succeed in life, fighting against a disease, fighting in your workplace, fighting within your family, fighting against anxiety or depression. But do not worry; if God gave Joshua victory over 31 battles, no matter how many battles you have, know that God can give you victory also. God will be with you in each of your fights. He has never failed anyone. The fight may be intense, but victory is guaranteed with Him.

Do not overthink your battles. Instead, cultivate a new attitude. Believe in God. Trust Him. God will fight for you.

Key Takeaways

- Don't waste time overthinking your life's problems, but instead develop a new mindset. Face your problems head-on and look for solutions.
- Learn to control your anger, because in the long term, anger as a reaction to stress is harmful to your physical and mental health.

- When you're living in the moment, it's much harder to dwell on the past or be concerned about the future. Mindfulness will assist you in becoming more aware of the present moment.

- Paying attention to your thoughts can assist you in being more conscious of your negative mental patterns. You can educate your brain to think differently with practice. Building healthier behaviors over time can assist you in developing the mental muscle you require to become less stressed and create a new mindset.

- Always have faith in God. He will grant you victory.

Time to Take Action

Sometimes the best way to overcome feelings of unworthiness, anger, or stress is to ride them out, especially if you feel as if you're out of viable options or have too much to deal with.

Keep fighting on—get dressed and do what you have to do, with the view that something positive might present itself to you. Life has a way of knocking even the best of us down, but that very same life also frequently surprises us with new ways of looking at things, better ways of solving our problems, and opportunities to get over what was seemingly an impossibly large obstacle.

You've made it this far and have learned many strategies for managing your tendency to overthink, anxiety, and stress. The last chapter will look at steps to help you master your emotions and live a purposeful life.

CHAPTER EIGHT

STEPS TO MASTER YOUR EMOTIONS AND LIVE A LIFE OF PURPOSE

"Set your mind on things above, not on things on the earth."

Colossians 3:2 (NKJV)

Sky's emotional rollercoaster

Let's look at an example of recognizing moments when something triggers our emotions, which is the first step to mastering them:

Sky was in her room doing homework when her mother walked in and asked if she had finished all her chores for the day. She quickly replied that she hadn't, which was why she was doing homework. When her mother left, Sky was left with an odd feeling. She was almost angry, and she wasn't sure why.

Later that same day, when Sky was in the kitchen making a grilled cheese sandwich, her father walked in and asked her if she needed help. A little annoyed, she replied that it was okay, that she was doing it herself and didn't need any help. Once again, she felt almost angry, and she wasn't sure where those feelings were coming from. She didn't think much of it, blaming it on being tired, and continued with her day.

At dinner time, when the family was gathered at the table, Sky's brother looked at her with a frown and asked if she was okay. Perplexed, Sky asked why he was asking that. Her brother replied that she looked angry or something, which made Sky even more furious. She left the table feeling annoyed and puzzled. She wasn't sure where any of these feelings were coming from, but she was growing incredibly frustrated.

Sitting on her bed and trying to read a book, she realized something must have triggered her. She wasn't sure what it was, but something about the interactions she'd had must have annoyed her for some reason.

Sky lay in bed that night and thought about the possibilities of what could have triggered her. After that day, every time she had an interaction that generated a feeling she wasn't expecting, she tried to get to the root of it, asking herself: *Why does this bother me? Why am I feeling like this?*

All of us occasionally feel like Sky did in this story. We get upset, frustrated, or angry and we don't understand why, but we realize that it must have something to do with our interactions with others throughout the day. When that happens, it's time to sit down and reflect on *why* you feel the way you do.

What Is an Emotion?

For many years, psychologists and philosophers have engaged in spirited debate on the nature of emotions.

Generally speaking, emotions result from interacting with others in a specific setting and culture. Various theories in neuroscience explain how a human being's brain can generate emotions by combining bodily perceptions and cognitive appraisals. Suppose something shocking happens to you today; it is natural and very normal to develop emotions such as sadness or anger.

Today, there are two main scientific approaches that can be employed to explain what emotions are: cognitive appraisal theory and James–Lange theory.

Cognitive appraisal theory says that emotions are judgments on how the situation you are in currently meets the goals you have set. According to this theory, positive emotions such as happiness express goals being fulfilled (Nelson-Coffey, 2022). On the other hand, sadness and negative emotions depict unfulfilled goals and disappointments in life and be a form of anger towards a stumbling block to your goals.

The James–Lange theory of emotion, developed by psychologists William James and Carl Lange, argues that emotions are just perceptions of various changes in your body in different situations, and thus emotions arise as a result of a certain physiological state.

These two theories can be integrated to develop a unified definition of emotions. We can, therefore, describe emotions as one's mental state, associated with the nervous system and linked to the chemical changes that take place in the body. These chemical changes are usually linked to feelings, thoughts, and behavioral responses. Emotions can also be termed negative or positive experiences linked to certain patterns of physiological functions in the body. The bottom line is that emotions are part of our reaction to the cognitive, behavioral, and physiological changes we undergo.

What Is Emotional Mastery?

Emotional mastery is the act of becoming aware of and learning to control one's emotional states (how one feels at a given instant) and utilizing them to one's benefit.

The emotional mastery process begins with identifying and understanding your feelings. Once you have assessed what you're feeling, reflect on what triggered the emotions and identify the thoughts that continue to add fuel to your unhappiness.

If these thoughts can't be resolved, you need to seek out healthier ways of responding to situations so that you can feel better about yourself and your life.

Let Go of Your Negative Emotions

If you have a negative thought process in your mind today, it isn't baseless. It has its roots in the very same survival instinct that enabled our ancestors to survive in the most dangerous situations. However, there is a line beyond which even helpful things can become toxic. If you let your brain run wild without any control, it will keep playing out fear-inducing scenarios, preventing you from taking action. Your mind knows that the safest bet for survival is to remain in your shell. The outside world is unpredictable, and there are forces beyond our control. However, becoming a slave to this mentality is also dangerous.

Negative thought patterns arise in your mind as a natural response to certain situations. The extent of the negative thoughts depends on your perception of the threat. Most of the time, there is really no threat at all; you're simply scared to take action, and your mind starts showing you the worst possible outcomes. This leads to inaction, procrastination, fear, and anxiety. If you fall into this trap, you are destined to fail. Inaction will get you nowhere. If you want to move forward in your life to grow, change, and improve, you need to act.

Excessive negative thought patterns are a part of mind clutter. Your mind is filled with too much negativity, and this is reflected in negative thinking. This can be a dangerous thing if it goes unchecked. It can make you indecisive, frightened, and weak, afraid to take a chance on something new. Your risk-taking ability will falter, and you'll become too fearful to make any decisions at all. This is a terrible state to be in the first place. You'll lose control over your life, and instead, your anxiety will begin deciding how you live your life. This will take a toll on your personal and professional life, health, family, relationships, career, and more.

Transform Negative Emotions into Positive Ones

It is essential to replace negativity with positivity; however, that's not as easy as it sounds. Most people misunderstand the whole idea of negative thinking. Happiness does not necessarily depend on the presence or absence of negative thoughts, but rather, on how we handle these negative thoughts.

Despite the setbacks and obstacles you face, it is essential to try to maintain a sense of optimism. The benefits of avoiding negative thinking are more significant than most people think. In fact, research suggests that positive thinkers enjoy life more than pessimists do (De Meza & Dawson, 2020). When it comes to physiological and psychological health, as well as stress levels, optimistic people are way ahead of the game. Thinking positively is an excellent way to heal, but first you need to stop listening to your mind's anxiety-driven falsehoods.

It's also helpful to try to figure out the origin of your negative thoughts. Remember, negative thoughts stem from wrong assumptions and beliefs; therefore, merely ignoring them is not good enough. You need to challenge those thoughts and replace them with positive ones. Everyone is worthy of love and happiness, and that includes you—don't forget this.

Control Your Emotions

Emotions are the most pervasive, compelling, and potentially unpleasant force in our existence. Our emotions guide us daily to take risks because we're enthused about fresh possibilities. We weep because we've been wronged, and we make sacrifices out of love. Our emotions, without a doubt, have great control over our reasoning minds in dictating our thoughts, intentions, and actions. However, when we react to our emotions too quickly or with the wrong feelings, we frequently behave in ways that we subsequently regret.

You might find that your emotions swing dangerously from one extreme to the other. Maybe you're on the verge of fury over a small argument with your spouse, but then in bliss thanks to your favorite TV show or a hug from your child. Like many other aspects of life, emotions benefit from moderation and a reasonable perspective. This doesn't mean it's a bad thing to fall head over heels in love or excitedly jump for joy when receiving good news. These are wonderful, joyous parts of human life. On the other hand, however, you must treat negative emotions with utmost caution.

Negative emotions such as fury, envy, and resentment tend to spin out of control easily, especially when provoked. These emotions can spread like weeds over time, training the mind to function on negative emotions and taking control of your daily life. Have you ever met someone who is always angry or hostile? They weren't born with that personality. They simply allowed certain emotions to simmer within them so long that they became inbred sentiments that arise far too frequently.

So, how can we avoid functioning on the wrong types of emotion and master our emotions even in the most trying of situations?

In our darkest moments, faith in God is our saving grace. Pray and ask God to reveal the best path forward when you're overcome with emotion.

"Trust in the Lord with all your heart

And do not lean on your own understanding.

In all your ways, acknowledge Him,

And He will make your paths straight."

Proverbs 3:5-6 (NKJV)

Use Your Emotions to Grow as a Person

i. Control your emotions to gain confidence.

There is a strong connection between confidence, emotional control, and the conquering of psychological habits. Over the years, through all of the surveys, interviews, and studies conducted on this topic, this is the most common and repeated truth from both participants and researchers alike: no matter what a person is trying to attempt, confidence is key!

Many different life factors can affect a person's self-esteem and confidence, with adolescence taking the largest toll on a person's view of themselves. However, you always have the opportunity to take action to improve your self-esteem and confidence levels and thereby improve your overall life satisfaction and path to reaching your goals.

ii. Record your emotions to become more aware of your feelings.

Keeping a journal is a great strategy to help organize your thoughts. People tend to underestimate the power of noting down their thoughts every day. Journaling enables you to rid your mind of negative emotions that you might not otherwise be aware of. It enhances your working memory and guarantees that you can more effectively manage stress.

Similarly, the habit of noting down your daily experiences in a journal helps you express the emotions that may be bottled up within you. This creates mental and emotional space for you to experience new things in life. The end result is that you can relieve yourself of anxiety and negativity and explore new experiences with a positive mindset.

iii. Don't be inhibited by what people think of you.

If you truly want to beat negative thoughts and negative self-talk, identify where it comes from. People around us often condition us into believing something bad about ourselves. Even seemingly harmless or subtle negative comments or pieces of criticism can impact our sense of self-worth. The voice of others slowly and insidiously becomes our inner voice of critical self-talk. Never let someone else's perception of you define your reality or become the foundation of your self-talk.

Are there people around you who view your life, or their own, in a predominantly negative light? Are you an unwilling victim of someone else's negativity? While it isn't uncommon for negative self-talk to originate within us, it can often be traced back to our conditioning and the beliefs, actions, and words of the people around us. Critical talk originating from another person's low confidence or self-esteem is highly challenging to deal with. Run miles away from such negative and destructive people to change your outlook on life, and begin to view it more positively and constructively.

Avoid slipping into the trap of negativity laid down by others. Stay away from chronic whiners and habitual complainers. Don't validate other people's complaints by chiming in. According to a Warsaw School of Social

Psychology study, people who are always complaining experience reduced life satisfaction, more extraordinary negative emotions, stunted positive thinking, and lower moods (Karim, 2020).

Tips for Developing Mental Toughness

Mental toughness is a personality trait that enables an individual to effectively face and overcome challenges, pressure, and stressors and still perform at his or her best regardless of the situation. Developing mental toughness will help you take charge of your emotions and life.

Do not get upset quickly, and stay calm and relaxed even in a stressful environment. Pray about your troubles. Believe that you can make a difference and that your life will impact the lives of others.

Stick to your goals, and evaluate them from time to time according to the facts and God's plan for your life.

Cultivate the habit of arriving on time, exercise regularly, and maintain a healthy lifestyle. Be true to your word. You don't need other people's approval to know what you're capable of. Whatever task is assigned to you, try to deliver with flying colors.

Do not be easily influenced or intimidated. See a challenge as a chance to showcase your God-given talents. Look at every problem and obstacle as a stepping stone to inspire and motivate you to push harder towards your goals. Don't give up quickly. Instead, strive to be better—welcome challenges as opportunities for self-development. Be willing to improve and learn something valuable from every difficulty you encounter. Move forward with God on your side. Through mental toughness, you can use your emotions to grow as a person.

Build a Solid Inner Life

Having an "inner life" is a vital component of your personality to help you face tough situations. "The inner life thus is something that seems to be much fuller than just doing what ethical reason demands; it seems to involve a whole sense of a moral space in our lives that needs to be filled... Certainly, it involves a certain appreciation of the fullness of life itself" (Springsted, 2020).

Your inner life involves your state of mind, what you think about, how you address those thoughts, and the enduring qualities of your mind. Ultimately, your inner life manifests itself in your behavior. Behavior, actions, and words are all ways of expressing what's going on in your mind. You may tend to behave certain ways in certain situations, and in this way, you're expressing what's happening in your inner life.

Related to your inner life is the concept of having inner strength. Some believe that inner strength is primarily about motivation and drive, while others believe it is mainly about spiritual discovery. If we take a more tangible approach, we can define inner strength as a set of abilities and skills that enable you to survive and thrive in your surroundings. It also entails a mindset that motivates you to strive for growth and innovation.

To develop inner strength, and thereby a healthy inner life, you must first take the time to learn more about yourself, including your aspirations, values, limitations, and personal goals. Building inner strength is, in some ways, a voyage of self-discovery and self-growth, a path to becoming a better version of yourself.

The Holy Spirit has the power to build you up and produce in you a strong inner life so that you can experience happiness and peace. Remember what the Apostle Paul said:

"But the fruit of the Spirit is love, joy, peace, longsuffering, kindness, goodness, faithfulness, gentleness, self-control."

Galatians 5:22 (NKJV)

Try to cultivate these fruits of the Spirit in yourself, and you will develop inner strength and a blessed inner life, which will, in turn, enable you to share that happiness ad peace with others.

Be yourself

Contentment is another element that is critical for mental toughness. To develop happiness, you have to learn how to be satisfied with what you have. This doesn't mean you should abandon your ambition or the desire to achieve greater success. Instead, it means you should make the effort to be grateful for the positives that currently exist in your life. After all, the only way you can truly appreciate the fulfillment of your dreams is if you first understand and accept your life the way it is.

In addition to appreciating what you have, you should be happy with who you are. Again, this doesn't mean you should settle for your current flaws and not try to improve your character, but it does mean you need to learn to appreciate who you are and the talents God has given you. There will always be issues you want to fix within yourself and things you know you could do better, but you have to love yourself, flaws and all, in order to truly improve.

When you learn to appreciate the good parts of your personality, you can pursue self-improvement with a sense of pride, hope, and optimism about who you'll become as you begin to fulfill your true potential. This occurs when you:

- Take time daily with God.

- Take time for yourself.
- Discover your identity: you are loved, you are blessed, you are unique, you have a bright future.

Discover your calling to overcome your challenges

The world is full of adventures and excitement, and only those who are confident and mentally healthy can fully explore and enjoy them. Mentally tough people are always on the go, so they discover many exciting new experiences. They learn new skills, try different activities, eat different cuisines, travel to other countries, venture into deeper conversational waters, meet new people. Mentally tough people enjoy their lives more than those who are afraid and unwilling to leave their comfort zones.

If you want to live a healthy lifestyle and overcome the challenges that come your way, you have to train yourself to see the world in a different light. The only way to do that is to step out of your comfort zone and explore! Only then will you realize that the world is a much better and more exciting place than you ever imagined it would be.

When your views of the world become positive, your mind will be healthier and stronger as well, and you'll be better equipped to overcome the hardships you may face. Eventually, you'll be able to strive harder to achieve your goals because you know that the world is not so scary after all, that everyone has a place and a role in society and in their community, and that success, joy, and peace are not at all elusive.

Several decades ago, scientists discovered that each person has a unique heartbeat. It's based on the volume and form of your heart, the direction of your valves, and your physiology. Out of the 7 billion people on this Earth, your heartbeat is unique. You are unique in the whole universe. This is just one indication to show you that you are unique in God's eyes. He takes a particular interest in you. Just believe it! God loves you. You are precious in His eyes.

God tells us:

"See, I have inscribed you on the palms of My hands; Your walls are continually before Me."

Isaiah 49:16 (NKJV)

Do not worry about the difficulties and stresses that arise in your life. You are in God's Hands. It's time to wake up, to build your inner life and develop your mental toughness. Remind yourself that you are blessed and God loves you.

Paul said:

"Blessed be the God and Father of our Lord Jesus Christ, who has blessed us with every spiritual blessing in the heavenly places in Christ."

Ephesians 1:3 (NKJV)

Do not let your negative emotions enslave you. Do not lose your joy by overthinking your situation. See the big picture: You have been created by God for a unique purpose. Your dreams are bigger than whatever challenges you may face. You have a mission in life. You are unique on this Earth, and you have a bright future. When you are tempted to feel discouraged, remember these words:

"The Lord has appeared of old to me, saying:

Yes, I have loved you with an everlasting love;

Therefore with lovingkindness I have drawn you...

There is hope in your future, says the Lord..."

Jeremiah 31:3, 17 (NKJV)

Key Takeaways

- Emotions arise from our physiology, our situation, and our interactions with others. If we allow negative emotions to take over, they can impact our health and wellbeing.

- Emotional mastery is key to helping you become mentally tough. You need to be able to recognize and control the emotions you're feeling. Writing your emotions down via journaling can be helpful, as well as reinforcing positive self-talk and turning to God in prayer.

- Mental toughness consists of control of emotions and behavior, commitment to your goals, confidence in yourself, and facing challenges without fear or trepidation. Mentally tough people experience and enjoy life's adventures to the fullest.

- A strong inner life, involving mental peace, clarity, and connection to God, will give you the mental toughness you need to transcend your moments of difficulty and experience the fullness of life.

Time to Take Action

As we have covered in this chapter, your brain can have a hard time sorting out emotions from logical reasoning, so it can be tricky to achieve emotional mastery even when you think you know the source of your feelings. We like to think we're in control, but the truth is, our unconscious mind has a much more profound impact than we might think.

Therefore, be gentle with yourself. Emotional mastery and behavioral change won't happen overnight. Take small steps toward your goals each day on the path to mental toughness and a peaceful inner life, and don't be discouraged if you still sometimes feel overwhelmed by negative emotions and thoughts. Keep trying to replace the negativity with positivity, and stay close to God so that He can give you the help you need.

CONCLUSION

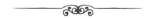

I hope that through reading this book and implementing the suggestions contained within, you become mentally strong, positive, and free from all fears and anxieties. Now that you have gained the knowledge contained in these pages, you know how to break your bad habits of overthinking and replace them with new, constructive ones. Don't stockpile your subconscious mind with negativity, but instead, gather positive thoughts and experiences to store in your memory and draw from in difficult times.

Let's look back at what we've learned in this book:

In Chapter One, we looked at overthinking in general and the factors that cause you to overthink. Then we addressed the various forms of overthinking and how you can rescue yourself from this trap.

In Chapter Two, we saw the consequences that overthinking has on our lives, mentally, physically, and socially. But then, we found out that all is not lost—there is still hope, even for the worst overthinker.

Chapter Three brought forward a variety of ways to eliminate overthinking, and we went further and addressed why you need a happy life that is not filled with negative thoughts. Endurance and becoming unbreakable under God's refuge crowned this chapter.

Everything starts in the mind, and that is why Chapter Four brought us to mental clarity. The brain is relatively tiny, but a lot happens there, and we addressed the importance of mental clarity in your life. Because stress kicks in when the mind is overanalyzing, achieving mental clarity is a crucial step towards eliminating overthinking.

Chapter Five addressed the concept of stress management. We examined the causes of everyday stressors in our lives and strategies for managing that stress.

Mental clutter is a key source of stress; thus, in Chapter Six, we looked at ways to declutter our minds and life. We looked at how to identify our core values.

In Chapter Seven, we discovered ways of cultivating new attitudes and addressing our anger. We go further. In particular, we discussed how DBT therapy can assist in the journey of managing anger and other negative emotions.

Finally, in Chapter Eight, we reached the peak of our journey, where we addressed living a purposeful life by mastering our emotions and finding our inner strength. We can conclude that the call to this journey starts with you.

Practice all the exercises and good habits found in these chapters to maintain your physical and mental health. After reading this book, you should:

- have the skills to control your life and desire to make positive changes;

- through God's grace, feel secure that no challenging situation can stop you;

- make the right decisions and spread love and joy to all your loved ones;

- be stable and calm, without going to extremes;

- focus on achieving your goals and create some time to pamper yourself;

- fill your heart with joy and not with the grief of sorrow and misery;

- take time to meditate on God's Word;

- take care of your mind and body and exercise daily, for this marks the beginning of a healthy life;

- cultivate your relationships, which are the number one predictor of your future wellbeing; and

- always be close to God, who is the controller of our lives.

Remember, there are two types of change: Rapid, superficial change can cause a temporary feeling of happiness, but eventually lands you right back where you started; on the other hand, continuous, incremental growth through small changes will enable you to create lasting positivity in your life. The single most important question here is: What will you do differently from now on? Take action to produce mental and behavioral change *now*. This is the core of all self-improvement.

Do not surrender to overthinking, anxiety, and fear. Develop your inner life daily. Balance your life in such a way that you can experience joy, love, hope, and peace in the emotional, physical, spiritual, and psychological dimensions. Do not overthink or shy away from challenging situations; instead, have faith that with God's grace, you will make it through.

"I can do all things through Christ who strengthens me." Philippians 4:13 (NKJV)

HEARTFELT THANKS & A SPECIAL REQUEST

You had countless books within reach, yet you chose mine. For that, I'm deeply grateful.

Share Your Light

Could you spare a moment to leave a review on Amazon? Your insights could guide others through the maze of Overthinking and Relationship Anxiety, offering hope and clarity.

Why Your Voice Matters

Your honest feedback is a guiding light, helping shape future books and empowering others on their journey. Whether it's a moment that resonated or how this book has impacted you, your perspective is invaluable.

Thank You for your trust and for considering sharing your thoughts. Together, we can illuminate the path to freedom from Overthinking and Relationship Anxiety.

>> Leave a review on Amazon US <<

>> Leave a review on Amazon UK <<

References

Abraham, M. (2020). *How anxiety can impair communication.* CalmClinic. Retrieved from https://www.calmclinic.com/anxiety/impairs-communication

Acenda Integrated Health (n.d.). *4 benefits of healthy relationships.* Acenda Integrated Health. Retrieved from https://acendahealth.org/4-benefits-of-healthy-relationships/

Ackerman, C. (2018). *What is neuroplasticity? A psychologist explains [+14 tools].* PositivePsychology. Retrieved from https://positivepsychology.com/neuroplasticity/

American Psychiatric Association. (2013). *Diagnostic and statistical manual of mental disorders (5th ed.).* Washington, DC: American Psychiatric Association.

American Psychiatric Association (2023). *What are anxiety disorders?* Psychiatry.org. Retrieved from https://www.psychiatry.org/patients-families/anxiety-disorders/what-are-anxiety-disorders

American Psychological Association. (n.d.) *Anxiety.* Retrieved from https://www.apa.org/topics/anxiety

Ankrom, S. (2023). *9 breathing exercises to relieve anxiety.* VeryWell Mind. Retrieved from https://www.verywellmind.com/abdominal-breathing-2584115

Anthony (2021). *What are the 5 major types of anxiety disorders?* Mind My Peelings. Retrieved from https://www.mindmypeelings.com/blog/types-of-anxiety

Aronov-Jacoby, S. (2022). *The benefits of self-awareness.* Humber River Health. Retrieved from https://www.hrh.ca/2022/01/27/the-benefits-of-self-awareness/

Bartholomew, K., & Horowitz, L. M. (1991). Attachment styles among young adults: A test of a four-category model. *Journal of Personality and Social Psychology, 61*(2), 226–244. doi:10.1037/0022-3514.61.2.226

Baum, I. (2021). *7 mistakes you're making when trying to get your partner to communicate better.* Well+Good. Retrieved from https://www.wellandgood.com/communication-mistakes-relationships/amp/

Beck, J. S. (2011). *Cognitive behavior therapy: Basics and beyond (2nd ed.).* Guilford Press.

Beckwith, A. & Parkhurst, E. (2022). *The mental benefits of decluttering.* Utah State University, Mental Health Education Extension. Retrieved from https://extension.usu.edu/mentalhealth/articles/the-mental-benefits-of-decluttering

Betz, M. (2022). *What is self-awareness and why is it important?* BetterUp. Retrieved from https://www.betterup.com/blog/what-is-self-awareness

Blue, E. (2018). *Diffusing emotion bombs: Managing anxiety and conflict avoidance in relationships.* Medium. Retrieved from https://medium.com/relationship-by-design/emotional-bomb-diffusion-aa99221a4f1

Burns, D. D. (1999). *Feeling good: The new mood therapy.* Harper Collins.

Caporuscio, J. (2020). *What is relationship anxiety?* Medical News Today. Retrieved from https://www.medicalnewstoday.com/articles/relationship-anxiety

Cassidy, J., & Shaver, P. R. (Eds.) (2016). *Handbook of attachment: Theory, research, and clinical applications (3rd ed.).* Guilford Press.

Cherney, K. (2022). *Effects of anxiety on the body.* Healthline. Retrieved from https://www.healthline.com/health/anxiety/effects-on-body

Cherry, K. (2023). *11 signs of low self-esteem.* VeryWell Mind. Retrieved from https://www.verywellmind.com/signs-of-low-self-esteem

Choy, Y., Fyer, A. J., & Lipsitz, J. D. (2007). Treatment of specific phobia in adults. *Clinical Psychology Review, 27*(3), 266–286. doi:10.1016/j.cpr.2006.10.002

Christopher, F. S., & Cate, R. M. (2018). Gender roles, power, and relationships. In T. D. Fisher, C. M. Davis, W. L. Yarber, & S. L. Davis (Eds.), *Handbook of Quality-Related Measures* (4th ed., pp. 447–454). Routledge.

Chukuemeka, E. S. (2022). *Effects of overthinking on your mental, emotional, and physical health.* Bscholarly. Retrieved from https://bscholarly.com/effects-of-overthinking/

Clark, D. A., & Beck, A. T. (2010). *Cognitive therapy of anxiety disorders: Science and practice.* Guilford Press.

Cleveland Clinic (2021). *How to do a digital detox for less stress, and more focus.* Cleveland Clinic Health Essentials. Retrieved from https://health.clevelandclinic.org/digital-detox/

Cloitre, M., Stolbach, B. C., Herman, J. L., Van der Kolk, B., Pynoos, R., Wang, J., & Petkova, E. (2009). A developmental approach to complex PTSD: Childhood and adult cumulative trauma as predictors of symptom complexity. *Journal of Traumatic Stress, 22*(5), 399–408. doi:10.1002/jts.20444

Colino, S. (2022). *Why decluttering is important for self-care (and when it isn't)*. Everyday Health. Retrieved from https://www.everydayhealth.com/healthy-living/why-decluttering-is-important-for-self-care-and-when-it-isnt/

Cuncic, A. (2023). *Negative thoughts: How to stop them*. VeryWell Mind. Retrieved from https://www.verywellmind.com/how-to-change-negative-thinking-3024843

Daisy (2020). *What is mental clutter? (And how to clear it)*. Simple Not Stressful. Retrieved from https://simplenotstressful.com/blog/mental-clutter

Davidson, R. J., & McEwen, B. S. (2012). Social influences on neuroplasticity: Stress and interventions to promote well-being. *Nature Neuroscience, 15*(5), 689–695. doi:10.1038/nn.3093

Davis, K. (2023). *How does cognitive behavioral therapy work?* Medical News Today. Retrieved from https://www.medicalnewstoday.com/articles/296579

Delap, D. (2022). *The physical effects of clutter on your brain and body*. Psychology Today. Retrieved from https://www.psychologytoday.com/us/blog/minding-your-mess/202207/the-physical-effects-clutter-your-brain-and-body

DeMartini, J., Patel, G., & Fancher, T. L. (2019). Generalized anxiety disorder. *Annals of Internal Medicine, 170*(7), ITC49–ITC64. doi:10.7326/AITC201904020

DPS Staff (2021). *10 ways to practice self-talk*. Delaware Psychological Services. Retrieved from https://www.delawarepsychologicalservices.com/post/10-ways-to-practice-positive-self-talk

Ein-Dor, T., Mikulincer, M., Doron, G., & Shaver, P. R. (2015). The attachment paradox: How can so many of us (the insecure ones) have no adaptive advantages? *Perspectives on Psychological Science, 10*(6), 665–685. doi:10.1177/1745691610362349

Eisenberg, N., Cumberland, A., & Spinrad, T. L. (1998). Parental socialization of emotion. *Psychological Inquiry, 9*(4), 241–273. doi:10.1207/s15327965pli0904_1

Eisler, M. (2019). *15 ways to declutter your mind.* Chopra. Retrieved from

https://chopra.com/articles/15waystodeclutteryourmind

Feeney, J. A., & Noller, P. (1990). Attachment style as a predictor of adult romantic relationships. *Journal of Personality and Social Psychology, 58*(2), 281–291. doi:10.1037/0022-3514.58.2.281

Feiring, C., & Taska, L. (2005). The persistence of shame following sexual abuse: A longitudinal look at risk and recovery. *Child Maltreatment, 10*(4), 337–349. doi:10.1177/1077559505276686

Feyoh, M. (2023). *29 journaling prompts for anxiety help in 2023.* Happier Human. Retrieved from https://www.happierhuman.com/journaling-prompts-anxiety/

Firestone, L. (2020). *Forgiveness: The secret to a healthy relationship.* PsychAlive. Retrieved from https://www.psychalive.org/forgiveness-the-secret-to-a-healthy-relationship/

Goldin, P. R., & Gross, J. J. (2010). Effects of mindfulness-based stress reduction (MBSR) on emotion regulation in social anxiety disorder. *Emotion, 10*(1), 83–91. doi:10.1037/a0018441

Gonsalves, K. (2023). *The 4 attachment styles in relationships + how to find yours*. MindBodyGreen. Retrieved from https://www.mindbodygreen.com/articles/attachment-theory-and-the-4-attachment-styles

Grossman, D. (2018). *The art of active listening*. The Grossman Group. Retrieved from https://www.yourthoughtpartner.com/blog/the-art-of-active-listening

Hall, J. (2020). *10 habits to keep your relationships strong*. Forbes. Retrieved from https://www.forbes.com/sites/johnhall/2020/05/31/10habitstokeepyourrelationshipsstrong/amp/

Hayes, S. C., Strosahl, K. D., & Wilson, K. G. (2012). *Acceptance and commitment therapy: The process and practice of mindful change (2nd ed.)*. Guilford Press.

High Focus Treatment Centers (2021). *Learning to challenge negative thoughts*. High Focus Treatment Centers. Retrieved from https://www.highfocuscenters.com/learning-to-challenge-negative-thoughts/

Hofmann, S. G. (2011). *An introduction to modern CBT: Psychological solutions to mental health problems*. John Wiley & Sons.

Holland, K. (2022). *Everything you need to know about anxiety*. Healthline. Retrieved from https://www.healthline.com/health/anxiety

Holland, K. (2020). *Positive self-talk: how talking to yourself is a good thing*. Healthline. Retrieved from https://www.healthline.com/health/positive-self-talk

Hoshaw, C. (2022). *What is mindfulness? A simple practice for greater wellbeing.* Healthline. Retrieved from https://www.healthline.com/health/mind-body/what-is-mindfulness

Howard, T. (2021). *The importance of showing gratitude to your partner.* Utah State University, Relationships Extension. Retrieved from https://extension.usu.edu/relationships/faq/the-importance-of-showing-gratitude-to-your-partner

Hutchinson, A. (2022). *What is graded exposure therapy?* Ovrcome.io. Retrieved from https://www.ovrcome.io/amp/what-is-graded-exposure-therapy

Ivory, D. (2022). *How to practice mindfulness in daily life.* Mindful. Retrieved from https://www.mindful.org/mindfulness-how-to-do-it/

Iyarn (2020). *Vulnerability for building stronger connections.* Iyarn. Retrieved from https://iyarn.com/blog/vulnerability-building-stronger-connections/

Izuakam, J. (2023). *What is your attachment style?* The Guardian: Life. Retrieved from https://guardian.ng/life/what-is-your-attachment-style/

Jenna (2023). *What is mental clutter and how can you reduce it?* Tidymalism. Retrieved from https://tidymalism.com/what-is-mental-clutter/

Johansson, R., Andersson, G., & Paxling, B. (2012). A randomized controlled trial of internet-based cognitive behavior therapy, self-help booklet, and no treatment for social anxiety disorder in Japan. *Cognitive Behaviour Therapy, 41*(2), 106–116.

Katz, L. F., & Windecker-Nelson, B. (2004). Parental meta-emotion philosophy in families with conduct-problem children: Links with peer relations. *Journal of Abnormal Child Psychology, 32*(4), 385–398. doi:10.1023/b:jacp.0000030292.36168.30

Kendler, K. S., Eaves, L. J., Loken, E. K., Pedersen, N. L., Middeldorp, C. M., Reynolds, C., Boomsma, D., Lichtenstein, P., Silberg, J., & Gardner, C. O. (2011). The impact of environmental experiences on symptoms of anxiety and depression across the life span. *Psychological Science, 22*(10), 1343–1352. doi:10.1177/0956797611417255

Keng, S. L., Smoski, M. J., & Robins, C. J. (2011). Effects of mindfulness on psychological health: A review of empirical studies. *Clinical Psychology Review, 31*(6), 1041–1056. doi:10.1016/j.cpr.2011.04.006

Knight, A. (2023). *Why overthinking is bad for your health? – Insomnia, anxiety, depression & decreased productivity*. Fischer Institute. Retrieved from https://fischerinstitute.com/overthinking-is-bad-for-health/

Knobloch-Westerwick, S., & Alter, S. (2017). Idealized media images and women's satisfaction with their relationships: Perceiving high idealized media images negatively predicts satisfaction. *Communication Research, 44*(5), 672–696.

Kumar, V. K. (2023). *Attachment theory*. StatPearls Publishing.

Lebow, I. H. (2021). *6 neuroplasticity exercises for anxiety relief*. Psych Central. Retrieved from https://psychcentral.com/anxiety/how-to-train-your-brain-to-alleviate-anxiety

Leonard, A. (2022). The impact of trauma on mental health. *Journal of Trauma and Recovery, 10*(2), 123–145.

Leonard, J. (2020). *What is trauma? What to know*. Medical News Today. Retrieved from https://www.medicalnewstoday.com/articles/trauma

Lindberg, S. (2021). *What are the types of anxiety disorders?* Healthline. Retrieved from https://www.healthline.com/health/anxiety/types-of-anxiety

Lindberg, S. (2023). *How does your environment affect your mental health?* VeryWell Mind. Retrieved from https://www.verywellmind.com/how-your-environment-affects-your-mental-health

Lok, A., Frijling, J. L., & van Zuiden, M. (2018). Posttraumatic stress disorder: Current insights in diagnostics, treatment and prevention. *Ned Tijdschr Geneeskd, 161*(3), D1905.

Los Angeles Christian Counseling. (2020). *16 characteristics of a happy couple.* LA Christian Counseling. Retrieved from https://lachristiancounseling.com/articles/16-characteristics-of-a-happy-couple

Madison, R. (2020). *6 exercises to strengthen emotional intimacy in your marriage.* First Things First. Retrieved from https://firstthings.org/strengthen-emotional-intimacy-in-marriage/

Mandriota, M. (2022). *All about the cycle of anxiety: What it is and how to cope.* Psych Central. Retrieved from https://psychcentral.com/anxiety/cycle-of-anxiety

Mantell, M. (n.d). *Vulnerability exercises to get more fulfilling relationships.* Mike Mantell. Retrieved from https://mikemantell.com/vulnerability-exercises/

Markowicz, J. (2021). *Attachment styles and hope for your relationship.* GoodTherapy Blog. Retrieved from https://www.goodtherapy.org/blog/Attachment-Styles-Hope-for-Your-Relationship

Mayo Clinic Staff. (2019). *Social anxiety disorder (social phobia)*. Mayo Clinic. Retrieved from https://www.mayoclinic.org/diseases-conditions/social-anxiety-disorder/symptoms-causes/syc-20353561

McDermott, N. (2023). *What are the attachment styles—and how can they impact your relationship?* Forbes Health. Retrieved from https://www.forbes.com/health/mind/what-are-the-attachment-styles/

McLean, K. (2021). *Understanding codependency (anxious attachment)*. Kennedy McLean Counselling & Psychotherapy Services. Retrieved from https://www.kennedymclean.com/amp/understanding-codependency-anxious-attachment

Mental Health Foundation (2022). *Anxiety*. Mental Health Foundation. Retrieved from https://www.mentalhealth.org.uk/a-to-z/a/anxiety

Mental Health Foundation (2022). *Physical health and mental health*. Mental Health Foundation. Retrieved from https://www.mentalhealth.org.uk/explore-mental-health/a-z-topics/physical-health-and-mental-health

Mikulincer, M., & Shaver, P. R. (2016). *Attachment in adulthood: Structure, dynamics, and change (2nd ed.)*. Guilford Press.

Mind (2021). *Anxiety and panic attacks*. Mind. Retrieved from https://www.mind.org.uk/information-support/types-of-mental-health-problems/anxiety-and-panic-attacks/

Morin, A. (2023). *How to stop overthinking*. VeryWell Mind. Retrieved from https://www.verywellmind.com/how-to-know-when-youre-overthinking-5077069

Morris, Y. S. (2016). *What are the benefits of self-talk?* Healthline. Retrieved from https://www.healthline.com/health/mental-health/self-talk

Nash, J. (2022). *24 best self-soothing techniques and strategies for adults*. Positive Psychology. Retrieved from https://positivepsychology.com/self-soothing/

National Health Service (2022). *Overview - Cognitive Behavioural Therapy (CBT)*. NHS. Retrieved from https://www.nhs.uk/mental-health/talking-therapies-medicine-treatments/talking-therapies-and-counselling/cognitive-behavioural-therapy-cbt/overview/

National Health Service (2023). *Post-traumatic stress disorder (PTSD)*. NHS Inform. Retrieved from https://www.nhsinform.scot/illnesses-and-conditions/mental-health/post-traumatic-stress-disorder-ptsd

National Institute on Aging (2020). *5 tips for dealing with social anxiety as you age*. Retrieved from https://www.nia.nih.gov/news/social-anxiety-tips

National Institute of Mental Health (2023). *Anxiety disorders*. NIMH. Retrieved from https://www.nimh.nih.gov/health/topics/anxiety-disorders/index.shtml

Nazish, N. (2017). *How to declutter your mind: 10 practical tips you'll actually want to try*. Forbes. Retrieved from https://www.forbes.com/sites/nomanazish/2017/11/19/how-to-declutter-your-mind-10-practical-tips-youll-actually-want-to-try/?sh=145fba0f24f1

Newman, M. G., & Llera, S. J. (2011). A novel theory of experiential avoidance in generalized anxiety disorder: A review and synthesis of research supporting a contrast avoidance model of worry. *Clinical Psychology Review, 31*(3), 371–382. doi:10.1016/j.cpr.2011.01.008

Nwokolo, C. (2022). *5 damaging health effects of overthinking*. HealthGuide. Retrieved from https://healthguide.ng/health-effects-of-overthinking/

Pattemore, C. (2021). *How to set boundaries in your relationships*. Psych Central. Retrieved from https://psychcentral.com/blog/why-healthy-relationships-always-have-boundaries-how-to-set-boundaries-in-yours

Peterson, T. (2015). *Anxiety and overthinking everything*. Healthy Place. Retrieved from https://www.healthyplace.com/blogs/anxiety-schmanxiety/2015/12/anxiety-and-over-thinking-everything

Peterson, T. (2018). *Safety behaviors with social anxiety: Helpful or harmful?* Healthy Place. Retrieved from https://www.healthyplace.com/blogs/anxiety-schmanxiety/2018/7/safety-behaviors-with-social-anxiety-helpful-or-harmful

Phelps, B. (2020). *10 benefits of happy relationships*. WebMD. Retrieved from https://blogs.webmd.com/relationships/20200715/10-benefits-of-happy-relationships

Pietrangelo, A. (2023). *How to be happy: 27 habits to add to your routine*. Healthline. Retrieved from https://www.healthline.com/health/how-to-be-happy/

Pinnacle Recovery (2019). *What are the 4 R's of anxiety?* Pinnacle Recovery. Retrieved from https://pinnaclerecoveryut.com/what-are-the-4-rs-of-anxiety/

Poplin, J. (2022). *Decluttering & self-care: The benefits of letting go*. The Simplicity Habit. Retrieved from https://www.thesimplicityhabit.com/decluttering-and-self-care-the-benefits-of-letting-go/

Powell, A. (2022). *Relationship anxiety: Signs, causes, & 8 ways to overcome*. Choosing Therapy. Retrieved from https://www.choosingtherapy.com/relationship-anxiety/

Qhek, J. (2022). *The truth behind safety behaviours*. Chill By Nette. Retrieved from https://chillbynette.com/the-truth-behind-safety-behaviours/

Rapee, R. M., & Heimberg, R. G. (1997). A cognitive-behavioral model of anxiety in social phobia. *Behaviour Research and Therapy, 35*(8), 741–756. doi:10.1016/S0005-7967(97)00022-3

Ray, S. (2023). *Conflict resolution: Process, strategies & skills*. Project Manager. Retrieved from https://www.projectmanager.com/blog/conflict-resolution-strategies

Reid, S. (2023). *Setting healthy boundaries in relationships*. HelpGuide. Retrieved from https://www.helpguide.org/articles/relationships-communication/setting-healthy-boundaries-in-relationships.htm

Richards, L. (2022). *What is positive self-talk?* Medical News Today. Retrieved from https://www.medicalnewstoday.com/articles/positive-self-talk

Robbins, T. (2023). *Why do I overthink everything?* Tony Robbins. Retrieved from https://www.tonyrobbins.com/mental-health/how-to-stop-overthinking/

Robinson, L., Segal, J., & Jaffe, J. (2023). *How attachment styles affect adult relationships*. HelpGuide. Retrieved from https://www.helpguide.org/articles/relationships-communication/attachment-and-adult-relationships.htm

Rodriguez, L. M., DiBello, A. M., Øverup, C. S., & Neighbors, C. (2015). The price of distrust: Trust, anxious attachment, jealousy, and partner abuse. *Partner Abuse*, *6*(3), 298–319. doi:10.1891/1946-6560.6.3.298

Roncero, A. (2021). *Automatic thoughts: How to identify and fix them*. BetterUp Blog. Retrieved from https://www.betterup.com/blog/automatic-thoughts

Rosenbaum, S., Tiedemann, A., Sherrington, C., Curtis, J., & Ward, P. B. (2014). Physical activity interventions for people with mental illness: A systematic review and meta-analysis. *Journal of Clinical Psychiatry*, *75*(9), 964–974. doi:10.4088/JCP.13r08765

Ryder, G. (2022). *What is trauma?* Psych Central. Retrieved from https://psychcentral.com/health/what-is-trauma

Salaky, K. (2017). 9 surprising benefits of being in a good relationship. *Insider*. Retrieved from https://www.insider.com/health-benefits-of-being-in-a-relationship-dating-someone-2017-10

Schwartz, B. (2022). *Self-soothing: What it is, benefits, & techniques to get started*. Choosing Therapy. Retrieved from https://www.choosingtherapy.com/self-soothing/

Scolan, D. (2021). *Rumination*. The OCD & Anxiety Center. Retrieved from https://theocdandanxietycenter.com/rumination/

Segrin, C., & Flora, J. (2011). *Family communication (2nd ed.)*. Routledge.

Sharma, S. (2022). *6 simple neuroplasticity exercises to rewire your anxious brain*. Calm Sage. Retrieved from https://www.calmsage.com/neuroplasticity-exercises/

Shea, M. (2021). *Try greeting your anxiety with the 4 Rs*. Shine. Retrieved from https://advice.theshineapp.com/articles/try-greeting-your-anxiety-with-the-4rs/

Simpson, J. A., Collins, W. A., Tran, S., & Haydon, K. C. (2007). Attachment and the experience and expression of emotions in romantic relationships: A developmental perspective. *Journal of Personality and Social Psychology, 92*(2), 355–367. doi:10.1037/0022-3514.92.2.355

Smith, S. (2021). *20 benefits of healthy relationships*. Marriage.com. Retrieved from https://www.marriage.com/advice/relationship/benefits-of-healthy-relationships/

Smith, S. (2021). *How important is intimacy in a relationship?* Marriage.com. Retrieved from https://www.marriage.com/advice/intimacy/how-important-is-intimacy-in-a-relationship/

Smith, S. (2021). *The importance of communication in relationships*. Marriage.com. Retrieved from https://www.marriage.com/advice/communication/importance-of-communication-in-relationships/

Soken-Huberty, E. (2023). *10 reasons why self-awareness is important*. The Important Site. Retrieved from https://theimportantsite.com/10-reasons-why-self-awareness-is-important/

Solvere Living. (2023). *Six ways to declutter your mind mentally and emotionally*. Solvere Living. Retrieved from https://solvereliving.com/blog/six-ways-to-declutter-your-mind-mentally-and-emotionally/

Spielberger, C. D. (1972). *Anxiety: Current trends in theory and research*. Academic Press.

Stanborough, J. R. (2020). *How to change negative thinking with cognitive restructuring*. Healthline. Retrieved from https://www.healthline.com/health/cognitive-restructuring

Stress & Development Lab, Harvard University. *Identifying negative thought patterns*. Harvard University. Retrieved from https://sdlab.fas.harvard.edu/cognitive-reappraisal/identifying-negative-automatic-thought-patterns

Stritof, S. (2022). *How to deal with jealousy in a relationship*. VeryWell Mind. Retrieved from https://www.verywellmind.com/overcome-jealousy-in-your-marriage-2303979

Sugden, L. (2022). *7 neuroplasticity exercises to rewire your brain*. Heights. Retrieved from https://www.yourheights.com/blog/health/neuroplasticity-exercises/

Swaby, M. (2019). *12 ways to recognize negative thoughts*. Benevolent Health. Retrieved from https://benevolenthealth.co.uk/12-ways-to-recognise-negative-thoughts/

Szymanski, D. M., & Kashubeck-West, S. (2014). Mediators of the relationship between social support and well-being in Latina breast cancer survivors. *Journal of Counseling Psychology, 61*(3), 358–369.

Thompson, J. (2022). *9 neuroplasticity exercises to boost productivity*. WorkLife. Retrieved from https://www.atlassian.com/blog/productivity/neuroplasticity-train-your-brain/

Toshi N. (2023). *Overthinking – To what extent can it damage your life?* PharmEasy. Retrieved from https://pharmeasy.in/blog/overthinking-to-what-extent-can-it-damage-your-life/

Tuca, A. (2023). *16 digital detox tips that actually work in 2023.* ThemeIsle. Retrieved from https://themeisle.com/blog/digital-detox-tips/

Van Overbeek, G., & Scholte, R. H. (2007). Effects of a cognitive-behavioral self-help program and a computerized structured writing intervention on depressed mood for Internet-based self-help coping with bereavement. *CyberPsychology & Behavior, 10*(6), 845–851.

Vidakovic, F. (2023). *50 journal prompts for anxiety – To feel less anxious.* Inspiring Life. Retrieved from https://www.inspiringmomlife.com/journal-prompts-for-anxiety/

Walters, M. (2022). *10 healthy habits that should be a priority in your marriage.* The Dating Divas. Retrieved from https://www.thedatingdivas.com/10-healthy-habits-that-should-be-a-priority-in-your-marriage/

WebMD Editorial Contributors. (2023). *Anxiety disorders.* WebMD. Retrieved from https://www.webmd.com/anxiety-panic/guide/anxiety-disorders

Wegner, D. M. (1994). Ironic processes of mental control. *Psychological Review, 101*(1), 34–52. doi:10.1037/0033-295X.101.1.34

Whelan, C. (2022). *How to manage low self-esteem.* Healthline. Retrieved from https://www.healthline.com/health/low-self-esteem

Witmer, S. (2023). *What is overthinking, and how do i stop overthinking everything?* GoodRx Health. Retrieved from https://www.goodrx.com/health-topic/mental-health/how-can-i-stop-overthinking-everything

Woods, E. (2021). *How your partner's past relationships & partners affect you*. Pure Health Center. Retrieved from https://purehealthcenter.com/how-your-partners-past-relationships-partners-affect-you/

Zaki, J., & Williams, W. C. (2013). Interpersonal emotion regulation. *Emotion, 13*(5), 803–810. doi:10.1037/a0033839

Made in United States
Troutdale, OR
04/20/2024

19328304R00261